June 3, 2008

Paul & Linda

Best wishes

I hope you enjoy reading my book

Rich and Eli

Growing Up In **Mama's Club**

Growing Up In Mama's Club

A Childhood Perspective of Jehovah's Witnesses

Richard E. Kelly

Parker Ridge Publishing   Tucson, Arizona

Readers may contact the publisher at:
parkerridgepubs@aol.com
www.richardekelly.com

This edition was prepared for printing by
Ghost River Images
5350 East Fourth Street
Tucson, Arizona 85711
ghostriverimages.com

Cover illustration by Terri VandeVegte
sheltiemom023@att.net

ISBN 978-0-9795094-2-1

Library of Congress Control Number: 2007910129

Printed in the United States of America
Third Edition
Printed: March 2008

10 9 8 7 6 5 4 3

Contents

Dedication

This book is dedicated to my sister, Mary Lyn Kelly, who was brutally stabbed to death in 1998. At forty-nine years of age, just when it appeared she had put her life in order, she was killed by an abusive third husband.

My sister and I were raised as Jehovah's Witnesses (the Club). The Club's negative views of education and the role of women, and my mother's compliance with its doctrines, hadn't prepared Mary Lyn for adult life, as was the case with many of our contemporaries.

If my story helps save one person from a similar fate, I'll be pleased. I love and miss you, Mary Lyn.

Note to Reader

The following story is a memoir covering the span of time I was involved with Jehovah's Witnesses, which I refer to as the Club. I have tried, to the best of my knowledge, to accurately describe both the people and events during this emotionally challenging sixteen-year period of my life. Writing this book has helped me make sense of a childhood in which I struggled to win the praise of my mother while staying true to myself.

In this story, I frequently use dialogue to make people come alive and bring the reader more into the scene. I believe my choice of words accurately reports the essence of those events at which I was not present but which were related to me by my parents or their friends. At times, I use words and the peculiar Club phrases that I used as a child. And I have changed the names of most of the people and some of the places described in this book.

I describe a number of very vivid and detailed scenes that occurred during Mama's five-month conversion process. And yet, I was only four years old at the time. While I can clearly remember some of the events, I must give much of the credit to Mama's good memory and oral history skills. She comes from a long line of excellent storytellers.

I have also included a glossary of words and jargon used by the Club from 1948 to 1964, italicizing my first reference to them. Some readers may find the short history of Mama's Club at the end of the book helpful.

Acknowledgements

I am grateful to my wife, Helen; son, Keith; daughter, Kim Waalkes; and adopted daughter, Bente Skalstad, for their love, critique, and encouragement. This book would not exist without them.

A special thanks to my editor, Sherry Sterling, for her English grammar skills, inquisitive mind, and sense of humor. She is a jewel.

I could not have succeeded without the counsel and participation of my cousins Lynn Vona, Ron Stansell, Dan Evans, and Maxine Stansell. If one could pick his relatives, they would top the list.

I also want to thank Jan Wintz and Jackie Hendershott, my Tucson and Grand Rapids bridge partners, respectively. Both Jan and Jackie have become good friends and their proofreading and suggestions have greatly improved the grammar and clarity of this story.

Special kudos go to the multitalented Terri VandeVegte for her proofreading skills, helping to make this third edition possible.

Thank goodness for friends like Cheryl & Don Brown, Dan & Debby Dykstra, Tom Cabeen, Chuck Vona, Joyce & Bill Hodges, Ellie Kleinheksel, Herb Olney, Dean & Norine Kasten, Larry & Diane Davies, Darrell Miller, Bob Mihallik, Bob & Claire Rogers, C. J. Maurer, Harald Rishovd, Amy Kelly, Jon Waalkes, Charles & Barbara Hedgepeth, Cindy Haworth, Nancy Linnon, John Meulenberg, Emil Marx, Richard & Suzanne Clark, Priscilla Johnson, Sue Lamos, Ken & Claudia Minette, Sissy Printz, and Rich Higuera. I will always appreciate their suggestions and kind words.

I want to acknowledge the inspiration of six still innocent, beautiful, vivacious, and independent granddaughters: Hannah and Katrina Kelly, Erika and Annie Waalkes, and Ingvild and Silje Rishovd.

I am particularly grateful to the late Irene Lasater and her Wednesday Writing Group. Without her guidance and patience, I would not have completed this project. She was a saint to everyone who knew her.

And, I would like to extend a special thanks to my very good friend, John Hoyle, a website consultant, and Michele DeVoe Lussky, a high-energy freelance writing consultant, for their excellent suggestions, helping to significantly improve this third edition of *Mama's Club*.

Introduction

Before I reached the age of twenty, God was supposed to destroy the world. Mama didn't know the exact day or hour it was coming, but she knew that *Armageddon* was going to be the war to end all wars. She also believed that only a select, small group of people would survive the worldwide holocaust, and so she orchestrated all of our family's activities to ensure we'd be in that elite group.

Mama obtained her view of future events when I was four years old. During her indoctrination period, I imagined she was joining a club like the one in Little Lulu comic books. Several years later, Mama was convinced that as long as she paid monthly dues, membership privileges entitled her and her family security in an insecure world and everlasting life in a new world to come. She called this new religion of hers *the truth*. I called it Mama's Club.

While the Club was a safe haven for Mama, that wasn't the case for me. I was forbidden to celebrate birthdays, Christmas, and other holidays. I was made to feel guilty when I challenged Club beliefs. Because I sought Mama's acceptance so desperately, I lived two lives: one trying to be true to myself, and the other attempting to appease her. My feigned piety would haunt me for years to come.

When promised dates for the end of the world didn't materialize, only to be replaced with new ones, I was embarrassed for

Mama. She rationalized what amounted to be false prophecy as a decision by God to delay Armageddon so more people could accept the truth.

Regardless of Mama's attempts to indoctrinate me, I still admire those who seek the truth. However, I question anyone who claims to have found it.

"Religion claims to be in possession of an absolute truth; but its history is a history of error and heresies. It gives us the promise and prospect of a transcendent world—far beyond the limits of our human experience—and it remains human, all too human."
- Ernst Cassier, *An Essay on Man*

Hard Knocks
Chapter 1

It happened over fifty-five years ago. And still, I hear the booming knocks at my front door. They weren't ordinary knocks, for they set in motion a series of events that dramatically altered the rest of my life.

Before taking my afternoon nap, Mama read a story from my favorite comic book. Her animated delivery of Little Lulu's adventures of finagling her way into the boys-only club or Lulu's imaginary tales of Old Witch Hazel was the best part of my naptime routine. On that particular day, I was awake in bed for a long time, thinking about Lulu and how she'd outfoxed Tubby and Iggy into getting admitted to their exclusive club.

I had just fallen asleep when I heard a hard "knock, knock, knock" at the front door. Knocks so loud, I heard them clearly from the far back bedroom of our newly built bungalow-style home in West Los Angeles. It was November 1947, and though I was only four years of age, I sensed something was wrong. We rarely had visitors. When I heard a second series of knocks, louder than the first, I sat straight up in bed. The knocks echoed through the house like someone was trying to break the door down. After a third round, I ran to the living room in time to see Mama opening the door.

I gasped with fright. Framed in our front door casing was the biggest and scariest person I'd ever seen. It was a giant, and she was wearing a dress. Perched on her gigantic head was a pile of coarse, graying black hair tightly braided and twisted round and round, like a coiled snake. A black straw hat, shaped like a hamburger bun, and two long knitting needles held everything in place. Dark brown stern eyes bulged from her head, and thick bushy eyebrows arched up and down when she talked. A huge pocked nose was anchored in her pale white face, although her wrinkly cheeks were daubed with two circles of thick pink rouge. She had an enormous mouth, large yellow teeth, and a thin silver mustache that glimmered in the sun. She wore a long-sleeved black dress stained with perspiration and big pointy black shoes, just like the ones Old Witch Hazel wore. As I remember her now, she could have doubled for the late professional wrestler, André the Giant, in drag, although she didn't have his disarming smile.

Dickie sitting on the bed where he first heard Mrs. Edwards' knocks.

When Mama first opened the door, the lady violently thrust her long right shoe one step up, locking it onto the threshold of our front door. Mama couldn't have closed it, even if she had

Mama's house in Los Angeles.

12

wanted to, with that big doorstopper clamped in place.

"My name is Mrs. Lena Edwards and I've come to bring you some good news," were her first words. With eyes trained on Mama's, she continued, "We hear so much bad news in the world today that people don't know where to turn. But there is a book I go to for help, and it tells what God plans to do with the mess we've gotten ourselves into." In a voice that sounded like static screeches from a crystal radio set stuck between channels, she went on to say, "This book tells about a government that God set up in heaven in *1914*, and it will soon bring peace and order to our world. But before that can happen, the war to end all wars, Armageddon, must be fought. When it finally ends, the Devil, his demons, and all nonbelievers and evildoers will be destroyed. Only then will the earth be restored to paradise conditions, and no one will ever die again."

I looked up and saw that the lady had Mama's undivided attention. While Mama focused on the message, I couldn't take my eyes off the messenger. Her arms and hands, perpetually in motion, often blurred my vision. Tiny white gobs of spittle formed in pockets of her mouth, and occasionally caught and elongated between her big puffy lips as inky black perspiration stains originating from her armpits moved down the sides of her dress. Intermittent showers of spit fluttered from her mouth as she spoke in her ear-piercing voice. This abuse to my senses was complemented by a heavy dose of cheap perfume, no doubt used to disguise her overactive sweat glands. As she talked, her long bony fingers swiftly found the page she wanted in her black book. For emphasis, she'd thump a finger on the spot from which she was reading. I wondered if this wasn't a magic book like the one Old Witch Hazel used when casting spells on people. While reading, she slowed down her speech, emphasizing one word at a time, lowering the pitch of her voice as best she could.

She repeated over and over that we were living in the last days, that Armageddon was very near, and that only a select group of people would survive. To conclude, the lady said millions now living will never die. But to be in that number, you had to read the

Tim, Mama, and Dickie a few months before
Mrs. Edwards' first visit.

black book, do what it said, and join with other people who believed that the end of the world was near. I got the feeling that this woman belonged to an exclusive club, like the one Little Lulu and Tubby were in, and she wanted Mama to join. She even included me in her presentation, asking Mama, "Would you like that boy of yours to grow up in a world where he wouldn't age after he reached his thirtieth birthday?"

Mama didn't respond, but she was thinking.

"Well, I'm here to tell you, it is possible that you and your boy will never die and could live forever in that *new world*."

The odd lady stayed at our home for thirty minutes, although it wouldn't be her last visit. That half hour, and the strange events that occurred during the next five months, would significantly impact the next sixteen years of my life and have a profound and lasting impact on Mama.

A Story of Hope and a Better Life
Chapter 2

That fateful day of hard knocks at our front door ushered into Mama's world a new and exciting way to look at and live her life, one that several months before she had been questioning was even worth living. Of course, I had no way of knowing how depressed Mama was. And she had no way of knowing that her circumstances fit the profile of those people who found a home with this message. That day was the turning point in Mama's life, and she made certain that the story was part of our family history.

Mama loved to share that story, telling it over and over again while I was growing up. Occasionally, she would add a nuance or two to keep it fresh and alive. But otherwise, the central theme of hope and a better life was always the essence of her tale, painting scenes that captured the beauty of a world she had come to love.

The most memorable version of her story was the very last one she would ever share with me. I was fifteen years of age and our family was living in Norfolk, Nebraska at the time. I had missed school that day due to a bad cold. Shortly before noon, Mama called up to my room, asking if I wanted to come down for home-made chicken noodle soup. It didn't take me long to respond. As I descended the stairway, wafts of Mama's delicious cold remedy beckoned me to the kitchen table. I sat down and slowly sipped the warm broth, feeling better with every spoonful.

I enjoyed Mama's medicine, and she made small talk as she tidied up the kitchen, managing to make me laugh several times. She had a good sense of humor when she was so inclined, and that day she had definitely found my funny bone.

When she finally joined me at the table, I noticed she was holding our King James Version of the Bible. It was the first Bible she had ever purchased, just weeks after that knock at our front door. Normally, she used the Club-translated version of the Bible, which was first published in 1950. The King James Version, however, held sentimental value for Mama, as it played a significant role in her story. Whenever I saw her bring it out, I instantly knew what was coming next. Another clue that she was nearing her preaching mode was her "holier than thou" look. As a younger kid, I'd figured that was the kind of face she thought a preacher should wear when someone's faltering faith needed a boost. But that day, I also saw an undeniable "I love you, Dickie" twinkle in her eyes, which I could never get enough of. Then she asked, "Do you remember that day when Lena Edwards first knocked on our door?"

I thought briefly about saying something that might disrupt the direction I figured this conversation was going. However, my better judgment prevailed, fueled by the combination of having been programmed with good manners for years and not feeling well that day. Yet I did feel well enough to deliver a pinch of teenage sarcasm by answering, "How can I forget?"

Not detecting my sarcasm, she responded with another question. "But do you have any idea how low and despondent I was? I don't ever remember feeling so alone and hopeless. I had nowhere to turn, and you kids needed better direction and guidance than I was giving you. I just don't know what would have happened to our family had Sister Edwards not stopped at our door that day."

While Mama talked, I wondered if she was describing a bad case of depression, and I considered what might have happened had she gone to see a good doctor instead.

"It was like I was there physically, but my energy for living was gone. That's when I decided to pray, asking for God's direction. Every day, sometimes five and six times a day, I tried talking to Him, begging for His help. I had been doing that for three months when I got the knock at our door."

As Mama spoke, I had to admit that I enjoyed seeing her happy and feeling so alive. Telling the story seemed to energize her. Besides, her enthusiasm was infectious. I could detach my personal feelings under the right circumstances. Her words exuded the pure joy she felt, as if she were listening for the first time to what she believed was a life-giving message.

"Dickie, you have no idea of the levels of joy that went through me, beginning to imagine that this visit and message might be in response to my fervent prayers."

Reminiscing about that momentous day, she snickered at the appearance of this first messenger, saying, "I'm sure you must have thought those people bringing the truth were all freaks. But it just goes to show you, you can't judge a book by its cover. That reminds me—when Lena left the house after the first visit, you thought she was reading from a black book. But that was my fault, having never read the Bible to you before then."

I interrupted her by asking, "But weren't you turned off by how loud and obnoxious she was while reading from the Bible? It gave me the creeps."

A tepid smile accompanied her response. "Dickie, it's never been a messenger thing for me. In fact, I think that's part of your problem with not seeing the truth like I do. I've never judged the person sharing God's truth. It has always been the message that attracted me, like the first words she read to me from Psalms 37:29 and Isaiah 11:6-9."

She asked me to listen carefully and see if I could feel God speaking to me while she read, "'The righteous shall inherit the land, and dwell therein forever. The wolf shall dwell with the lamb, and the leopard shall lie down with the kid; and the calf and the young lion;...and a little child shall lead them. And the cow and the bear shall feed; their young ones shall lie down together; and the lion shall eat straw like the ox. And the sucking child shall play on the hole of the asp, and the weaned child shall put his hand on the cockatrice' den. They shall not hurt nor destroy in all my holy mountain: for the earth shall be full of the knowledge of the Lord, as the waters cover the sea.'"

She explained that to her, those words were like gentle spring rains on a parched desert land. She believed God was personally inviting her to enjoy a much better life, and she felt a joy unlike anything she had ever experienced before.

Mama's version of the story that day didn't include the part about her having three children at the time; I was the oldest at four years of age. Or that she was married to a man who didn't have the best fathering skills. She also hadn't yet told me that he wasn't my biological father; that would happen a year later.

She left other key factors out of her story that day. Like how hardworking my stepfather was, sometimes working over sixty hours a week. That he had a gambling problem and it wasn't uncommon for him to squander a good portion of his paycheck. That we were living in a brand-new house and more money was going out than coming in. Mama had been facing a serious financial dilemma.

She had other stresses, including being 900 miles removed from any of her family members, all of whom lived in a remote part of eastern Idaho. She'd also survived the emotional ordeal of conceiving and delivering a child out of wedlock in the 1940s.

Mama had planned to raise me as a single mother, but three months before I was born in October 1943, she had a stroke of good luck. She met a handsome Air Force Lieutenant, Jack Kelly, who fell madly in love with her in spite of her pregnancy. I was two months old when they were married. In March 1944, they moved with me to Los Angeles, California, to leave behind the stigma associated with a mother and her illegitimate child and to start a new life together. Mama's overwhelming shame at once being an unwed mother was a great burden for her to bear. She was also living a lie telling people I was Jack's son.

My half-brother, Tim, and half-sister, Susan, were born in February 1945 and December 1946, which didn't help Mama adjust to this new environment. She didn't have the support system she needed. Although she thought of herself as an intelligent, independent thinker, and as someone who didn't rely on other people, she was tired and lonely, and she needed emotional and spiritual support.

But the straw that broke Mama's spirit came shortly after Susan was born. Mama wasn't conscious at Susan's birth. She had been sedated with a heavy dose of ether, going to sleep an hour before Susan came into this world. In fact, Mama didn't see her daughter until four hours later, when the sedation wore off. Several years later, she learned that many of Susan's brain cells had been destroyed. Doctors called these children whose mothers were unconscious during the birthing process "twilight babies." If Susan wasn't being cuddled or sleeping, she went on daily crying jags that lasted for hours, making life a living hell for anyone within earshot.

Mama continued to recall that pivotal day eleven years earlier. This time, her version of the story included the part where Lena read from Matthew 24:14. Before reading it to me, she asked me to listen carefully: "'And this gospel of the kingdom shall be preached in all the world for a witness unto all nations; and then shall the end come.'

"Dickie," she added, "I knew she was fulfilling Bible prophecy right there on our doorstep."

I listened, but didn't say a word while Mama continued. "And though some people are frightened and skeptical, hearing that the time of the end is marked by a violent worldwide battle between the forces of good and evil, a war so fierce that nothing like it has or will ever occur again, they must put their faith and trust in God. That is exactly what Lena showed me would happen when she read from Revelation 16:14-16, 'For they are the spirits of devils, working miracles, which go forth unto the kings of the earth and of the whole world, to gather them to the battle of that great day of God Almighty. Behold, I come as a thief. Blessed is he that

19

watcheth, and keepeth his garments, lest he walk naked, and they see his shame. And he gathered them together into a place called in the Hebrew tongue Armageddon.'"

I maintained my silence.

"Dickie, those readings from the Bible ushered pure life-giving air into lungs that were for all practical purposes dried up and dead. I experienced a spiritual high when Lena read from Revelation 21:4, where it says, 'And God shall wipe away all tears from their eyes; and there shall be no more death, neither sorrow, nor crying, neither shall there be any more pain: for the former things are passed away.'" When she asked if I would like to live forever in that world, I couldn't speak a word, I was so excited at the prospect. I finally nodded my head and she put her Bible away in her large book bag and pulled out *The Truth Shall Make You Free* book. She explained that it would help me come to a better understanding of God's word and of what I needed to do to survive Armageddon and to live forever in God's righteous new world.

"As good as everything had sounded, I was suddenly engulfed by a dreadful feeling, thinking that something may be wrong. It occurred to me that this may be just another book peddler. Deciding to turn to God for help, I said a silent prayer, asking for a sign. Almost instantly, it came to me that if this was just another book salesman, money would be requested. If it was from God, there would be no charge. Anxiously waiting for what would come next, I heard it clearly when she told me that the book could be mine for a small contribution of fifty cents.

"I felt like my stomach had just been ripped apart with a sharp knife and all the sweet pure air that had uplifted my spirits just went 'poof' leaving me feeling like an empty fool. Still reeling from disappointment, my voice wavered while telling her I didn't have the money. But then a modern-day miracle occurred. Without the slightest hesitation, she said if I would read the book and ask for God's help in understanding it, she would leave it for free."

Mama told me that a spiritual rush encircled her almost immediately, explaining that this first encounter with the truth helped her understand the Pentecost and how fellow believers must have felt when God's Spirit descended upon them for the first time.

I started to get nervous, knowing what would come next. A good salesman would call it the "trial close" portion of his presentation. Mama never failed to make her story blend seamlessly into something I should do to get reconciled to the loving God she trusted and worshipped. So I said I was tired and needed to go back to bed. She reluctantly stopped, releasing that day's opportunity to wrap me in the Club's safety net and her world to come.

As I slowly walked away, I thought about how much I wished she had spent more time investigating the Club's history of false prophecy and doctrinal flip-flops and gotten a second, educated opinion on its convoluted theology. However, ten years before, I knew that in her depths of despair, she needed to believe in something far bigger than herself and to believe that she was an important part of God's plan. For Mama, it was the first day of a totally new and wonderful life, immortalized now in her story of hope and a better way to live.

She didn't start telling that story, however, until several years after her conversion. When Mrs. Edwards first left our house, Mama didn't have the faintest idea of what she would ultimately have to learn and do before she could join the Club or the crisis it would create for our family during the next five months.

Mama Finds the Truth
Chapter 3

Mama's motivation to read and learn from the book she now believed was a gift from God could not have been any greater. But doing it alone was not easy, as it read like a service manual filled with words and terms with which she wasn't familiar. Several times she even tried praying beforehand, but it didn't help. Six days passed and Mama was about to give up.

But Mrs. Edwards knew where we lived and had no intention of letting her prospect get away. One week after her first visit, she again appeared at our home. This time it was more chaotic. She arrived before naptime when Susan, Tim, and I were giving Mama fits by crying and screaming. Then we heard those trademark knocks. They were so loud that Susan stopped crying immediately. I suspect Mama's heart flip-flopped hearing the unmistakable sound of God's messenger. She jumped out of her chair, picked up Susan from the crib, eye-checked Tim and me, raced for the door, and swung it open in one swoop, catching Mrs. Edwards' next knock in midair.

"Oh, am I happy to see you!" gushed Mama. "I tried to read the book. Honest I tried. But for some strange reason I couldn't make sense of it all by myself."

I suspect Mrs. Edwards could hardly believe her ears. Most of the time people weren't the least bit interested and even asked her to leave. I imagine this never fazed her, as she was one of the bluntest, most opinionated, aggressive, and focused people I have ever met. In social settings she was offensive, loud, and obnoxious. But as a door-to-door evangelist working directly for God, she was in a league of her own. Given the slightest lull in a conversation, or the tiniest hint of encouragement from a prospect, she could preach up a storm. Now Mama was giving her a rare green light and she wasn't about to disappoint her or the host of angels that she believed were watching over her.

"Yes, Mrs. Kelly, I can help you. Would it be all right if I come inside?"

"Of course," Mama replied.

Mrs. Edwards' unusual physical presence and screechy, loud voice shocked Susan, Tim, and me into a manageable state. I wouldn't have dared interrupt her, although I doubt I could have even if I'd tried. We ultimately made the next hour fairly simple for her to work Club magic on Mama.

"Mrs. Kelly, whenever two or more people meet to learn about God's plan for the future, it is necessary to pray, asking for His guidance and direction. Since this is what we will be learning about in your new book, I'd like to have you bow your head while I pray. Dear *Jehovah!*"

I remember once questioning Mama about the history of the word "Jehovah" in the King James Version of the Bible. Even a cursory knowledge reveals the stretch of the translator's imagination: he invented the word. She recognized that it probably wasn't how God's name was pronounced, but reasoned that at least the Club was trying to do the right thing by differentiating Him from all the false gods. When I asked if I could call God "George" instead of Jehovah, she told me to shut up and said I was making a mockery of His name.

In fact, all members of the Club call God "Jehovah." They believe He wants them to be on a first-name basis with Him. The way they see it, God is no different from most of the people He created. They use questions to get you to see it their way: "Do you like it when someone forgets your name? How do you think God feels when we don't call Him by His name?"

Mrs. Edwards prayed: "Please bring your Holy Spirit into Mrs. Kelly's house today. Help her see your truth. Help her learn your grand plan for her and her family. We now ask for your guidance and direction as we study this book in the name of your only begotten son, Jesus Christ. Amen!"

She reached into her weather-beaten, black leather briefcase and pulled out a well-worked Bible, a copy of the same book Mama had, and then two booklets, handing one to Mama. She explained that it contained only questions, and the answers were found in the book.

Mrs. Edwards then directed Mama to the first chapter in the book, and showed her how to match it up with the appropriate questions in the booklet. She read the first two out loud, "What reward can faithful followers of God's Word expect? When will this happen?" Next, she slowly read the first paragraph, asking Mama to find the answers. She gave her a pencil, instructing her to underline them in the book. After the reading, she again asked the questions, encouraging Mama to tell her the answers. And Mama didn't disappoint her, responding with, "Everlasting life on a paradise earth, and it will happen in the generation of those people living in 1914."

"Yes, Mrs. Kelly, you got them both right," Mrs. Edwards praised her up and down, like Mama did for me when I ate all my vegetables. Several times, Mrs. Edwards suggested they read together from the Bible when a particular verse was cited in the book. She rationalized that this made Club assumptions, like "1914 marks the time of the end," or "Millions now living will never die," unassailable truths. Before an hour was up, Mama had correctly answered the questions for the first chapter of the book.

That day officially marked the beginning of what Mama called her spiritual journey, sweeping our family into the maelstrom of cult-like beliefs and a non-mainstream lifestyle.

When I was older and read Mama's book, I read the entire

chapter in the Bible from which she quoted and not just the selected verses. Read this way, it was clear to see how unique and unusual the Club beliefs were. I only wish Mama had asked Mrs. Edwards to do the same.

Before leaving, Mrs. Edwards read Matthew 24:45, asking Mama to listen very carefully. "Who really is the faithful and discreet slave whom his master appointed over his domestics, to give them their food at the proper time?" Mrs. Edwards answered the question, explaining that the organization that published the book Mama was now studying was this faithful and discreet slave. In fact, she asserted, it was the only group that God worked with, having exclusive rights for understanding the Bible.

Mama accepted this bold and egoistic assumption because as she told me many years later, "It says so here in the Bible." I wish she would have researched the very short history of this group (less than seventy years at the time) or the Club's first two outspoken presidents. Although I'm sure she'd tell me it was the message and not the messengers in which she was interested.

Two weeks after Mrs. Edwards' second visit, Mama had read her new book from cover to cover, underlining all the answers. She was studying the book with Mrs. Edwards twice a week, covering an entire chapter every visit. She also had built up the courage to tell Papa about what she was learning, although that didn't go as well as she had expected.

Our Last Christmas
Chapter 4

In mid-December 1947 Mama said she was as happy as she had ever been. She was learning new things every day, had a purpose for living, and was developing a relationship with God that she had once only dreamed about. Though Papa didn't see things the same way as Mama, he wasn't trying to discourage her—yet.

Mama's energy for doing household chores and fixing well-balanced meals had increased dramatically since she started to study the Bible with Mrs. Edwards. She dressed up before Papa came home from work, asked how his day went, and listened to what he said. And Papa clearly noticed.

It was Mama who suggested that they purchase a fresh Christmas tree to help them properly celebrate the birth and life of Jesus Christ. While Papa wasn't a churchgoer, he loved the glimmer and spirit of Christmas. On Sunday, Papa's only day off, they purchased a tree, set it up in our living room next to the fireplace, and decorated it with lights and tinsel. Later that night, they wrapped presents and spread them enticingly around the tree for us kids to feast our eyes on early Monday morning, though we'd have to wait until Christmas day before opening the gifts. The thrill and magic of the sight of that tree still lingers pleasantly in the recesses of my mind.

Unfortunately, that is not how it struck Mrs. Edwards when she came for the twice-a-week study of the Bible she and Mama had on Tuesday and Friday afternoons. Of course Mama had no way of knowing how offensive this would be to one of the most hardcore of the Club's members. And Mrs. Edwards let Mama know her thoughts on this matter as soon as she walked into the house.

"Why Gail, what in heaven's name have you gone and done? You've been making such good progress and now you go and undo it all by placing the ultimate of pagan symbols right in the middle of your home! Don't you know that Christ was not born on December 25th? Furthermore, we are clearly told in God's Word to celebrate his death, not his birth." Then she reached for her Bible, quoting verses to support her assumptions. Mama didn't say one word in rebuttal, as if she knew Mrs. Edwards was probably right, and she needed time to think.

"Well, what do you want me to do about it, Lena?"

"You must remove this unclean abomination to the Lord, now!"

"I'm not certain that would be the right way to handle this matter. I want to consult with my husband first. As you know, he's a nonbeliever and could make it very difficult for me in the future."

"Then talk with him about it as soon as possible. Show him why it's wrong and how detestable this is to Jehovah. In fact, let me give you the name and telephone number of a Club *elder*. It might help to have a man talk with him."

Then Mrs. Edwards positioned herself so that she didn't have to look directly at the brightly decorated Christmas tree and suggested they begin their Bible study for the day. Mama had all the answers underlined in the book. So that part was easy. But more than once her mind drifted to a more pertinent issue. How and when would she inform Papa of this new development?

She waited until we kids were asleep that night before sharing her revelation. "Jack, Mrs. Edwards was here today and showed me from the Bible that Christmas is a pagan holiday. In fact, true Christians don't celebrate it. She thinks it could harm my spiritual health if we keep that tree in our house."

28

At first Papa thought Mama was joking. When it finally dawned on him that she was dead serious, he went ballistic. He informed her that the tree was staying and he and we kids would celebrate Christmas with or without her. He also made it very clear that Mrs. Edwards was never to set foot in our house or yard again. "Do you hear me, Gail? I don't want her on my property. Gail, are you listening?" Mama went silent. It was a familiar ploy of hers, and it frustrated the dickens out of Papa as he never won at that game.

Papa was a bread and pastry salesman, employed by Helm's Bakery. He sold his wares from a company truck in the residential neighborhoods of Santa Monica, Culver City, Venice, and West

Dickie wearing Papa's Helm's Bakery hat and jacket.

Los Angeles. His job was similar to the Good Humor Ice Cream man. The only difference was that he sold fresh-from-the-oven dough-nuts, pies, cakes, cookies, and bread instead of ice cream.

Six days a week, he left the house at 5:00 a.m., long before we kids were up. He drove his truck into the main plant and stocked it as full as possible. On his route, he used a special whistle to let homeowners know he was in the area. His goal each day was to sell everything in his truck. Sometimes he was out until 6:00 p.m. On other days he'd get lucky and finish his work at 1:00 p.m.

On this particular Wednesday, his customers were in a buying mood, and he arrived home close to 1:30 p.m. However, shortly before that, we heard the now infamous knocks of Mrs. Edwards. It was not *book study* day, but she had stopped by to see how the conversation had gone the previous night with Papa.

She had only been there a minute when he pulled in our drive-

29

way with his bright blue and yellow Helm's truck. He got out, glared at the small red and white Nash car parked in front of our house, and spotted the large ungainly woman talking to Mama. He moved quickly to our front door.

"Who are you?" he demanded.

"I'm Mrs. Edwards, and I'm..."

"Get out of here! Do you hear me? I want you to leave and never come back, you home-wrecker! Get out! Get off my property!"

When people think they are doing God's work and held only accountable to Him, they are not quick to respond to the direction of mere mortals, which she clearly considered Papa to be. She not only didn't budge an inch, she attempted to explain why she had every right to be there.

Papa grabbed her arm forcibly and pulled her away from the door and off the porch. He literally dragged her standing up until they were at her car, all the time yelling that she was never to come back.

Papa was like a wild man, flushed with adrenaline and rage. Tim, Susan, and I were crying hysterically. And yet, Mama didn't react in kind. She maintained a quiet demeanor through it all, never once chastising Papa for his very physical display of anger. Then she asked him to take care of us kids (which was the last thing we wanted), told him that she needed to take a long walk alone, and she would fix a nice dinner when she got home in an hour or two.

The next day, Mama called Mr. Allen, the Club elder that Mrs. Edwards had told her about two days earlier. She told him that she had been studying the Bible with Lena Edwards for the last six weeks and shared all the events leading up to and including the physical removal of Mrs. Edwards from our home.

Surprisingly, Mr. Allen could not apologize enough for Mrs. Edward's actions. He made it very clear that her comments about the Christmas tree were absolutely inappropriate. He encouraged Mama to go ahead and celebrate Christmas with her family and that no harm would come from it. He agreed with Papa that Mrs. Edwards should not be allowed to come back to our house. But he did recommend that Mama meet with Fern Morrison, who could commence studying the Bible with her on Friday. Needless to say, Mama was elated and agreed.

As it turned out, Mrs. Morrison was one of the kindest, sweetest persons I've ever known. While definitely a true believer, she practiced her religion with compassion and kindness. She was soft-spoken and fit the profile of a perfect grandmother. She packaged the Club's message in such a palatable way, without screaming or talking down to Mama, that I often shudder, wondering how my response to the Club might have been different had she been my first exposure to it.

We had a great Christmas that year, although Papa had no idea that it would be our last. His intention was to help Mama quit this Club nonsense; he just needed a little more information. With it, he believed he could put together a plan and then everything would go back to the way it was—the way it should be.

Papa Needs More Information
Chapter 5

Before Papa could gather the final bits of information he needed to put his plan into action, Mrs. Morrison invited Mama to her first Club *meeting*, on Sunday, January 10, 1948. Mama excitedly thought about it for a day before deciding. When Papa came home from work on Saturday afternoon, she informed him of her decision. She also planned to take us three kids with her. He could join us if he wished. Reacting rather passively to the news, he suggested he could get some chores done around the house while we were gone. But he knew that as soon as we left, he'd go next door to find out more about the Club from our neighbor, Bud O'Brien.

Club members don't call the building in which they worship a church. They prefer to differentiate themselves from all other religions by calling it a *Hall*, or more precisely a *Kingdom Hall*.

The only difficulty Mama had in getting to the Hall at Venice Beach was transportation. Mrs. Morrison said that if Mama could get us there, someone would drive us home. The first service started at 1:00 p.m., so the four of us left our house on Globe Avenue shortly after 11:30 a.m. We walked a quarter of a mile to the corner of Sawtelle and Venice Boulevards. There we waited for fifteen minutes before a streetcar stopped for us to board. Mama paid the fee and we found our seats. The near empty streetcar invited investigation.

Tim and I changed seats several times, ending up in the back row where we were entertained by long bursts of oleo-yellow sparks generated from the jolts of electricity that powered our streetcar.

It was nearly eight miles to Venice Beach. When we arrived at our stop, we walked a block towards the Pacific Ocean and came to what appeared to be an old storefront building, most likely a hardware store at one time. Near the door was a sign that read:

Venice Beach Kingdom Hall
Meetings held:
Sunday 1:00 p.m. – 3:15 p.m.
Tuesday 8:00 p.m. – 9:00 p.m.
Thursday 7:30 p.m. – 9:30 p.m.

Mama opened the door and to her pleasant surprise, she was greeted by the outstretched arms of Fern Morrison.

What Mama didn't know was that Mrs. Morrison had nervously paced the sidewalk in front of the Hall for the previous fifteen minutes. She had wanted to be the first to greet her. There was always the risk that a potential convert could get cold feet when welcomed by an unfamiliar face and never come back. And then there was that loose cannon, Lena Edwards. Who knew what she might do. But nature had called and Fern had to go, scurrying back into the Hall. She was on her way out again as Mama entered.

"Gail, I am so glad to see you! Welcome! Welcome! Welcome! Come on in. I want you to meet...." Before it was over, she introduced us to almost everyone there. Tears of joy welled in Mama's eyes.

I had never been in a church before, but I had seen pictures. And this definitely wasn't a church. It was just as the Club calls it, a Hall. The wood floor was scarred and grooved, without the slightest hint of stain or varnish. One hundred well-shellacked, wooden folding chairs were organized in rows, five on the left and five on the right, with an aisle in between. At the end of the Hall, on the far left side, was a stage with a floor-mounted microphone, podium, and two chairs. On the far right side, unpainted plywood walls rose to the ceiling, encasing a single unisex bathroom and a large storage area. A bolted, brightly marked red exit door separated the stage and the bathroom. Behind the rows of chairs, on the left side, a large mahogany stained piano stood jammed against the wall. And, of course, near the entrance door was a large metal box with the words *contribution box* painted on it in big bold letters, which served as a reminder that the *spiritual food* dispensed at this Club cafeteria wasn't free.

While the Hall appeared Spartan and austere, the energy of the people inside, about fifty when we entered, made the long room come alive. They were talking loudly, laughing, and acting as if they were all part of a big family, with one exception. Sitting conspicuously alone to the far left and center sat a very familiar person. When I first spotted her my heart nearly stopped. It was Mrs. Edwards reading her Bible. I felt more comfortable moving as far away from her as possible.

Shortly before the first service began, Mrs. Morrison suggested to Mama, "Why don't Dickie and Tim sit with me, while you and Susan take a seat in the row ahead of us." The meeting started on time and a man said that Brother Brown would speak on the topic, "Babylon the Great, the Mother of All Harlots."

As Brother Brown stood up from his seat in the audience, walked to the stage, and put his notes and Bible on the podium, I thought he may have dipped his skin in rich milk chocolate. It was definitely very brown and I wondered if that's how he got his name. For the first few minutes, I was fascinated by the musical cadence of his voice and animated delivery. Frequent bursts of laughter and a contagious smile added to the show. Eventually, he focused on all that's wrong with other religions, just as Mrs. Edwards had.

When we got restless, Mrs. Morrison gave Tim and me coloring books and crayons. Before long, the talk was over and the audience clapped. Then Brother Brown said we'd take a break and reassemble in fifteen minutes. Mrs. Morrison stood up, asking Tim and me if we would like to go to the party store with her to buy pop and candy. Needless to say, we bolted out of our seats, eager for the change of scenery.

While we were gone, Mama talked with an old German Club member, Brother Kapp. He had survived Hitler's concentration camp during World War II and held Mama spellbound with his story. He explained that it wasn't just the Jews who were incarcerated, but hundreds of loyal Club members as well. Mama was impressed by this man of faith and wanted to hear more, asking if she could talk to him on the phone sometime. He gave her his number, encouraging her to call.

Once we were back in our seats, a man called Brother Allen welcomed everyone to a one-hour study of a magazine called the *Watchtower,* the official house organ of the Club. He asked if anyone needed a copy. Several people raised their hands, including Mama. After copies were provided, he asked us to bow our heads and had what seemed to be a very lengthy conversation with God. Afterwards, he told us to stand and sing song number 57, "Take Sides with Jehovah." Mrs. Morrison handed Mama a songbook. The piano suddenly came to life and the singing commenced. Definitely not recordable, but the eighty people now in attendance seemed to enjoy the experience. As off-key as most of them were, none could compare to the bellows from Mrs. Edwards. She was the loudest and could not carry a tune.

The *watchtower study* was organized much like Mama's twice-a-week book study. The only difference was that the questions were printed on the bottom of each page. Brother Allen asked the questions, people in the audience raised their hands, he'd call a name, and they'd shout out the answer. Two or three different members would comment on the paragraph being covered. When no further comments were forthcoming, another man came to the microphone and read the paragraph.

I was comfortably buried in my coloring book, about half an hour into the meeting, when my heart again nearly stopped. I heard Brother Allen say loud and clear into his microphone, "Yes, Sister Kelly." Then the shaky crackling sounds of Mama's voice broke the momentary silence with, "The good news of God's Kingdom will be preached in all the world and then the end shall come." I nearly froze with fright, never really sure why. Mind you, Mrs. Edwards was called upon to answer several questions before and it hadn't bothered me.

While we were at the meeting, Papa went next door to talk with Bud O'Brien. Unfortunately, he was out playing golf and wouldn't be back until late in the day.

A few days after Christmas, Papa started asking several of his fellow Helm's Bakery drivers whether they had ever heard of the Club. Most of them had and weren't bashful about sharing what they knew, though it was never positive. The most common thread was that Club members were religious fanatics who knocked on people's doors all the time. Other than that, most of the guys didn't know much. It wasn't until he talked with Bud O'Brien, our next door neighbor, that he found someone who professed to understand what these people believed. In fact, he claimed to know all about the Club. He had just read a book about them written by an ex-member of the Club. Bud's priest had also warned him about talking to members of the Club when they came to his door. After he explained this, Bud looked right into Papa's eyes and said, "So Jack, why are you interested in those commies?"

Papa was caught off guard and started to stammer, not wanting him to know that Mama was getting in pretty deep with these loonies that Bud was now intimating were communists. "Well, you know, if they should come to our door, I'd like Gail to know how to deal with them."

"Listen Jack, talking here at work is not the time or place for this type of thing. You stop over at the house some Sunday on our day off and I'll give you the lowdown."

Over the next few days, Papa started asking customers about the Club. He was even documenting what he heard. He hoped to confront Mama with these facts, putting his plan to work. While he had made no progress on this Sunday, at least he knew where to get the needed information, and he was confident that by the next weekend he'd have what he needed. He would then save Mama with the truth about this dangerous cult. She'd see the folly of her ways and be eternally grateful for his protective efforts. But it was Papa who would have the surprise of his life before the next week was over.

The Ultimatum
Chapter 6

Early the next morning, while walking to his truck, Papa spotted Bud loading his truck with fresh pastries and said, "Hey, did Michael tell you I stopped by your house yesterday?"

"Yeah, Jack, sorry I missed you. I had a lousy game of golf. Sure wished I'd stayed at home."

"I was hoping you could fill me in on what you know about the Club," he said, careful not to let on that Mama had been studying with them for over two months. Or worse, that she'd attended her first meeting the day before, and was so overjoyed by the experience that she planned to go again.

"Jack, why don't you come over Sunday afternoon?"

"That'll be great. I'll be there," Papa said before walking to the far end of the bakery commissary to find the giant decadent cream puffs that were available only on Mondays. As he strolled, he felt good about how things were developing. He had already started a list of things that he'd heard about the Club and wondered if it would be a good idea to give a copy to Bud. It included:

• Don't celebrate Christmas, Easter, Halloween, or birthdays
• Bud says they're communists
• Don't believe that Jesus is equal to God
• Won't serve in the armed services or fight for their country

- Won't salute the flag or say the Pledge of Allegiance
- Believe only 144,000 chosen ones will go to heaven
- Knock on people's doors trying to convert them
- Are very clannish
- Don't vote in local or national elections
- Hold communion once a year and only those with the hope to live in heaven can partake of it
- Don't believe in hell — when you're dead, you're dead
- Are home-wreckers
- The first two presidents of the Club were egomaniacs, allowing no one to challenge their authority

He figured that after talking with Bud on Sunday, his list would grow substantially. Maybe Bud would even give him some Bible verses to counter the Club's silly assumptions. Papa figured that would appeal to Mama. Yes, he'd make a copy of his list and give it to Bud Tuesday.

Unfortunately, the next five days didn't go very well for Papa. Each evening after work, he'd harp to Mama about items on his list. He just couldn't wait to win her back with reason. But every time she countered with, "So show me from the Bible why they're wrong." Frustrated because he hadn't done the needed research, he could only count the days until he would get Bud's help. In the meantime, the more he nagged, the more Mama's resolve strengthened.

On Saturday, when Papa arrived home from work, Mama had a nice lunch ready. Halfway through the meal she told him, "I'd like to start attending all the meetings at the Hall. That means you'll have to take care of the kids on Tuesday and Thursday nights. I'll have them ready for bed, so it won't be any work for you."

Instantly, battle lines were drawn at the Kelly house. Papa jumped out of his chair, pointed his finger at Mama, and yelled, "Over my dead body you will!" While his list wasn't complete, he quickly found it, dropped it on her lap, and screamed, "This is why you aren't going to attend the Sunday meetings either!"

Mama struck back with a vengeance. She challenged his intellect and skills as a father. Tim and Susan were crying, while I sat speechless. Neither parent seemed to be listening to what the other was saying. Suddenly Papa stopped speaking, turned around, and walked out the front door. We heard his truck motor start up and watched him back out of the driveway.

Papa was gone for over six hours. He knew what he had to do now, having rehearsed it in his mind over and over. His original plan had gone up in smoke. It was now do or die. He'd have to make this new plan work.

Mama was in bed when he walked into the house, though she was still wide awake. He entered their bedroom and turned on the light.

"Gail, I've had a lot of time to think about this and I know what I have to do. At first, I wanted to document information about this new religion of yours to help us both look into it objectively. I'd hoped to have my list ready by next week. Unfortunately, I've gone and jumped the gun, spoiling that. And so it's plan B, and now you must decide. It's me or that damn church of yours! Do you hear me? If you don't stop this religious nonsense, I'm going to leave you. It's all up to you. What are you going to do? It's me or your church, what will it be?"

Mama got out of bed, trying to get Papa to lower his voice. "Jack, please quiet down and let's talk. I made a mistake at lunch-time. Please forgive me."

But Papa was undaunted in his pursuit. "Gail, what's your decision? It's either me or your church! You can't have us both. Tell me now. Otherwise, I'm leaving you tonight and never coming back."

"Jack, let's talk about this tomorrow after we've had a good night's sleep."

"Okay Gail, obviously you've made your decision. I'm leaving."

He turned around and stomped through the hallway adjoining the bedrooms. He opened the closet door and grabbed a large suitcase from the top shelf. While trying to ease it down, it slipped out of his hands and crashed to the floor, waking me up. He picked it up, carried it back to their room, and started packing. They didn't seem to notice me entering their bedroom. Crying, Mama begged him to reconsider. I remember seeing his luggage full of clothes and then hearing the sound of metal on metal as the latch locked into place.

He stood up, suitcase in hand, and asked Mama again, "Gail, what will it be, me or those religious fanatics?"

Mama didn't answer. She only cried and pleaded for him to reconsider. He stood there for several seconds scowling. Then he marched out of the bedroom, down the hall, through the living room, and toward the front door. He turned around, giving Mama his final ultimatum, "Gail, this is your last chance. What will it be, me or the church?"

Suddenly, Mama stopped crying. She wiped away the tears and took a long deep breath. With her eyes fixed on Papa, she calmly announced, "Jack, please just do one thing before making your final decision. I know you wanted to talk with me about what you've learned. And I'd like to give you that opportunity, but first I need to make a telephone call. Can you wait for me to do that?"

It was clear that Papa was thinking seriously about what he should do next. He was holding tightly onto his suitcase when Tim staggered into the living room and innocently asked, "Where are you going, Papa?" That's when Papa started to cry, dropping his suitcase and rushing toward his firstborn son.

Holding him tightly in his arms, he said, "Tim, at the moment, I'm not going anywhere. Your mama has to make a telephone call."

Mama found her purse, retrieved a telephone number, and started dialing. After hearing two rings, the sound of an older man's voice spoke into her ear, "Hello."

"Is this Brother Kapp?"

"Yes it is. Who am I talking to?"

"My name is Gail Kelly and I met you at the Kingdom Hall last Sunday."

"Oh yes, I remember. What can I do for you?"

"My husband and I have a crisis on our hands and we need help. Can we come to your house and talk? This is an emergency. It can't wait and we'll have to bring our kids."

"Gail, my roommate and I will be happy to see you. Now don't you worry about a thing. We'll put this matter into Jehovah's hands and everything will work out fine."

A Conversion
Chapter 7

Papa walked into Brother Kapp's small metal trailer house a nonbeliever and left three-and-a-half hours later a changed man. He'd had an epiphany, although he'd never use that word. He'd say it was God's Holy Spirit and he was the modern-day Saul of Tarsus. Papa had never heard of Saul before that night, but he quickly related to him. Those familiar with their Bibles know the story: Saul was persecuting the early Christians when God sent Jesus to give him an "attitude adjustment." Temporarily blinded, he saw the truth, converted, and changed his name to Paul. Like the converted Saul, Papa became a believer that night.

I believe he and Mama celebrated his epiphany within the next twenty-four hours. And I don't think the celebration was spiritual in nature, unless they prayed before and after. For you see, my sister Mary was born a month premature on September 17, 1948.

My parents told me and my siblings what happened that night many times. The story was like an expanding accordion, with new details added all the time. That momentous event was an important milestone in their spiritual journey together, and they made the story an integral part of our family history.

After getting directions to Brother Kapp's trailer park close to the beach, near Washington and Pico Boulevards, Mama hung up. She explained to Papa that Mr. Kapp was a survivor of one of Hitler's concentration camps and she wanted the three of them to talk about the things on Papa's list. He agreed. Papa woke up Susan, Mama dressed, and we all crowded into the Helm's bakery truck.

It was cold that night and the truck was unheated. It only had a seat for the driver, so the rest of us sat on the damp metal floor for our twenty-minute ride. A light rolling fog coming off the Pacific Ocean greeted us at the trailer park. Once out of the truck, Mama made it crystal clear that we were in a quiet zone. Susan was dead to the world and the last thing Mama wanted anyone to do was wake her up.

Several hours before our arrival, Klaus Kapp and his room-mate, Juergen Toitch, had baked bread and oatmeal raisin cookies. Homemade vegetable beef barley soup for the week ahead was slowly simmering in a large metal pot. While not intentional, Mama couldn't have cooked up a better environment.

She knocked lightly at the door and it opened almost immediately. She again made the "please be quiet" sign and whispered, "Is there a place Susan can sleep?" Brother Kapp motioned for her to follow him to the back bedroom where a just-borrowed crib was wedged between the wall and a double bed. Soon they were both back in the living room making proper introductions.

Our hosts were in their mid-fifties, though they looked twenty years older, and they spoke with thick German accents. Klaus enunciated his words very clearly while Juergen slurred his, making it difficult to understand what he was saying. They had both been imprisoned early on during Hitler's reign of terror and ended up in Auschwitz a year before the war was over. While they bore the physical scars of life in a concentration camp, their love of life wasn't dampened. They were smiling, happy, caring people–the polar opposites of Lena Edwards, with not a pretentious or arrogant bone in their bodies. Brother Kapp was a good listener, while Brother Toitch was slow to catch on to what was going on in the world around him.

After the initial introductions, they offered us still-warm cookies and bread. Tim and I had milk while the adults drank hot tea and coffee. Up to that point, Papa wore his "mean-stern-tough-guy, nobody's-going-to-pull-the-wool-over-me" mask he donned to show who was in control. But while warming his tummy, he had time to size up these two old men, who looked like harmless overgrown elves. He started to relax, thinking he'd soon have his way with them. Before long, he was smiling and feeling quite comfortable.

After Tim and I finished our cookies, buttered bread, and milk, Mama told us we'd have to go to sleep in the back bedroom. She made it clear that we were to stay quiet and not get up. If Susan woke, we would be in big trouble. Brother Kapp said that he'd turn on the furnace fan to help drown out the adult conversation. Once Mama tucked us in bed, Tim fell asleep immediately while it took me a while. My mind was racing, wondering what they were talking about.

The four adults seemed to hit it off right from the start. The men treated Papa with respect and dignity, and whenever Papa expressed a concern, they listened carefully before responding. In the end, Brother Kapp did the bulk of the talking. Mama hardly said a word.

Papa first expressed his displeasure about the Club policy related to the military and not fighting for one's country. He was proud to have been an Air Force Lieutenant during WW II. Brother Kapp let him vent. When he ran out of gas, he asked Papa what he would have done had he been living in Germany when Hitler came to power and told to join the military. Papa didn't answer.

Klaus said that this is what happened to him many years ago, and then he read aloud several Bible verses that he used to help him make the right decision. Because of his decision, he was put into prison where he served hard time before being transferred to Auschwitz. He unbuttoned his shirt and showed where he had been beaten and burned several times. "Why do you think I endured that kind of torture and abuse?" he asked Papa before answering, "Because I put my trust in a Higher Power and His laws take precedence over mere mortals." He had Papa's attention.

When Papa brought up the flag salute issue, he wasn't as accusatory as he'd been about the Club's stance on the military. He was now merely inquiring as to why they choose not to salute the flag. And in the Club's way, Brother Kapp responded to a question with another question. "And what would you have done had you been living in Germany in the late 1930s and told to raise your right hand and shout 'Heil Hitler'?" Papa said he wouldn't have done it. "You know why I wouldn't and didn't? Because my marching orders are laid out clearly in the Scriptures," said Brother Kapp, before sharing more Bible verses.

Unnerved, but impressed that such common, unassuming people could defend their beliefs so skillfully, Papa reconsidered his initial harsh judgment. Apparently Mama had seen more in this group of people than he had first given her credit for.

He asked, "How do you people defend yourselves when you're called communists?" Both Kapp and Toitch politely laughed and explained how often Jesus, his apostles, and the early Christians were falsely accused of being subversives and troublemakers. They explained that the Bible made it very clear that God's people would be treated that way. They told him all Club activity was banned in the Soviet Union and that hundreds of faithful Club believers had been executed during the Stalin years. They spoke about the need for a theocracy, not communism, as the only way to bring about a permanent lasting peace for mankind.

They asked Papa if he had any concerns about Mama's work habits, mothering skills, or attention to his needs since she'd started studying the Bible with the Club. He confessed that he'd seen a big positive change and was grateful.

When Papa asked about Club beliefs regarding heaven and a paradise earth, Kapp responded in the Club way: "What do you think God's intentions for Adam and Eve were? Would they have died a natural death and then gone to heaven?" Now Papa was really paying attention. What they said made sense; even he knew that had Adam and Eve been faithful to God, they would have lived forever on a paradise earth.

Klaus shared Bible verses that he said proved true Christians would be persecuted and spoken poorly of during the last days. He let Papa read the verses out loud, and it had the desired effect, as he started to think that these people just might have something. But he didn't like Lena Edwards and wanted them to know it. Kapp and Toitch listened attentively before acknowledging that she was a very unusual and strange person. They said her methods were questionable but she'd had a very difficult life. Abandoned by her parents and her husband, she was now solely responsible for the support of her thirty-year-old, severely retarded daughter, as well as herself. And to make matters worse, she was almost deaf in both ears. "The real issue isn't about this poor woman who could use hearing aids and better people skills, it's our relationship with God that matters most." Papa wished he hadn't brought up the subject.

They discussed the Club's position on holidays and birthdays. Kapp read aloud the only two instances in the Bible where birthdays for Pharaoh and Herod were mentioned. And although he acknowledged that nowhere were we told not to celebrate them, he asked if those references were positive or negative. Papa had to admit that giving the decapitated head of John the Baptist on a platter as a birthday gift to Salome wasn't something of which God would have approved. They told Papa about the pagan origins of Christmas, Easter, and Halloween, explaining that the Club's position was based on issues of conscience.

When Papa asked about going *house-to-house* to proselytize for new converts, Kapp asked him what he would do if he knew the end of the world was coming in the next fifteen years, and that the only way to survive was to follow specific directions that weren't provided by mainstream Christianity. They read more Scriptures and asked him how he thought the early followers of Christ were able to attract so many new followers.

While growing up in Mama's Club, I learned how easy it is for well-intentioned people to use the Bible to support what the Club wanted them to believe. Papa's parents had revered the Bible, but they never read it to him as a child. He was naïve to the fact that to seasoned Club members, the Bible was like a piano on which they could play any tune they wanted to support even the most preposterous assumptions.

There wasn't anything phony about Klaus or Juergen. They appeared to have a very good relationship with their God. And the more Papa spent time with them, hearing them talk, observing the confidence of their convictions, the more he liked them. And he wanted them to like him.

Papa exorcised old beliefs that night. He cried several times. Before leaving, he had agreed to a one-on-one, weekly book study with Brother Kapp on Wednesday nights and a visit with his family to the Kingdom Hall later that day.

Mama's Test
Chapter 8

My parents didn't have four hours of good sleep before they were awakened by three fully rested kids. Fortunately, the rejuvenating powers of an epiphany, topped off by caffeine, eliminated the negative symptoms for them. When the phone rang at midmorning, Mama was wide awake and well into her day. It was Fern Morrison calling to let her know she'd just heard the good news.

Several of the Club members had met at the Hall before going in the *door-to-door work*. Brother Kapp had told everyone the news about Papa, including his plan to be at the meeting that day. Apparently Sister Edwards spoke up saying she could take us to the Hall, living only two blocks away in a trailer park. The only hitch was how Papa might feel about it.

Mama asked Fern to wait while she spoke with Papa. A few seconds later she reported, "Fern, the only thing he's concerned about is when we should be ready."

At noon Papa went next door and told Bud O'Brien he'd done considerable research on the Club in the last few days and no longer needed his help. He thanked him for his interest, suggesting that they get together in the near future to share what he had learned.

Sister Edwards' tiny 1946 Nash pulled into our driveway shortly after noon. As we piled into the car, I thought it strange that only a few weeks before she'd been physically escorted off our property and now, not only was she back, but her car was on our driveway and not the street where she'd always parked in the past.

Papa was a chain-smoker, enjoying nonfiltered Camels or Lucky Strikes. When all of us had finally squeezed into Lena's small car, Papa pulled out a cigarette, lit it, and exhaled. He smoked it down to a tiny stub, crushing it out in an ash tray that had never been used. Sister Edwards must have received strict instructions on how she was to behave, for she didn't say a word. It was only when Papa lit a second cigarette that Mama asked him to roll down the window.

In those days, Club members were admonished not to smoke. Today, they are *disfellowshipped* if they do. At any rate, Lena Edwards hated smoking. She wouldn't allow it in her home or car. More than that, in her indifferent rigidity, she preferred black-and-white solutions to issues and situations, having little tolerance for shades of gray. But to do something that may have caused Papa to alter his positive attitude about the Club would have been a cardinal sin. If Brother Kapp endured being beaten and burned for his faithfulness, Sister Edwards could endure a little gray smoke.

Our second meeting at the Hall was uneventful, even though everyone there must have known the story of Papa's miraculous conversion. Kapp and Toitch greeted Papa like a long-lost son. They bubbled with pride, introducing him to everyone they could. Papa enjoyed being the center of attention.

By the first of February, Mama was attending all five weekly meetings. Papa was attending the two on Sunday and one on Tuesday. Before the month was over, they were both attending all five. But Mama had learned that this wasn't enough. If she was going to join the Club, she'd have to regularly participate in the door-to-door work, knocking on people's doors as Lena Edwards had done on hers three months before. And while she would be mentored for a while, she would ultimately have to do it alone in order to become a member.

Selling was never one of Mama's strong points. If she had taken a personality profile, she'd find that door-to-door sales would be the last thing she should ever do. So this kind of ministry was a big test for her. She prayed and prayed, finally making a decision (with Papa's full support) in mid-February.

Getting a babysitter for Tim and Susan was the next obstacle. That was resolved when one of the neighbors offered to help out, although Mama didn't tell her why she needed help. My parents decided I would go with Mama, perhaps for moral support or maybe on advice that it would be good training for me.

A Club elder picked us up in the morning and drove us to a private home. Eventually, ten adults gathered. Brother Allen started a fifteen-minute service with a prayer, followed by a Club thought for the day, which came from a book they called the *Yearbook*. He shared several tips on getting people to purchase the latest issues of the *Watchtower* and *Awake!* for five cents each. Then they divided us into four car groups, giving the drivers *territory assignments*. Mama and I were asked to go with Lena Edwards. Everyone left the house in a collegial mood, wishing each other success for the morning's work ahead.

Dickie, shortly after going into the door-to-door work with Mama.

As we neared the car, now without a man or "brother" in charge, Lena took control asking, "Gail, do you have enough magazines?"

"Yes, Lena, I have ten of them. I think that'll be enough."

"No, it won't! You should be better prepared. Take six of mine."

Mama quietly accepted them before we climbed into the car. After closing the door Lena asked, "Do you have your *field service record* to keep track of where you *place* magazines and mark down *not-at-homes*?"

"Yes, Lena."

Lena kept the inquisition alive with, "So Gail, did you remember to bring handbills for Sunday's public talk at the Hall?" (A special talk, "Religion Is a Snare and a Racket," was being given at every Kingdom Hall around the world.)

"Yes, Lena, I've got plenty of them."

Once the car was moving, all conversation stopped. No small talk. No words of encouragement. Just road noise. As we drove, I noticed we were headed back home. Soon we were at Charnock and Sawtelle. Then we turned south on Globe Avenue, driving past our house. We stopped at the end of the block, ten houses away from where we lived. Mama, with knots in her stomach, felt the early symptoms of a panic attack.

Sister Edwards, oblivious to how Mama was feeling, barked, "Gail, you call on all the homes in your block. I'll do the ones south of it. It should take about an hour. We'll meet back at the car when you're done."

Mama went into shock. Her face turned ashen white. With trembling lips, she pleaded, "Lena, since this is the first time I'm going in the door-to-door work by myself, I'd prefer to make calls in another neighborhood."

Lena looked at Mama in sheer disbelief, while her eyes glared in disgust. There was a long silence and then, "Gail, do you love Jehovah God or don't you?"

Mama didn't say a word. She looked away from Lena and stared out the car window for a long time. Then she opened the door and asked me to get out. I did what I was told, and Lena jumped out and huffed to the back of her car. Mama grabbed my hand, took me to the sidewalk, and we started walking. I thought we were going back to our house.

We had breezed past five homes before she tightened her grip on my hand and came to an abrupt stop. She slowly turned us around. Lena was following us in the middle of the street, halting when Mama stopped and turned. She looked like a giant ogre of shame, attempting to glare some sense into her onetime pupil.

Her bulging eyes seemed to say, "Gail, it isn't too late. But you better darn well decide real quick who you're going to take marching orders from! It's either Jehovah or Satan the Devil!" They both appeared to be frozen in time until Mama made the first move. She slowly backtracked, one small step at a time, dragging me along as we walked past Lena, without saying a word.

Mama didn't stop until we were on the front porch of the first house on the block. She waited for a few seconds, said a silent prayer, and rang the bell. Mrs. Mallory opened the door.

"Why Gail, how good to see you. So what do I owe the pleasure of your visit?"

"Daphne, I'm here to share some good news with you. Unfortunately, that's not what we get from our newspapers today. But that doesn't have to be the case. I have with me two magazines that offer hope and a wonderful promise for the future."

"Gail, you've got to be kidding! When did you get hooked up with those fanatics?"

"Daphne, if you'll take the time to carefully read these two magazines, I think you'll see it differently."

"Gail, you're nuts. I'm sorry, but I'm not interested in that garbage," Mrs. Mallory said before slamming the door.

Suddenly, Lena Edwards wasn't the issue. Mama's spiritual adrenaline was flowing again. Isn't this how Jesus and his disciples were treated? She was a player now, fulfilling Bible prophecy. Like Job, Abraham, Jonah, and other faithful believers, she had passed a significant test. Before the morning was over, she had called on every home on both sides of our street. She placed twelve magazines, recording the addresses of the six homes where they were purchased and of eleven not-at-homes.

That day, I enjoyed the small talk and attention Mama gave me between calls. But that was it. Too many times, I watched her being received with disgust and anger. I told her the next time she went door-to-door, I wanted to stay home with the babysitter.

Later that month, Papa went in the door-to-door ministry without incident. But then, he had been selling all his adult life and loved that kind of work. Fortunately, it would be over a year before I had to go again.

In March, both Mama and Papa were baptized by full water submersion, dedicating themselves to serving Jehovah God for the rest of their lives. They now believed God was best served by doing what the Club told them to do, such as going to five one-hour meetings a week, doing door-to-door work at least twelve hours a month, and attending three *assemblies* a year. Supposedly, this made God happy. But even that was not enough.

My Grandparents
Chapter 9

Mama was two months pregnant when my parents were baptized. Six months later, my sister Mary Lyn was born, making it possible for Mama to tell people she had four kids, four years and under. This, coupled with the fact that she averaged fifteen to twenty hours going in the door-to-door work a month, and that she went regularly to all five weekly meetings, held her in high esteem at the Hall. She was even asked once to share this story at a three-day *circuit assembly*. The Club didn't hesitate to use guilt as a means to an end.

Fortunately, my life wasn't all Club activity. In August, I started my first year of school. Mama hired a babysitter, dressed up in a new maternity outfit, and walked me the half mile to Charnock School. And though I wouldn't be five until October 19, I was more than ready. Entering the classroom and meeting my teacher was a dream come true. It was only when Mama told me she had to leave and then began crying that I had second thoughts.

When she left the room, I panicked and ran after her. She was already outside the ten-foot-high chainlink fence that surrounded the two kindergarten classes before I caught sight of her. I started yelling and had climbed to the top of the fence when Mama finally heard my cries. While coaching me down, she reminded me what a big boy I was. She had cried because of how proud she was of me. Mama left the second time without incident. After that, school was always a joy and a welcome escape for me. Learning was fun and exciting. And I was able to put into practice things I learned, unlike my lessons at Club meetings.

One of the first things I did at school was to exert my independence. Mama had drilled into me that I wasn't to salute the flag or recite the Pledge of Allegiance. She reasoned it was a form of idol worship and Jehovah wouldn't look kindly on me if I did. She read Bible verses to me that seemed to support her position, making it clear what the penalty for disobedience was. I wasn't old enough to challenge her logic, but I was pretty sure that the consequences couldn't be that severe. Mama had an unequaled ability to exaggerate if she thought that was how she'd get your attention. I listened to what she said, but when it came time each morning to show support for our flag and country, I was one of the most enthusiastic participants. My concern wasn't what God might do, it was what Mama would do if she caught me.

In addition to attending school, my other childhood passion was spending time with my maternal grandparents, who lived in Robin, Idaho. Grandpa was a dry wheat farmer and cattle rancher, and he and Grandma lived on a made-for-the-movies landscape that was nestled in the Bannock range of mountains. Two spring-fed streams with feisty brook trout bordered their property to the north and south. While Mama had the Club and its promise of a paradise earth to come, the area of the world where my grandparents lived was my paradise.

I had lived with my grandparents in Robin for the first five months of my life. A few days after I was born, my grandparents convinced Mama that they should raise me. This made it possible for Mama to move to Denver, Colorado, where she and Jack Kelly could be together. Jack and Mama were married in December. In March 1944, Mama had second thoughts and informed my grandparents that she wanted to bring me up in Los Angeles, California, with help from her new husband.

For two to three weeks every summer while growing up, I vacationed with my grandparents at their home—my version of heaven here on earth. In addition, Grandma and Grandpa visited our family in Los Angeles several times during the winter months.

Our trip to Robin in the summer of 1948 was particularly important for Mama. While she'd told her parents about joining the Club, and given them yearly subscriptions to the two Club magazines and copies of her two favorite books, she believed they needed some personal attention to help them see and accept the truth. She wanted nothing more than to spend eternity with them on a paradise earth. In fact, informing relatives of what God has in store for the future is another of the Club's initiatives. Mama hadn't done so yet because

Grandpa, Dickie, and Rex in Robin, Idaho.

her extended family lived so far away. Her plan was to start first with her parents, Vern and Mina Evans.

Papa couldn't go with us on this visit. Traveling by train was a big challenge for Mama with three children and one on the way. But she was on a mission, for during the trip she told me: "Wouldn't it be nice if Grandma and Grandpa started going to the Hall like we do? We don't want them to be destroyed at Armageddon with the nonbelievers, do we?"

I never answered. It wasn't something I wanted to talk or think about. It really bothered me that she said stuff like that. I adored my

59

grandparents, thinking they were the best in the world.

Our last stop on the train was Downey, Idaho. My grandparents were there on our arrival and drove us twenty-five miles on winding, dirt roads to their ranch. It took over an hour to get there, but the journey wasn't a burden. I was going home. And being so far from everything, we wouldn't have to attend any Club meetings. That alone made it paradise.

During our stay, I spent most of my time outdoors: fishing for brook trout with Grandpa, riding with him on his favorite horse, Old Silver, helping him milk cows, playing cowboys and Indians with Tim, digging for black flint arrowheads near the cottonwood stream, playing games with my cousin, Danny, and imagining what it would be like to live with my grandparents.

Grandpa Evans and Dickie on Old Silver, two summers before Mama's conversion.

with Tim, digging for black flint arrowheads near the cottonwood stream, playing games with my cousin, Danny, and imagining what it would be like to live with my grandparents.

Grandpa was my hero and I couldn't spend too much time with him. When we were in the house, Grandma read and played cards with me. And when Mama wasn't looking, Grandma would let me take sips of her Coca Cola. Occasionally, I'd hear adult conversation about God, the Bible, and how much Mama wanted Grandma and Grandpa to join the Club with her. I was glad they never included me in those conversations.

Although my grandparents didn't overtly object to Mama's new religion, it definitely didn't interest them. They were happy she'd found a community for emotional support, but it wasn't a group they wanted to join.

The only serious concern they had was related to blood transfusions, knowing the Club taught that God forbids it. If Mama chose to let one of their grandchildren die to appease this new God of hers, my grandparents told her they would consider her an unfit mother. Mama told them about blood substitutes and the health risks related to transfusions. In Mama's mind, it was an issue of following God's requests and the subsequent reward of a resurrection and everlasting life in a new world, versus a short wretched life in this old world prolonged by an infusion of another person's blood. And besides, the chance that she'd have to make a decision like that was very improbable. After all, she had healthy kids. She couldn't convince them, and they knew it was hopeless to try to change her.

From that point on, my grandparents avoided conversation related to Mama's newfound beliefs. Unfortunately, it didn't stop her. Once, I was sitting on the steps leading to my bedroom in the basement, eavesdropping on a late-night conversation, when Grandpa pounded his fist on the table in exasperation saying, "God damn it, Gail, give it a rest!" It wasn't something I should have heard, and yet when I crept quietly back to my bed and thought about it, I knew Grandpa was probably right.

In spite of Mama's zeal to make them her first converts, my grandparents decided to split two weeks of their winter vacation with our family and Grandma's sister, Aunt Martha, in East Los Angeles. They arrived at our house first, on December 24, planning to spend seven days. We were hardcore Club zealots by that time. Christmas was a pagan holiday, our family wasn't going to condone any part of it, and all our relatives were duly informed of our position.

Early on Christmas Day, Grandma and Grandpa, unbeknownst to my parents, wrapped and placed presents near the fireplace. I was the first one up and walked into the living room where my grandparents slept on the couch the night before. When Grandma saw me, she whispered loudly, "Hey, Dickie, look what Santa's brought you."

Flabbergasted when I spotted the pile of gifts, I wasn't sure how they got there. I excitedly rushed over to find my presents and started opening them. The first was a large yellow truck, the second a complete set of Tinker Toys. This was a dream come true. My grandparents seemed to be enjoying the experience as much as I was. Then Grandma said, "What do you think Tim will do when he hears that Santa Claus has been here?" I jumped up and ran to our bedroom, telling Tim the good news. He was opening up his presents when Mama walked into the room.

She let out a gasp. I knew we were in trouble, well aware of the pagan origins of Christmas. But it wasn't Tim and me she was angry with, it was Grandma and Grandpa. You'd have thought they had just given us blood transfusions. Mama claimed it was righteous indignation when she yelled, "What right do you have to interfere with decisions that Jack and I make! I'm not your ward and I won't tolerate your wanton disregard for Jehovah God!" She told them how terrible they were. Lena Edwards couldn't have done it better. Tim and I cried. My grandparents didn't say a word. In less than an hour, they dressed, packed, and left. I wouldn't see or hear from them for eight months.

Later, Mama tried to justify her reaction. But the damage was done, and it would have a lasting impact. Oh, how I wanted to believe that Mama was right, but conflicts were already forming in my young mind that would ultimately alienate us. However, if given a choice at the time, I would have anesthetized myself to believe like her.

The Memorial
Chapter 10

Soon I learned how to amuse myself at Club meetings. And that wasn't easy, for after Papa started attending meetings, I wasn't allowed to color or write when someone was speaking from the platform. My parents figured I was old enough to learn and should listen. While Tim, Susan, and Mary fell asleep during the meetings, I couldn't in that environment.

It wasn't what was being said from the platform that captured my attention, it was how it was said. Adding to my amusement was the wide range of unusual people that the Club attracted. I was always eager to catch what one of them might do during the meetings.

Our family always sat in the second row from the front on the right-hand side. That meant anyone who needed to use the restroom during the meeting had to walk directly in front of us. You'd think the bathroom's location would have discouraged most people. Surprisingly, a lot of them had weak bladders or other problems and were oblivious to their amusement value. Even when out of sight, their audible bodily functions didn't go unnoticed. Brother Toitch was particularly good. He'd walk by, disappear, and then you'd hear several long toots like a tugboat blowing its horn in rapid succession. Just when you thought he was done, he'd outdo

63

himself on his second or third round. I'm sure it could be heard in the rear of the Hall. When he'd go back to his seat, I could hardly contain myself, although he must have felt much better.

Once, a teenage girl sauntered into the restroom holding a large brown paper bag. She was in there for twenty minutes, not afraid to use the flusher several times. When she came out, her hair was wet and done up in oversized, pink pin curls. A long sheet of soiled toilet paper attached to one of her heels trailed behind.

On another occasion, an older woman hurriedly passed us. She couldn't have been in there more than a second when I heard the flusher go. There was a long pause for several minutes. A lengthy series of flushes followed one right after the other. Then I noticed water slowly seeping from the bottom of the door. When I pointed it out to Mama, she went for help. Apparently, the lady had put several thick sheets of paper towels in the toilet, clogging it. Somehow, she thought flushing it over and over again would eventually solve the problem.

Shortly after the flushing episode in late March, Papa decided to look for a new job. He wanted to spend more time in Club activities and working six days a week was making it difficult. Within two weeks, he found a job with Farmer Brothers Coffee Company. He was hired to sell and deliver coffee and related products to restaurants, making twice the money while working only five days a week. Mama attributed his good fortune to the fact that he had put God's interest first. Because of the extra income, we purchased our first car early in April. We no longer had to depend on others to take us to meetings or in the door-to-door work. It was in that car that we drove to the Kingdom Hall for the 1949 *memorial.*

Members of the Club were required to attend a special one-hour evening service held once a year in March or April, called the memorial. It always set the annual attendance record for any of the meetings held worldwide. In Club circles, it was considered the most important meeting of the year.

My first recollection of the service was the one on April 12, 1949. Normally, we went to someone's home for a one-hour book study. This day, Mama informed me, we'd go to the Hall to celebrate the memorial. She explained its purpose and why it was so important to attend. If there is a Religious Dogma Hall of Fame, the explanation for the memorial would be the centerpiece.

Mama tried her best to share with me the rather complicated spin that the Club gives to support this special meeting. Not then being familiar with how communion was observed weekly or monthly in most churches, I didn't grasp how strange it all was.

The Club believed that God's last earthly kingdom was destroyed in 607 B.C., when Jerusalem was ransacked by nonbelievers. When that happened, God decided He couldn't depend on humans to run things. He'd have to set up a kingdom in heaven to rule over the earth. But He wouldn't do it right away. He planned to wait for 2,500 years, or the year 1914 to be exact. If His son successfully passed a test living as a perfect man for thirty-three years, He'd make him the permanent king of His kingdom. He'd also give him *144,000* angels to help rule. They would have once lived as people here on the earth, been tested during their lifetime, found worthy, died, and then resurrected to heaven when God was ready for them.

God's son, whose name became Jesus Christ when he was born of the Virgin Mary, passed all the tests the Devil could throw at him while he was alive. A few days before his death on a large wooden stake—not a cross as the clergy misinform people—he got together with his faithful apostles. He told them he'd have to die, but he'd be resurrected in three days. And approximately 1,900 years later, he'd be inaugurated as the king of God's heavenly kingdom.

If his apostles proved faithful like him, they'd be resurrected as well, although they'd have to wait hundreds and hundreds of years. But they were going to be the twelve cornerstones of his kingdom, each responsible for 11,999 fellow rulers. This group would help Jesus rule over a paradise earth where perfect human beings would live forever.

But while they were alive, the apostles had to meet and celebrate once every year. It was mandatory. Then Jesus showed them what they had to do. First he took some unleavened bread, gave thanks, broke the bread, and handed it to his apostles saying, "Take and eat; this is my body." Then he poured rich red wine into a cup, saying, "Drink from it, this is my blood, which will be poured out for the forgiveness of sins." Using the Jewish lunar calendar, he showed them how to determine the exact month and day to meet, telling them it had to be done after 6:00 p.m. If they followed his instructions, their resurrections would take place on or about 1914.

Jesus reminded his apostles of God's plan to populate the earth with perfect, God-loving people, as was his original intention when he put Adam and Eve in the Garden. Faithful followers mentioned in the Old Testament, like Moses, David, Daniel, Esther, and Ruth, would be resurrected shortly after Armageddon and live forever on a paradise earth.

Jesus explained that after his death and up to 1935, God would put the heavenly calling into the minds and hearts of these chosen people. Why He would pick some and not others, He never told them. But they all knew it had nothing to do with anyone being better or worse than the billions of people who would eventually be rewarded with everlasting life on earth.

Hundreds of years passed after Jesus instituted the memorial of his death. In the late 1870s, the so-called Christian churches were teaching that everyone goes to heaven and holding communion as often as fifty-two times a year. Because of this misinformation, God wasn't even close to having 144,000 tagged for the heavenly calling. He was thousands of people short. But He was impressed with a former haberdasher turned Bible student, Pastor Charles Taze Russell. God talked to him, revealing His dilemma. The pastor listened and accepted His challenge. God also told him we're living in the time of the end and that the memorial needed to be celebrated properly. Russell began to mass-produce books, booklets, and magazines, informing people that the churches were telling them lies, while he alone told the truth. He attracted and organized people into a Club, trying to restore the early church as it was in the time of Jesus and his Apostles. He reinstated the annual memorial, telling those in the Club that many of them were heaven-bound. If so tagged, they must partake of the emblems. The majority of his future followers will have the earthly calling, like Mama. They'll have to attend the memorial service but won't partake of the symbolic bread and wine. They'll just observe.

That's not exactly what Mama told me when I was five years old, but by the time I was ten, I knew that's what she and other Club members believed.

What she did tell me was that I must shake my head no when the bread and wine were passed to me. Eating and drinking of the emblems unworthily would bring instant damnation and certain death without possibility of a resurrection. But by observing this memorial of Christ's death, I would celebrate the most important event to have ever happened in human history. Because Jesus sacrificed his life for me, I probably wouldn't have to die.

At the memorial service, I listened to a half-hour sermon summarizing much of what Mama told me. I also watched intently as the bread and wine were passed, counting seven people at our Hall who professed to have a future in God's heavenly kingdom. One was a homeless man just off the street. He gulped down a full glass of wine when it was passed to him. When he wasn't struck dead on the spot, I suspected Mama had exaggerated, although he held up the service while they searched for a clean glass and refilled it. When the emblems were passed to Lena Edwards, she bowed her head each time, mouthed a short silent prayer, and then partook. She munched gingerly before swallowing what appeared to be a stale cracker. When the wine was passed, she sipped as little as she could put in her large mouth. I noticed that she was the only woman partaking, and if Mama was right, why in the world had God chosen Lena Edwards over Fern Morrison?

Three months before the memorial, Mama received a long letter from Grandma. In it, she apologized for the episode they helped create at Christmas. While they didn't agree with her beliefs, they recognized her right to decide how she and Papa would raise their children. They were wrong and said it wouldn't happen again, hoping we would make our annual trip to Idaho during the summer, which we did in late July in our new car.

In November, shortly after I turned six, Mama told me I was old enough to go into the preaching work. The *placard ministry* is how I was initiated. I had to walk the Venice Beach pier with her, wearing a bulky, double-sided cardboard sign. It covered everything but my head, shoes, and arms, and it advertised a special talk they were having on Sunday related to the sins of the Catholic Church and God's condemnation of that religious group. I reluctantly trudged up and down an area the size of a block, handing out handbills promoting the special meeting and hoping I wouldn't see someone I knew.

Towards the end of the year, Mama warned me that Armageddon might come in October 1954. She figured the number forty and the month of October had special significance in Bible chronology. When you calculated forty years from the time God set His kingdom up in heaven in 1914, it wasn't a difficult assumption to make, or so she reasoned.

Death and Near Death
Chapter 11

Mama thought before the decade was over, she'd be living in paradise, edging ever closer to perfection. While she believed that process would take a thousand years, thinking about it thrilled her, and it was often the topic of conversation with other Club members.

But in January 1950, she got some unexpected news. She was pregnant. That was the last thing she and Papa wanted or could afford. Mary had been easy. But the memory of Susan's difficult first years still haunted Mama. Who knew what a fifth child would bring? And Mama wanted to spend more time in Club activity, not less.

I overheard my parents talking about it and their options. That's the first time I heard the word, "abortion." They wanted to pray about it. And of course, they wanted to get advice from a Club elder. Two weeks later, Mama told me that she and Papa had to go away for the day and they wanted me to stay at a neighbor's home overnight. My siblings stayed with different families.

After spending a day and a night at the neighbor's house, Mrs. Randall told me, "You'll be staying with us for another day."

"Why?" I asked. She wouldn't tell me. I was upset by this news, thinking all kinds of crazy things—none of them good. I sulked across the yard to their large sandbox and played alone for over an hour. Though I needed to go to the bathroom, I was determined to hold it, but I had waited too long. Embarrassed, I removed my underwear and tossed it in the Randalls' trashcan. When I told Mrs. Randall that I wanted to go to my house to get clean underwear, she suggested I use one of her eight-year-old daughter's clean, pink, cotton panties. That wasn't an acceptable option, so I decided to wear nothing under my jeans.

When our family was finally reunited, Mama appeared to be in good spirits, saying that she and Papa had gone for a well-needed rest and that everything was fine. It would be more than fifty years before I'd hear another word about what Mama really did when I stayed two nights with a neighbor.

In June 2001, shortly after Papa passed away at eighty-two years of age, I spent time with Mama, telling her what I suspected. She didn't seem surprised, acknowledging that if she had to do it over again, they would not have aborted the baby. It was a different time and she didn't want to dredge up the past. Then she said, "I'm glad you told me, but how did you find out?" When I told her, she further confessed, "Papa and I talked to Brother Allen before we decided what we'd do. It wasn't a congregational matter and he said it should be left up to our conscience. Of course, today the *Society* (Club) has changed its stance on this matter."

What I didn't confess to her was how many times while growing up I had thought about that potential brother or sister and what he or she would be like. Why that embryo and not mine? Were five children too many for my parents? If Mama really believed Armageddon was so near, why couldn't she have toughed it out for a few more years?

Our family had to come to grips with another dilemna in early March, when a member of our family contracted a life-threatening disease.

We had gone in the door-to-door work that Saturday morning, selling the *Watchtower* and *Awake!* The *Awake!* magazine was relatively new, having replaced the *Consolation* in the summer of 1946. Its purpose was to rehash the world news, giving the Club's spin on events.

My brother, Tim, had just turned five and was well into his second semester of kindergarten. He wanted to learn to ride his bike without training wheels. After *field service* and lunch, Papa and I offered to help. Within thirty minutes he was riding almost as well as I did. Papa went inside while Tim and I rode around the block several times, stopping occasionally to show neighbors his new skills. Next, we challenged the dirt trails on a large empty lot in front of our house for over an hour.

At mid-afternoon, I proposed a race. "Why don't we start at the house and go around the block? You go toward Charnock Road and I'll head toward Regent Street. Let's see who gets back here first." Tim liked the idea. When we passed each other on Sawtelle Boulevard, he was significantly behind. Once I got back to the house, I waited several minutes for him. As he approached, I noticed his bike wobbling. When he tried to stop and dismount in our front yard, he crashed onto the grass. I waited for him to get up. His upper body moved, but his legs appeared lifeless, so I disentangled him from his bike and suggested we go inside.

"Dickie, I can't! I can't move my legs! Go get Mama!"

At first, I thought he was kidding. When I tried to help him up, he started crying. "Please Dickie, get Mama. I can't move my legs!"

I ran inside, yelling for help. Papa reacted first. He reached down and picked Tim up, seeming to think all he needed was to be put upright on his feet. When Papa let go, Tim fell hard, landing directly on his face.

Within minutes, Mama, Papa, and several of our neighbors were huddled around Tim. He was running a high temperature. Something was seriously wrong, although they thought his condition had something to do with the excessive amount of time he had spent riding his bike. His legs were completely limp and he couldn't move them. Our next-door neighbor offered to babysit Susan, Mary, and me, while my parents rushed Tim to the hospital.

Our neighbor fed us supper, gave us our baths, and entertained us. When it was well past our normal bedtimes, she took us to our house and put us in bed. We eventually fell asleep with her repeated assurances that everything was okay ringing in our ears.

When I awoke the next morning, I looked to see if Tim was in his bed. It hadn't been slept in. Then I heard my parents talking and ran to their bedroom. They had been crying. Their eyes were bloodshot and they had gotten little sleep, if any.

Mama was happy to see me. She gave me a big hug and said, "Dickie, we're so proud of you. Mrs. Arness said you were such a big help with your sisters yesterday."

"Where's Tim?" I interrupted.

"He's at the General Hospital downtown. He's resting now with good doctors and nurses looking after him."

"What's wrong with him?"

"Tim has polio. But he'll be okay. They believe they've caught it early enough and he'll fully recover."

"When will he come home?"

"We don't know for sure, but if everything goes well, he could be back home in three months."

Aware of how serious it was, I asked, "Can I go see him?"

"Only Papa and I can see him right now. But he'll be home before you know it."

It was over four months before he could come home. As it turned out, Tim had to spend his first two weeks confined in an iron lung. He was lucky as he eventually recovered all of his body movement.

During the early stages of his disease, I learned how morbidly afraid Mama was of dying. The Club helped eradicate this fear with its promise of skipping over death to eternal life. But in life-threatening situations like Tim's, the Club did little to nothing. Its position was that the door-to-door ministry saved lives and had the highest priority. No elders of the Club came to comfort Tim or my parents. They didn't pray for his recovery at meetings. Club members didn't prepare meals for our family. And because blood transfusions weren't an issue in Tim's case, they gave no advice. His care was solely in the hands of the doctors.

During the first few weeks, Mama didn't know whether Tim would recover or not. Without direction or support from the Club, she often broke down, crying hysterically. She repeatedly told me that I must not worry, saying, "If Tim does die, he'll be resurrected in the new world and never die again." Repeating that promise to me, I suspect, helped her cope with her own fears.

She told me about a twenty-room mansion in San Diego called *Beth-Sarim*. It was built and maintained by the Club for people like Moses, David, Abraham, Isaac—and Tim, if he should die. Beth-Sarim was to be used by the newly resurrected for initial orientation in the new world after Armageddon. Apparently, San Diego's climate was just right and the facilities adequate for the millions of faithful people who would be brought back to life in the very near future. It would be the "Ellis Island" of God's new world. Logistically, this wasn't possible, but then math was never Mama's strong point.

Several years later, I learned that in 1929 the Club built this palace to accommodate the faithful Old Testament prophets whom they expected to make a pre-Armageddon appearance in order to prepare believers for the Apocalypse. At least that's what the members were told. But the truth is Beth-Sarim was the primary residence for the second president of the Club, Judge J. F. Rutherford. In fact, official records list him as the sole caretaker.

Shortly after his death in 1942, the Club had second thoughts about how this lavishly decorated Spanish villa was meant to be used. They decided that its purpose would be best served after Armageddon, the version Mama shared with me.

I found it odd how God changed His mind each time the Club appointed a new president. When I confronted Mama with these facts, she said, "Dickie, that's a pack of lies," wanting to know where I got such information. I let her know that a man I met in the door-to-door work said that's what the Club was telling its readers in the 1930s. Several weeks later, I located a 1937 issue of the *Watchtower* and a copy of the 1939 book, *Salvation*. And sure enough, the man was right. When I asked Mama to read pages 86 and 311, she refused. She knew what she believed and had no intention of reading anything that wasn't current spiritual food from the Club. She shook her head in disgust, telling me that Bible prophecy informed us that God's people would be lied about in the last days. It seemed to embolden her convictions.

I knew she would ultimately believe only what she wanted to believe. It's like what Mark Twain once said, "The trouble with the world is not that people know so little, but that they know so many things that ain't so."

Advice from the Club
Chapter 12

At age five my sister Susan lagged significantly behind other children of the same age in her language skills and attention span. Mama figured that once she was involved in a structured learning environment that would all change. And it was with those expectations that Susan started second semester kindergarten in January 1951.

Unfortunately, Susan's problems didn't go away. Her teacher could hardly understand what she said. She required constant attention. Two weeks later, Susan's teacher and the school's principal asked to meet with Mama. They got right to the point, telling her, "Mrs. Kelly, we aren't trained or organized to teach your daughter properly. We believe she has some serious learning disabilities and may be mentally retarded. The public schooling system is not structured to help kids like Susan. We're recommending that she undergo extensive testing at UCLA, one of the best medical schools in the country, at no cost to you. They will evaluate her condition, determine her learning potential, and recommend a developmental plan that will prepare her for a productive adult life."

Mama wasn't surprised. She knew from the first time she saw Susan that something was wrong. While Susan had been delivered painlessly, the ether had put Mama in a deep sleep, from which she awoke three hours after Susan's birth. When she finally did see her, the extreme misshaping of Susan's head and pervasive black and blue bruises caused by the metal delivery prongs were telltale evidence. Mama thought about Susan's first two years and her constant crying. When it came time for Susan to start school, Mama surmised she was operating at the mental and emotional level of a two year old, maybe even less. She had hoped public schooling would help and struggled with the thought of how embarrassing it would be to tell people that her daughter flunked kindergarten. But there was hope.

During the next three months, Susan was questioned, observed, x-rayed, and probed by several UCLA doctors and technicians. They reported that the front part of her brain was permanently damaged. The doctors said the condition was called "no power of concentration."

They hypothesized three possible reasons for her condition: It may have been the result of a lack of oxygen to Susan's brain during the ether-induced birthing process, the misuse of forceps pulling her head out during delivery, or it could just be genetic. While they could never be certain, Susan's condition matched the symptoms of hundreds of children delivered pain free by several of Beverly Hills' obstetricians in the mid- to late-1940s.

Regardless of how it happened, Susan had severe brain damage. There was good news, though. She was teachable. It would be a tedious process, but she could learn to improve her speech and with extra attention, she could eventually learn to read, write, and do numbers at an eight- to ten-year-old level.

The doctors recommended a special school and identified several excellent teachers. They told Mama that there was much she and Papa had to learn in order to help Susan progress in her future education.

While the plan was promising for Susan, the extra work and time required of my parents would be particularly challenging with three other children and Papa's full-time job. But neglecting these basic duties wasn't what worried them. They were more concerned about the time it would take away from their participation in Club activities and the door-to-door work.

Once they quantified how much time would be involved, they sought advice from the Club. But the *congregation servant* at their Hall wouldn't give it. He told them to speak with someone higher up in the Club hierarchy.

The congregation servant's position was equivalent to the head pastor at most churches. He served as a volunteer lay minister while holding a normal job outside of the Club in a factory or office. He was also one of the Hall's three elders, the others in order of rank being the assistant congregation servant and the bible study servant.

Once every six months, a *circuit servant* visited our Hall for a week. Our congregation servant reported to him. The circuit servant's position was a full-time job, paid in part from the Club's headquarters in Brooklyn, NY, and from contributions from members at the twenty or so Halls he visited. His duties were to assess and report how the elders and other members at the Hall were doing according to standards set up at Club headquarters, give lectures, act as judge and jury in disputes, make changes in the Hall's hierarchy if necessary, encourage the congregation to spend more time in the door-to-door ministry, and give advice to members.

Only men could be elders or circuit servants. The Club taught that God has a hierarchy that begins with Jehovah at the top. Below Jehovah comes Jesus. Below Him come all the angels. Below them come men. Below men come women, the lowest of God's human creation. Because women were lower than men, they couldn't minister from the pulpit or make decisions on congregational matters.

In Club hierarchy, the congregation servant was at the top of the organizational chart at the Hall. He reported to the circuit servant, who, in turn, reported to the *district servant*. This man's job was to mediate doctrinal issues and be responsible for the approximately twenty three-day conventions held during the year, which were called circuit assemblies.

When my parents explained their dilemma with Susan to their

congregation servant, he suggested they meet with both the *circuit* and district servant at the *circuit assembly* in May.

During that meeting they explained Susan's condition, what the UCLA doctors had recommended, and the amount of time they would have to spend to help her. And that, in order to help her, they'd have to miss meetings and spend less time in the door-to-door work.

The district servant said, "Brother and Sister Kelly, we can't tell you what to do. But we can ask you several questions that may help. Do you think we are living in the time of the end?"

Despite the fact that Papa was supposed to be the head of our family, Mama was the de facto leader, and she answered all the questions. "Yes, of course. We know no one knows the exact day and hour. But we wouldn't be surprised if Armageddon comes and we're living in the new world before this decade is over."

"What do you think will happen to Susan if she makes it into the new world?"

"I know she'll be there, because we plan on being there. Once in that environment, she'll grow to perfection, having a mind far better than she would have had in this world, under the most ideal of conditions."

"What do you think Jehovah would want you to be doing with all your available time before Armageddon?"

"We should be preaching the good news of God's kingdom."

"That's right. And Brother and Sister Kelly, how will you keep fresh and alert to do your best in the door-to-door work?"

"We'll do it by attending all the meetings and assemblies provided by Jehovah's organization."

"Yes. Now you know, we can't advise you on what to do in this matter. But, hopefully, we've asked some questions that will help you make the right decision. And don't forget to ask for Jehovah's guidance in prayer."

Regrettably, Mama took their advice, although she'd swear on a stack of Bibles the decision was her own. She ultimately settled on a bare minimum of training for Susan, which was nothing more than free babysitting. She was so convinced that the new world would arrive before any of her children left home that she ransomed Susan's future for it.

Susan turned sixty on December 21, 2006. She has never left home. She lives with my mother in a large, comfortable house in a small town in Iowa. She can't read or write. She has no math skills. But she goes regularly to all five weekly Club meetings, to two three-day circuit assembliest a year, and to an annual three- to five-day *district assembly* held during the summer. She frequently joins Mama in the door-to-door work, although she doesn't say a word.

Susan can be compulsive at times and is prone to short bouts of depression. Her pronunciation skills make understanding her challenging for an untrained listener. She understands almost everything she hears. Unfortunately, she can't always repeat the words exactly as she hears them. She cannot cook, drive, handle her finances, or comb her own hair.

Susan is likeable, appreciative, thoughtful, and happy. She is interested in getting to know what other people like and enjoy. She is intuitive, and if she senses someone has a problem she will try to help. But if someone shows the slightest bit of disdain for her condition through body language, she'll clam up. If you didn't hear her talk, you'd never know she has a disability, as she takes great pride in her physical appearance.

If someone asked Susan, while accompanied by Mama, what her name and age was she'd say, "My name is Tutan Olibia (Olivia) Ketty and I tickty. Is dat right, Mom?"

Susan's pronunciation skills could be a bit racy at times. While vacationing with my grandparents, she loved to ride in the back of Grandpa's pickup truck. Unfortunately, she couldn't say her "tr"s, replacing it with an "f" sound. While Grandpa didn't use the resulting word, he never failed to snicker when Susan asked, "Gampa, can I go in da pickup x#&*?"

One of the stories Grandma loved to tell family and friends about Susan was when she was nine years old and unhappy with how Grandma had styled her hair. Grandma told her it looked just fine. But Susan insisted that it could be improved, saying "I vetty paticula." She said it several times before Grandma finally figured out that she was trying to say, "I am very particular." She laughed, thinking that this girl was much smarter than she had given her credit for.

Learning at School
Chapter 13

In February 1952 my third grade class visited the La Brea Tar Pits in downtown Los Angeles. We had studied weeks in advance about prehistoric animals and knew at this site we'd see some of the best-preserved fossils in the world. As we toured the grounds and looked at exhibits, I was awed by a world so different from mine. The lifelike displays and giant skeletal remains made it easy to visualize what this part of Southern California looked like 40,000 years ago. Mammoths and saber-toothed tigers were particularly impressive, since they were so much bigger and fiercer than their modern-day counterparts. I imagined their agonizing deaths, as they sank slowly in the eerie, steamy ponds of tar. While that thought bothered me, I was pleased to see their well-preserved skeletons.

I imagined living thousands of years ago in a strange, hostile jungle. It dawned on me that the world was always changing. Extinction of any species was a possibility. I was intrigued by archeologists' work helping us learn about the past.

While walking home from school, I told Tim what I had seen and learned. I suggested we ask Mama to take our family to the La Brea Tar Pits sometime. Maybe we'd see an archeologist pull out the bones of a giant elephant-like creature from the past. We could even bring a picnic lunch and play in the nearby park.

When I told Mama about our field trip and how I'd like our family to go, she wasn't happy. She told Tim and me, "Science is a false God to those people who rely upon it for answers. If scientists used the Bible, they'd know how old life is and that evolution is not true."

According to Mama, each creative day referred to in the first chapter of Genesis was 7,000 years long and God didn't start making fish and birds until the fifth creative day. He only began creating wild land animals on the sixth day, finishing that work day when He created Adam and Eve. Right now we were in God's Sabbath day, the seventh day, and He was resting. She calculated that the earliest a land animal could have existed would be approximately 13,000 years ago.

She went on to tell us, "People have only been here on this planet for a little less than 6,000 years. We know from the Bible that those 6,000 years will come to an end at Armageddon, which will come and go before you boys are old enough to leave home. Then there will be the thousand-year reign of Christ. During that time, we will grow to perfection and the earth will be restored to the paradise God intended it to be. After that, God's rest period will be over. When He starts His next work week, we can only guess what He may decide to create. To me, the future is far more important than the past."

And with that, Mama discarded my excitement about discovering what happened 40,000 years ago in the area in which we now lived. Even more, she relegated my interest in science to a form of idol worship.

Later that night, while Tim and I were in bed, I whispered, "Do you believe what Mama said about how old life is?" Though he didn't answer, I continued, "Tim, I have a hard time believing her. I saw with my own eyes bones of extinct animals that lived here in Los Angeles 40,000 years ago!"

Two days later Mama took me aside, saying, "Dickie, Tim tells me that you don't believe what I told you about God's creation and how long life has been here on this earth."

My heart started to pound. Feeling betrayed by my brother, I was angry, but managed a lame denial saying, "Mama, I don't know what you're talking about."

"I think you do, Dickie. And I'm not happy with a lot of stuff you're learning in school, particularly that science nonsense. If you start believing it, God may block His Holy Spirit from you. If that happens, your survival at Armageddon will be in jeopardy. But don't worry, I'm going to make sure that doesn't happen. You're old enough to join the *theocratic ministry school* and you can't get a better education anywhere. I'm going to ask Brother Jalotti to enroll you this week. What do you think?"

"Sure, if that's what you want me to do."

At Mama's Kingdom Hall, one of the five weekly hour-long meetings we attended was the theocratic ministry school. Held Thursday at 7:30 p.m., its purpose was to train boys and men to speak from the pulpit and in the door-to-door work. Women and girls could only observe. That would change a few years later, when females were allotted one ten-minute part, but they had to do it sitting down and give their message to another woman.

The meeting started with a fifteen-minute speech, then two ten-minute talks, and it closed with an eight-minute Bible reading. The first speech was called "the instruction talk" and was given by an experienced speaker. The skill level for the other three ranged from bad to good.

A man called the theocratic ministry school servant, whose job was to critique and commend the speakers publicly, presided. Using a special report card prepared at Club headquarters, he graded the speaker on only three things at a time. It could be for audience contact, appropriate introduction, voice modulation, pronunciation, gestures, preparation, good conclusion, enthusiasm, etc.

Club headquarters controlled all subject material. If you were assigned one of the three sermons, you were told what book or magazine to use in developing your topic. If you were assigned the Bible reading, your preparation of an introduction and conclusion came from a Club textbook.

Mama enrolled me in the theocratic ministry school in late February 1952. My first assignment wasn't until early April, so I had plenty of time to prepare. I was going to read chapters twelve and thirteen of 1 Corinthians. Mama wrote a short introduction and conclusion for me.

Aware that soon I would have to walk up onto that raised stage, speak into a microphone, and be the center of attention for eight minutes, I started listening to what was being said at the meetings. I saw how nervous some speakers were. Some never made eye contact with the audience. Many mispronounced words. But there were also good speakers who knew how to pause to make a point, change the pitch of their voice to command attention, and gesture wisely. Some even told human-interest stories, better connecting their listeners to the point they were trying to make.

If I was going to get involved, I wanted to be like the good speakers. I knew I'd have to practice my part over and over again to make it possible. And that's what I did, sometimes three times a day over a three-week period. I got so good that my eye contact with an imaginary audience was almost perfect. Mama also coached me. She told me that when I first got on stage, I should look at my audience without saying a word for two to three seconds. So I practiced that as well, getting up from my bed and looking at Tim's empty bed like it was the Hall filled with the eighty people who would be listening.

I was very excited about going to the meeting to give my first talk. But once we arrived at the Hall, I started to feel the flutter of butterflies in my tummy. When I told Mama about it, she said, "Dickie, don't worry. You'll do just fine. Remember now, take deep breaths and breathe out slowly. Don't worry about the messenger. You've got a great message to share tonight and Jehovah will help you."

When it came my turn to speak on stage, I'd already waited almost fifty minutes. Joe Jalotti, the theocratic ministry school servant, introduced me, explaining that this was my first speaking assignment. I would be critiqued on my appearance, how I talked into the microphone, and my utilization of the allotted eight minutes.

I walked on stage dressed in a new suit, white shirt, and bow tie purchased at Penney's a few days before. My shoes were polished and scuff free. Mama had greased my dark brown hair with Brylcreem, parting it smartly on the left side with a small wave in the front. I put my Bible and notes on the podium and looked at my audience. I saw Mama smiling, Tim standing so he could see me, Papa looking like he didn't care one way or the other, Susan and Mary sitting on my parents' laps, and Fern Morrison nodding her head approvingly. Even Lena Edwards had her head propped up higher than normal.

I wasn't nervous and delivered the introduction without using my notes, pausing for effect several times. During my Bible reading, I tried to pronounce all the words clearly and correctly. I particularly enjoyed reading 1 Corinthians 13:2-4, doing so with enthusiasm:

If I have the gift of prophecy
And can fathom all mysteries and all knowledge
And if I have a faith
That can move mountains,
But have not love
I am nothing.
If I give all I possess to the poor
And surrender my body to the flames
But have not love
I gain nothing.
Love is patient.
Love is kind.
It does not envy,
It does not boast,
It is not proud.

Looking directly at my audience while I read, I noticed how pleased they appeared to be as they followed along in their Bibles. I got the distinct feeling that both the words and I were responsible for that, and I liked it.

I delivered my conclusion and started walking off the stage. When the audience clapped more generously than normal, I was grateful that Mama had enrolled me in this school.

It was time for my critique. Brother Jalotti said, "Young Brother Kelly, you made an excellent presentation. It's hard to believe that someone your age, with no public speaking experience, could do so well. You spoke for seven minutes and fifty-five seconds and that was excellent use of your time. Your appearance was outstanding, although I suspect Sister Kelly had something to do with that. You also spoke directly into the microphone at all times. The only criticism I have is that we'll have to wait six more weeks before we hear from you again."

I loved hearing those words. For the first time, I enjoyed something at Mama's Club. After the meeting, I was congratulated over and over again. My little ego was massaged beyond its wildest dreams.

The harsh reality of my success sank in when Brother Allen told Mama, "He may only be eight years old, Gail, but he's ready for the door-to-door work. Can you imagine the positive impression he'll make? People will listen to what that boy has to say."

The Stump Speech
Chapter 14

While I was taking a more active role in challenging Mama's beliefs, Tim was embracing them. His experience shaped his conscience and ultimately severed any chance for us to develop a close, trusting relationship.

Whenever I shared with him my concerns or doubts about Club beliefs, he appeared to listen and never challenged me, but he also never told me what he thought. Instead, he tattled to Mama. The consequences took a turn for the worse when Tim's second grade class met in my room for the Pledge of Allegiance one day. After his class lined up in the back of the room, my teacher led us through our morning patriotic ritual. I participated with my normal enthusiasm, never thinking that Tim might see or hear me. Of course, he reported back to Mama.

When I got home from school that day. it didn't take long before Mama confronted me with my unfaithfulness. I denied it. But she was having none of that. Tim had just told her the full story and relayed a conversation he had with a girl over a month before. She was curious about why he didn't salute the flag and I did. He hadn't said anything about it before because he wasn't sure it was true. But now he knew.

My brother was a spy and I felt betrayed. But that wasn't my problem now. I had lied and gotten caught. I started crying, wishing I had been honest with Mama when first confronted. I told her several times that I was sorry and wouldn't do it again.

She must have thought I was talking about saluting the flag, for she gave me a big smile and hug and said, "Dickie, we all make mistakes. I know it's difficult for you to be so different at school, but I'm looking out for your eternal life. Now you must promise to Jehovah that you'll never pledge allegiance to the flag again. Can you do that?"

It would have been easy to say "yes," but this was something new. She had never phrased an order like that before, and it bothered me to be forced to make Jehovah a promise. When she repeated the question, I finally answered, "I promise not to do it again." Of course, the "it" for me was "tell a lie," but for Mama, "it" was "the Pledge of Allegiance." And when she gave me another big hug, I decided not to clarify it for her.

Later, while alone in our backyard and feeling sorry for myself, I thought about each member of my family. I didn't like lying to Mama. Papa never played or talked with me—he only spanked me. Susan got too much attention. Tim was a tattletale. Mary was okay, but she'd never miss me. I wanted to be a normal kid with a normal family. I didn't like going to Club meetings. I wanted to run away from home. If my grandparents had lived close by, I'd run to them.

I was ready to explode. I jumped up, ran out of our yard, and crossed Charnock Road before ending up in a large open field behind the Manriquez home, a half mile away. I stopped at the edge of a large pollywog pond and decided to head for an area where about fifty mounds of dirt had been dumped over a year earlier. Eventually, I found an open area between two of the piles and hunkered down, out of sight from the rest of the world.

I stayed in that safe basin for almost two hours. At first, it felt good to be alone, like I was on some big journey. But it didn't take long for me to recognize the futility of my situation. I had no place to go but back home, although I decided not to leave my calm crater until it was nearly dark.

I never confided in Tim again. Any conversation we had was superficial. I knew he was smart, but he didn't mix well with other kids and was oblivious to my feelings. I often wondered if his time alone in an iron lung, the hospital, and the sanitarium where he recovered from polio had impacted his personality negatively. While growing up, he was always a loner, although he was far more sensitive to Mama's needs than I was.

In the summer of 1952 we took a three-week vacation. We first visited my grandparents for ten days and then traveled to western Idaho to spend time with Mama's sister Vera, her brother Ross, and their families. The main purpose for this trip, as Mama told our immediate family during our drive there, was to do some proselytizing. She hadn't given up on converting her parents, and this would be her first attempt at bringing her sister and brother into the truth.

While staying with my grandparents, I got much better acquainted with Daniel "Danny" Boone Evans. He was the son of Grandpa's younger brother, Dean Evans, and lived on a farm that adjoined my grandparents' property. Although Danny was a first cousin to Mama, he was only two years older than I was. During that visit we were inseparable. We played checkers, Sorry, Monopoly, and Canasta. He taught me how to play chess. We fished in Garden Creek and got lost in the unending forest of trees that bordered his property to the west. We searched for, and found, black obsidian arrowheads at an ancient Indian hunting site. Talking came easily for Danny and me, and we never ran out of things to say. He also accepted me for who I was.

We were playing Chinese checkers in his living room when Mama made an unplanned visit. Danny's mom, Camilla, who was Mama's favorite aunt, answered the door. The two of them talked about their families and people they knew. Then Mama started preaching. Camilla smiled and let her talk. When Mama pressed her, Camilla used a well-worn Bible to defend her beliefs. It didn't take long to see that neither of them was going to budge. But when Camilla was challenged on a specific doctrine, she always responded in a kind and loving way, while Mama responded to challenges by raising her voice and acting like she was insulted. That really embarrassed me.

Eventually, Camilla said, "Gail, you've got a beautiful family. We love all your kids. Dickie and Danny play so well together. And we're so proud of you. When you and Vera were growing up, you two had such a yearning for a more spiritual life. I see that you've found what you were looking for and that makes me happy. But I've got to get dinner going for my family right now. Perhaps we'll visit again before you have to leave."

Several days later, we traveled to Homedale, Idaho, where we stayed with Aunt Vera, Uncle Edwin, and their four boys. Perhaps because there were twelve of us under one roof, I never heard religion discussed.

On this visit, I got to know Aunt Vera's second-born son, Ronny, who was my age. Something clicked between us from the beginning. There was an openness and shared curiosity for life that made spending time with him special. The key was that we could talk with each other. He listened to what I said without passing judgment and I enjoyed hearing what he had to say.

While staying at Ronny's house, we made several afternoon trips to visit with my Uncle Ross, Aunt Jane, and their four children. Mama did her best to get them to see that she had the truth, but like all the other relatives on this trip, they weren't interested. In the car on our drive back home, Mama told us that she had no intention of giving up on any of her relatives. They were all good people and would eventually see that it was the truth. And I was grateful, for that meant I had two new friends.

Normally, I wouldn't have been allowed to play with Danny or Ronny. By Club standards they were *worldly boys,* and therefore, *bad association.* Since Mama joined the Club three years before, I had never played or talked with anyone outside the Club for any length of time. But because they were relatives and Mama hoped to convert their parents, I could spend time with them.

In September I started the fourth grade. Saddled with her isolation mentality and memories of my third grade science education, Mama would have homeschooled me had that been an option in those days. But she didn't have a choice.

I was assigned to Mrs. Magee's class. She was a hands-on teacher, who made sure her students knew the value of what they were learning. She also updated us daily on world events, making them relevant to our world.

Mrs. Magee believed that the only way a democratic society worked was when its citizens got involved. Voting was critical to making that happen. We learned about the upcoming presidential election and the two candidates, Dwight Eisenhower and Adlai Stevenson. She told us both men were qualified to succeed Harry Truman as the thirty-fourth president of the United States and wanted us to vote for one of them in a mock election. But she recommended that we first talk with our parents to get their advice.

I never told Mama about it, as I knew Club members didn't vote. They didn't believe in getting involved in worldly affairs. I once asked her why. She shared several Bible verses that made no sense to me, and said, "Now you can see why I don't vote. And besides, God's kingdom was set up in heaven in 1914 and it's the best government man could have. Why anyone would reject it over inferior man-made governments, I haven't a clue."

On several occasions, I overheard Mama talking about Eisenhower. She seemed to think his mother was a member of the Club, which it turns out she was, and I thought if Mama voted, she'd probably vote for him. So when Mrs. Magee asked for a show of hands of where we believed our families stood, I raised it for Eisenhower.

A few days later, she told our class, "Next week, we're going to hold mock presidential rallies during recess. This will involve all fourth, fifth, and sixth grade classes here at Charnock Road School. Two representatives from each of the six classrooms will be chosen to head the campaigns, one for Stevenson and one for Eisenhower. Those twelve students will also make short speeches, encouraging students to vote." It sounded exciting and I wondered who would be chosen from our room.

When Mrs. Magee announced that Betty Sisler would rally for Stevenson and Dickie Kelly for Eisenhower, I was stunned. I wasn't afraid to speak to groups of people but wondered what would happen if Mama found out. It was also possible that Tim could learn about it, although his third grade class wasn't going to be involved in the election. So I decided to talk with Mrs. Magee.

As class was being dismissed for the day, I said, "Mrs. Magee, I'd really like to give that speech and help lead the pep rally for Eisenhower. But I don't know what to say."

"Oh Dickie, I'd be pleased to help you. In fact, Betty asked me at lunch if I would help her. I'll write out three-minute speeches for both of you. I'll have them ready by tomorrow, so you'll have plenty of time to practice."

The next day, Mrs. Magee gave me my speech. It was neatly typed on two sheets of paper. The first time I read it, I was so excited. During my recess periods and lunchtime I read it over and over again. By the end of the day, I had it memorized.

I knew Mama would not have approved of what I was doing. I'd be in serious trouble if I got caught, but that didn't bother me.

When it was my day to speak I had an audience of 150 students, six teachers, and the principal. I started my speech yelling into the microphone. "It's time for a change." The Eisenhower supporters started yelling and clapping. I motioned for them to quiet down. Without using my notes, I told them how important it was that they vote in our mock election and why. I finished with, "Whether you're a Democrat, Republican, or just a concerned citizen, you need to vote on Election Day if you want democracy to work. Pick your candidate wisely and choose who you want to be the next president of the United States of America. I know who my choice is. I like Ike!"

The school yard erupted in cheering. Students started yelling back in unison, "I like Ike! I like Ike! I like Ike!" I was flushed with excitement.

Betty was asked to speak next. Nervous, she had to read from her notes. She delivered catchphrases like "You never had it so good," and "I love the Guv" in a monotone. Though the material was good, she never connected with the audience.

It took three days and six recesses for all twelve speakers to make their presentations. Two rallies were held at our Thursday morning recess, and that afternoon everyone voted. On Friday, our principal, Mrs. Connors, announced the results.

"We were very pleased with the mock election and rallies. You've done a wonderful job. We hope this exercise prepares you for the time you'll be old enough to vote. Now I'd like to announce the winner. You have elected General Dwight D. Eisenhower as your next president."

After the students let out a big cheer, Mrs. Connors continued, "I'm very proud of the Stevenson supporters as well. You put up a good fight and the election was very close. I noticed not one 'boo' from your group when I announced the winner. That is how the system should work.

"I also want to thank all twelve speakers for your talks and the way you campaigned. At no time was the opposing candidate attacked. While we may have differences of opinions on the candidates' policies, we need never attack their character.

"I'd like to give special recognition to one of our students. His speaking skills went well beyond what we're trying to teach here at Charnock Elementary. Richard Kelly, would you please come forward to accept this certificate of our appreciation for your involvement in this election?"

Not normally addressed by my formal name, it took me a second to realize that she was talking about me. I approached her and she handed me a certificate, asking everyone to give me a big hand. I was embarrassed and thrilled.

She asked me where I had learned to speak like that, and I was speechless. I wasn't going to tell her. When she asked again, I said that Mrs. Magee had helped me.

At the end of the school day, I put my award and several "I like Ike" buttons into my lunchbox, thinking I'd hide them somewhere or put them in the trash later in the day. The last thing I wanted was for Mama to find them.

Arriving home, Mama asked how my day had gone. She also wanted to know what I had in my lunch box.

"What do you mean?" I asked.

"Dickie, you've got some metal objects in your lunchbox. I can hear them."

I froze in fright, turned red, and couldn't speak.

"Dickie, what do you have in your box?"

"I got a speaking award from Mrs. Connors and my teacher gave me a bunch of 'I Like Ike' buttons."

"When did you give a speech and what was it about?"

"Mrs. Magee wrote out a three-minute speech for me about General Eisenhower."

"Did you tell them where you learned to speak so well?"

"No, Mama, because I know you don't believe in voting."

She asked me to bring my lunchbox to her and she opened it. After reading the certificate, she said, "Dickie, that's quite an honor. That had to make you feel very proud. And in one way, I'm proud of you, too. But I'm also disappointed. You know what you did was wrong, and I expect it won't happen again. Now take that paper and the pins and throw them in the trash."

I was amazed at her reaction. Normally, I'd get a strong lecture or a privilege would be taken away. At the time, I couldn't figure out why I had gotten off so lightly, although I think Mama recognized that I had clearly seen one of the benefits of my association with the Club. I wouldn't have been able to give that speech had I not been enrolled in the theocratic ministry school. But at the time, what was uppermost on my mind was that I had stood up to Mama and told her the truth.

The ultimate reward for my participation in the mock election came very early on Wednesday morning, November 5, 1952. When I awoke, the rest of my family was sound asleep. I got up and quietly tiptoed to the back door. No one heard me go outside. The morning air was cool and invigorating. I walked briskly down our asphalt driveway towards our copy of the *Los Angeles Examiner*. I picked

up the paper, unfolded it, and broke into a big, satisfied smile when I saw the front page head-line. There in large, bold print were the words, "Ike Wins in a Landslide."

Mary, Dickie, Mama, Tim, and Susan shortly before Dickie's stump speech.

Grandma Bean
Chapter 15

In January 1953, a few days after Dwight Eisenhower was sworn in as the thirty-fourth president of the United States, Mama told me that my Grandma Bean had sold her house in Johnstown, Pennsylvania, and was coming to live with us.

"Who is Grandma Bean?" I asked.

"She's your Papa's mother."

"Why do you call her Grandma Bean?"

Mama patiently explained to me the progression of Grandma Bean's names. She was born as Margaret Harris and had married Papa's daddy, Harry Kelly, becoming Margaret Kelly. They had two boys, Papa being the youngest. Two years after Papa was born, his older brother died choking on a peanut shell. Papa's daddy died unexpectedly four years later. With two deaths in the family within six years, Papa's mother had a nervous breakdown and couldn't take care of him. Papa had to live with an uncle and didn't see his mother for over two years. Then she married Frank Bean and became Margaret Bean. Shortly after that, Papa was reunited with his mother. He lived with them until he left home to join the Air Force. Mr. Bean had recently died, and except for an elderly sister, Papa was the only relative she had.

Now I was really curious and asked, "What does Grandma Bean look like?"

"Unfortunately, we don't have a picture of her. But if you'll come with me to my bedroom, I'll show you a large photograph of Papa when he was four years old with his biological father, Harry Kelly."

As I looked at the picture, I was struck by how much Papa resembled his father, and how much Tim, Susan, and Mary resembled Papa.

But Papa's father was dead and it was his mother who was going to come live with us and so I asked, "Whose room is she going to sleep in?"

"Papa and I are going to move Susan in with us, so Grandma Bean can sleep in the same room with Mary."

"When is she coming?"

"She'll arrive here by train towards the end of February."

"Does that mean she'll be a part of our family?"

"Yes, Dickie, and she can stay with us for as long as she wants."

If Papa was pleased or saddened by this new addition to our family, he never let on one way or the other. I suspect that Mama saw her as a potential convert and welcomed some help preparing meals and doing household chores. But since Mama had never met or even talked with her before, there was no way to know if she'd be a help or a hindrance.

Tim, Grandma Bean, Dickie, Susan, Mama, and Mary picnicking near Big Bear Lake, California.

Papa went alone to pick her up from the train station on Saturday, February 21. He called Mama to tell her that Grandma Bean had arrived safely and they'd be at the house soon. Mama hurriedly got us kids ready to meet her, dressing us up like we were going to the Hall. Papa's 1947 green Plymouth slowly pulled into the driveway and came to a stop. We were excited to finally get to see what Grandma Bean looked like. Papa got out first and walked in front of the car to the front passenger door. He opened the door and reached his arm in. A very pale white hand with light purple veins grabbed hold of it. He then helped lift an older woman to her feet. She had long, coarse, silver-white hair. It was braided in the back, hanging well past the belt she used to cinch her long, light green, silk dress. The skin on her face and arms was an ivory pink, much like the inside of an abalone shell. Remnants of freckles were clearly visible on cheeks daubed with light pink rouge. Her teeth were nearly perfect, though store-bought, with a dull yellow cast to them. But her best feature was a mammoth, contagious smile.

Mama came forward, shook her hand, and said, "So finally we meet. Welcome to the family, Grandma Bean."

Her voice crackled as she responded, "Gail, I'm so happy to meet you. Jack said you were an attractive woman and he wasn't kidding."

Papa was the next to talk. "Kids, I want you to meet your Grandma Bean."

Starting with Mary, she shook our hands and told us how pleased she was to meet us. But before giving me her perfunctory greeting, she hesitated. Perhaps it was because I looked so different. I was dark-complexioned with dark brown eyes and hair. My siblings were light-complexioned. Tim and Susan had bright red hair. Tim's eyes were deep blue and Susan's reddish-brown. Mary was a Marilyn Monroe blond with blue-green eyes. I could see Mama's discomfort with Grandma Bean's long pause, but she finally reached out and shook my hand, telling me how pleased she was to meet me. Then Papa pulled two large suitcases from the trunk and a box from the car and carried them into the house.

Mama had prepared a celebration meal, but as we ate, there was little conversation. Mama asked questions and Grandma Bean answered in as few words as possible. When we moved to the living room, there was still more silence than conversation.

Tim, Grandma Bean, Dickie, Susan, Papa, and Mary.

Grandma Bean made no attempt to engage anyone in conversation. Mama asked her to tell stories about Papa when he was a little boy. She declined, saying she couldn't remember any.

Perhaps she was tired from the trip and needed time to acclimate herself. But several days later, she still had made no effort to engage any of us in conversation. She and Papa didn't touch or make small talk. She was like a stranger living in our house.

By the end of two weeks, she had made no effort to help Mama with the meals or housework. Twice Mama asked if she'd take care of us kids while she ran errands. She declined both times saying she wasn't comfortable doing it. But she had paid for all of our groceries since she'd arrived and insisted she pay the monthly mortgage bill while she was living with us. And she had made absolutely no demands of any kind on my parents.

Just how and when Mama tried to convert her, I don't know. But by the middle of March, Mama told Papa that she just couldn't get through to her. Grandma Bean was a Baptist and had no intention of abandoning her faith. She didn't protest the religion her son had chosen and expected Mama to do the same with her.

Grandma Bean passed the first month and a half eating meals with our family, crocheting while sitting in the living room rocking chair, joining us on weekend drives to the San Fernando Valley, and listening to a small, ivory-colored radio that she brought with her from Pennsylvania. On Sunday morning, when we went to the Hall, we would drop her off at a large red brick Baptist Church on Venice Boulevard, and two hours later one of her fellow churchgoers would drive her home.

It was early in April when I discovered that this docile, detached old lady had some spark of life in her. Her radio gave her away. She loved baseball! When the major league baseball season started in 1953, she listened to delayed, simulated radio broadcasts of designated games, as well as to live coverage of the Hollywood Stars, a minor league farm club of the Pittsburgh Pirates, her favorite team back home. While the games were in progress, she kept a written record of everything that happened, which she called "keeping score."

I first discovered this passion of hers when I came home from school one day. Grandma Bean was listening to a baseball game, only it wasn't the Grandma Bean I knew. This person was animated and vibrant. It was like a light got turned on and she beamed with energy. After watching her for fifteen minutes, I knew this was a person and a game I wanted to get to know. So I started asking questions. I wanted to learn, and she was more than willing to teach me. Over the next two weeks, she explained how baseball was played, taught me how to "keep score," exposed me to the drama of the game, and told me who her baseball heroes were and why. I was hooked.

I knew that Mama didn't like me spending so much time with Grandma Bean. But I hadn't been giving Mama a hard time about going to the meetings or in the door-to-door work. She liked that. Furthermore, I had become friends with Georgie Alvarez, a boy my age whose family had started attending meetings at our Hall. So she left me alone.

On a Thursday evening shortly before I was supposed to get ready to go to the Hall, I told Mama that I wasn't feeling well and asked if I could stay home with Grandma Bean. I gave a convincing performance and Mama bought it. Ten minutes after they left,

I walked into Grandma Bean's room and asked if I could listen to the big game with her. Our Hollywood Stars were playing their crosstown rivals, the Los Angeles Angels. She gave me a big smile and told me she wouldn't tell my parents.

Towards the middle of May, she asked Mama if I could go with her to a Friday night baseball game at Gilmore Field. It featured the Hollywood Stars and the San Francisco Seals. I begged and pleaded with Mama to let me go. I knew that I was supposed to be going in the *magazine work* the next morning and she didn't like the idea of me staying up late the night before. So I told her I would spend three hours in the door-to-door work placing the *Watchtower* and *Awake!* the next day if she'd let me go.

Mama wasn't a fool and knew what I was up to. But she also believed that the more I went in the door-to-door work, the more likely I'd see it was the truth. For her, the more you participated in some Club activity, the greater your chances were for getting God's Spirit to help you.

Perhaps I sold my soul to the Club, but those three hours on Friday night with Grandma Bean were worth the price. Walking into that stadium during the first inning was a dream come true. It was my new world and Grandma Bean was leading me to it. The tall overhead lights made the playing field, grass, and players appear surreal; the cracks from the bats startled my senses, making me feel more alive than ever; and the sounds and smells from hawkers promoting their popcorn, peanuts, and hot dogs only enhanced the experience. Listening to a game on the radio was great, but this was like visiting the temple in Jerusalem during King Solomon's heyday.

Early in June, Mama decided Grandma Bean couldn't live with us anymore. She and Papa told her that she had to find a place of her own. I'm not certain how she took the news, but I never heard Grandma Bean say one bad word about my parents or the Club. The day she left, she told Papa that she wanted to leave her radio with me. She would buy a new one when she moved in with her older sister. After all, I was the only one who had taken the least bit of interest in anything she really enjoyed.

A week before my parents asked Grandma Bean to leave, I did something really stupid. After we had dropped her off at her church on Sunday morning and were on our way to the Hall, I naively asked, "Mama, could I go with Grandma Bean to her church sometime?"

Mama let out a shriek, turned her head to face me in the back seat of the car, and yelled. "Dickie, I can't believe you said that. Grandma Bean made her choice and she has rejected Jehovah God."

I tried to interrupt her, wanting to explain that I only wanted to see what the inside of her church looked like, but Mama just rambled on, "Now why would you want to go to her place of worship where they have all rejected Jehovah God as well? Her church and all churches teach lies. When Armageddon comes, they'll be the first to be destroyed. Now, don't let me hear you talk such foolishness again."

Mama used to tell me that she knew the Club was the only group with the truth because of the love the members had for one another. She claimed that anyone with an open mind and a pure heart could see it immediately. I always countered her by saying that it was conditional love.

I knew Club rules and its contempt for any person or group who didn't believe as its members did. And particularly for those who had a chance to hear the truth but rejected it. Club members' coldness and lack of common decency to the nonbeliever blatantly betrayed the love they claimed differentiated them from all other religious groups.

In fact, if a person became a Club member by getting baptized, he or she couldn't express an opinion contrary to the Club's stated beliefs. If they did–and didn't repent–they were disfellowshipped. Then they became a nonperson. I knew of a fifteen-year-old girl who openly challenged several of her parents' Club beliefs. When she refused to acknowledge her "wrongdoing," they told her that she could no longer eat her meals with them. She was forced to eat alone in another room.

After Grandma Bean left our house, no one in our family wrote or spoke to her again. When I asked if I could write to thank her for the radio, Mama told me that it wasn't a good idea, and that I should try to forget about her. But that wasn't about to happen. Grandma Bean had gifted me with her passion. This new world of baseball proved to be a welcome reprieve from the drudgery of the Club routine that I endured.

Six years later, when Papa was informed that she died, he didn't shed a tear. I asked my parents if Papa was going to her funeral and Mama spoke up with a firm "no." But she wanted me to know why and quoted Matthew 8:21, 22 where it says, "Another disciple said to him, 'Lord, first let me go and bury my father.' But Jesus told him, 'Follow me and let the dead bury their own dead.'"

It was becoming clear to me what was going to happen when I was old enough to disassociate from the Club.

Georgie, Sheila, and The Rod
Chapter 16

A few months before I first learned about Grandma Bean, three events occurred during a three-month period that helped me make sense of "who I was" in a Club world where conformity had a much higher priority than individuality.

In November, shortly after the 1952 elections, I started waking up at 5:30 a.m. Restless, I'd go quietly outside, get the newspaper, and read it in our living room. I had done it several times before Papa walked in on me. He informed me that the sound of the paper's pages turning had awakened him, and in the future I wasn't to get out of my bed until 6:30 a.m. At breakfast that morning, he told everyone in the family what I'd done, and made it clear that if I did it again, I'd be severely punished.

One of the key aspects of the Club experience for children was that *sparing the rod* was a no-no. Physical discipline was encouraged and Proverbs 13:24 was used by the Club to support its position. It states, "He who spares the rod hates his son, but he who loves him is careful to discipline him." Unfortunately, the Club emphasized the rod and not other forms of discipline. Because of that, excessive use of the proverbial rod was not uncommon.

Mama often slapped me in the face when I said something that displeased her. I resented that form of discipline. It made me

105

angry, not remorseful. As I got older I tried to dodge her blows, but I wasn't always successful.

Papa often spanked me with a belt hours after my infraction. And if he was angry, his anger was excessive.

As bad as my parents were at times, they were mild compared to some of the Club members at Mama's Hall. One man was a garage mechanic with massive hand strength. Whenever his four-year-old son started moving in his seat during one of our meetings, he'd tell him to sit still and listen. When it happened a second time, the dad would snap one of his muscular fingers into his forehead. The boy's head jerked back like a prize fighter's when dealt a knockout punch. It wasn't unusual to see some parents at the Hall spank babies less than a year old because they wouldn't be quiet.

The day after Papa threatened me with severe punishment, I awoke at my now normal 5:30 a.m. I tossed and turned for several minutes before deciding to take the risk. But this time, I read the paper on the front porch. It was still dark, so I quietly opened the front door and switched the porch light on.

I wasn't halfway through the comic section when I heard the door open. I looked up, saw Papa towering high above me, and froze in fear, aware of what was coming next.

He screamed loud enough for everyone in our house to hear, "What are you doing, boy? Do you know it's not even 6:00 a.m.? Get in your bedroom right now!"

I jumped up and ran to my bed. Then I heard Mama's voice, "What's going on, Jack? What are you yelling about?"

"That boy of yours has done it again! I told him less than twenty-four hours ago that he was to stay in bed until 6:30 a.m. Now he's gone and disobeyed me. He must be punished severely."

Mama saw the fire in his eyes as he picked out one of his biggest belts from the closet and, not liking that or the tone of his voice, said, "Jack, don't you talk that way to me. You're angry and you've got to calm down before you discipline Dickie."

Papa slapped his belt menacingly against their bedpost and replied, "Gail, that boy of yours is a bad one. If I don't do something now, he's going to turn into a juvenile delinquent."

"Jack, stop it! You're going to do something you'll regret."

Normally, Mama could control Papa when he was angry or his thinking wasn't clear, but not this day. When he entered my room, he was holding both ends of the belt in his right hand. His face was flushed blood-red and he had the eyes of a madman.

He was barely coherent as he yelled, "Dickie, you're going to get the spanking of your life! Now turn over on your stomach and take your punishment!"

"Please, don't! I don't deserve it. I won't do it again," I pleaded.

When I saw how futile my words were, I decided not to accommodate his unreasonable request. I sat straight up in my bed, pressed my back up against the wall, looked at him defiantly, and screamed, "I hate you! I hate you! I hate you!"

This only infuriated him. As he tried to dislodge me and turn me over, the buckle end of the belt slipped from his grasp. He stood up, reached his hand back as far as he could, and let loose with a violent swing. The buckle caught me directly in the forehead. A flash flood of blood raced over my eyes. Immediately, I turned my head toward the wall to protect my face. Again and again, he struck my back, neck, and arms. Then suddenly he stopped. Perhaps he saw the puddles of blood on my bed sheets or he finally heard Mama screaming, "Jack, stop it! Stop it! Stop it, before you kill him!"

When it was over, I felt no pain. I wiped blood from my eyes in order to see and looked first in disbelief at the bloodstained sheets and then the multiple lacerations on my arms. I only looked up at Papa when I heard him unleash an awful cry, begging and pleading for me to forgive him.

I suffered no long-term physical scars from the beating, and Mama convinced me that it would never happen again, which it didn't. But no one in our family was to tell anyone about this unfortunate event. Mama rationalized this order, saying, "We wouldn't want to say something that could bring reproach upon Jehovah's organization. After all, Papa is on the *congregation committee* (an elder) and he didn't mean to hit Dickie with the buckle end of the belt."

I knew Papa didn't mean to hurt me, so I was able to forgive him. But I wouldn't forget the disgust behind his words, "That boy of yours." In a fit of rage, Papa had seared them into my consciousness—I knew he wasn't my biological father. These words were far more powerful and lasting than any of his blows. And I would grapple with them for the next seven years before Mama finally acknowledged this truth.

The next month I met Georgie Alvarez. His parents had just bought a home in Culver City in an area where many members of our Hall lived. When we were first introduced at the Hall, I liked him right off the bat. We were both nine years of age, and I found it easy to talk with him. Within a few weeks, I learned that I could talk with him about my concerns with the Club without any reprisal and that he had his own concerns, which he shared with me.

Georgie was a charmer and could talk with adults as well as his peers. He seemed to always know what to say to make people feel good. Mama fell in love with him from the moment she met him, giving him her stamp of approval for *good association*. Little did she know that he was much smarter than I was at hiding his misgivings about the Club and far more worldly-wise too.

The first time he came to play with me at my house, he "worked the room," as I called it years later in my work life. He addressed Mama as "Sister Kelly," and took an interest in what she was doing and saying. He chatted briefly with all of my siblings and, had Papa been present, he would have charmed him for a few minutes as well. None of it was a façade. Georgie was comfortable with himself and genuinely interested in other people. When Mama told us to come to the kitchen table for a snack, he exuded sincere appreciation. You'd have thought he hadn't eaten in a week, the way he thanked Mama so profusely.

Georgie became Mama's nominee for the poster child of gratitude. Mama oozed joy while preparing him meals, serving them to him, and making small talk while he courteously consumed everything she put in front of him. I suspect if she had to choose between eating a bowl of creamy black walnut ice cream, receiving a beautiful bouquet of red long-stemmed roses, or putting food in front of Georgie, she'd opt for the latter.

When Georgie and I were alone, we fantasized about what it would be like to live with normal families—ones that didn't take religion so seriously—although Georgie's parents weren't nearly as fanatical about the Club as mine were. Eventually, I told him about the belt buckle incident and how Mama wanted to keep it a secret. He in turn told me about problems that he had with his dad.

I took no notice of Georgie's ethnic background until several months after we became friends. After one of our meetings, Georgie started up a conversation with a very homely girl named Arlene, who was a year older than we were. Her mother was a Club member and her dad a nonbeliever, and she didn't attend meetings very often. Georgie and Arlene must have talked for fifteen minutes before she had to leave.

Before Georgie joined me, Doug Crowell, who was the Hall bully when adults weren't around, stopped Georgie. He appeared to be giving him a lecture. When Georgie finally joined me, I asked what Doug had said.

"Oh, he warned me that Arlene's dad is prejudiced and that he hates 'spics.' It's just Doug being a jerk."

"So what's a 'spic'?" I asked.

"Oh, come on Dickie, you know what that means."

"No, Georgie, I don't."

Finally he explained, "It's a racial slur for Mexicans. You don't ever want to call Italians 'wops' or Mexicans 'spics,' because that insults them. But I'm not going to let Doug get me riled. I'm proud of my family history and who I am."

I later learned that Georgie's mother, Rosie, had Apache, Spanish, and Eastern European blood. His father's people had come from Spain and several indigenous southern Californian Indian tribes called the Chumash, Tongva, and Gabrielino. I was impressed, as I had no idea about my family history.

Several weeks after learning about Georgie's ancestry, I again ran afoul of Mama's rigid belief system, and it started at school. My teacher, Mrs. Magee, wanted us to make Valentine cards for our friends and family. After showing us how to design the card's cover, she showed us how to be creative and personal with our Valentine message. While I knew that Mama considered this kind of activity pagan, I figured no harm could come to me if I made cards for my classmates and the teachers and I didn't tell Mama about it.

On Friday, after working all week on our project, we exchanged Valentines. I not only received cards from most of the kids in my class, but from kids in other classrooms as well. I was flattered to have received so many cards and impressed by the variety of colorful cover designs. Art was never one of my strong points, but I appreciated that talent in others. Several of the Valentine messages were very personal, making me feel extra special. And for some reason, I figured that according to Mama, the sin was in making Valentines, not in receiving them. So I thought that both Mama and my sister, Mary Lyn, would like to see and read the Valentine cards I had received. Mary Lyn would particularly like the artwork and Mama the messages, learning that I was so well liked at school.

When I came home, I spread all of my Valentines on my bed and told Mary Lyn about them. She was admiring the artwork when Mama walked into the room. It took Mama a few seconds to assess what was going on before she gave both me and Mary Lyn that pained look in her eyes, and I knew immediately that this had been a bad idea.

"Why, Dickie, do you want to have any connection with this terrible holiday that honors the pagan goddess of love? It's just another trick of the Devil to keep people from worshipping the one and only true God, Jehovah. I'm very disappointed. Now what do you think would happen if Armageddon came at this very moment and you were sitting there with those idolatrous cards?"

She didn't wait for my answer. She scooped them up in a big pile and stuffed them into the trash bin. I knew that I had made a mistake and that Georgie wouldn't have been so stupid, but it hurt and I started to cry. I didn't want to live with Mama any longer and again decided to run away.

Slamming the front door behind me and running across the street was the easy part. But where would I go? I needed time and a place to think. That year the winter rains had filled the two vacant lots in front of our house with thick three-foot tall green grass. I knew where the neighbor kids had dug a good-sized hole in the ground weeks before and decided that would be the perfect place to hide while I worked out the details of my plan.

My foxhole sanctuary was very close to the property line of the corner house on Globe Avenue and Charnock Road, where new neighbors had just moved in. I had been sequestered in my secret hideout for nearly half an hour, making little progress on deciding where I was going to go, when I heard a girl's voice. "Hi, my name is Sheila Lawton. What's your name?"

Startled, I jumped up and turned around. In front of me stood a short heavyset girl wearing thick horned-rimmed glasses. I would later learn she was eight years old. She was also wearing a brand new Annie Oakley cowgirl outfit complete with hat, gun, and holster, and she wasn't the least bit threatening. So I told her my name.

"What are you doing in that hole?" she asked.

"I'm running away from home and I'm trying to figure out where to go."

Without the slightest hesitation, she said, "Would you like to play with me in my yard while you figure out where you're going?"

I didn't answer her question, but asked, "Do you live in that house?"

"Yes, would you like to see my dollhouse and new swing set?"

"Sure, but let's crawl through the grass to your yard. I don't want my parents to see me."

When we were safely hidden behind the high fence in her yard, I stood up and noticed how much taller I was than Sheila. While admiring her cowgirl outfit I asked, "Do you like playing cowboys and Indians?"

"Of course, silly. It's my favorite thing to do."

While swinging, we talked and talked. It was easy to talk with her. She seemed interested in what I had to say and we found out that we enjoyed doing many of the same things. Then she got right down to the issue at hand by asking, "So why are you running away?"

"My parents aren't happy with me. They're always telling me 'You can't do this and can't do that because God doesn't like you when you do.' I'm not supposed to play with kids who don't belong to our religion and if kids find out what religion I belong to, they don't want to play with me."

"Dickie, are you Jewish?"

"No, why do you ask?"

"Because I'm Jewish. A lot of kids at school won't play with me and my mom thinks that's the reason. But then it could be because I'm so smart."

"Sheila, I like talking and playing with you."

She smiled and said, "I like talking and playing with you, Dickie. But I don't think you're going to run away from home. Not at your age."

I confessed the physical futility of it, but told Sheila, "At least I can pretend and that helps." I went on to say, "When I'm alone, like I was in that hole where you found me, I pretend I'm a cowboy, and I live a long, long way from here. I imagine that I'm riding my horse all over the mountains of Idaho and don't ever have to go to Mama's Hall. And I pretend that when I go to school, I say and do things like all the other kids."

"Like what things, Dickie?"

"To begin with, I'd celebrate Valentine's Day. This past week, my classroom made Valentines and when I brought some cards home to show my mother, she jumped all over me. She thinks it's a wicked holiday and the Devil is behind it. She told me that God gets jealous and angry whenever He sees people sending Valentine cards because it doesn't bring glory to Him."

"Do you think God is like that?"

"Not really. But sometimes, I'm not sure. Mama says it doesn't matter what I think because I'm just a nine-year-old boy who doesn't have a clue what God's thoughts are. If I question her and tell her what I think, she says I think too much and I'm way too proud."

Over the next few years, both Sheila and Georgie proved to be good sounding boards for me. They were true friends who actively listened to my concerns—my lifelines in a sea of conflicts.

But Mama wasn't giving up on me quite yet. In spite of my resistance, she had high hopes that

Dickie and Sheila Lawton playing in the field across from Mama's house.

the Club's eight-day *international assembly* in New York City, held in July and August of 1953, would turn me around. And in fact, it did give me second thoughts. Perhaps I'd been wrong all along about the Club.

Yankee Stadium
Chapter 17

Mama believed her five weekly Club meetings provided almost the right amount of spiritual food to keep her healthy and active in the truth. To balance her spiritual diet, she attended three annual Club conventions: two three-day circuit assemblies and a four-day summer district assembly. It was at the latter, she believed, where some of the most nutritious spiritual meals were served.

In the summer of 1953, the Club decided to go all out and hold an eight-day international convention in New York City, at Yankee Stadium. It would be the largest gathering of Club members and the biggest spiritual feast in its seventy-four-year history.

The Club's president, Nathan H. Knorr, and vice president, Fred Franz, would be keynote speakers. New Club publications would be released for the first time. Hayden Covington, the well-known legal counsel for the Club, would be there as well. And more *new truths* than normal would be revealed for the first time.

Mama believed the "light of truth" got brighter and brighter as we moved closer to Armageddon. In other words, God progressively revealed more and more new truths to His earthly organization, the Club, as time inched closer to the end. With so many new truths about to be released at this coming assembly, Mama figured the new world was maybe just a year or two away.

115

Since God had to reverse Himself on the interpretation of the Bible hundreds of times during the Club's existence, it occurred to me that if God did indeed communicate exclusively with the Club, He was either the biggest teaser of all time or He was very confused, having to change His mind constantly.

For example, during the first sixty-six years of the Club's history, the Club encouraged its members to give blood to save lives. In a 1940 issue of the *Consolation*, a blood transfusion was spoken of favorably. But in 1945, God apparently changed His mind. Now, it seemed, He loathed the practice and Club members were told in a July *Watchtower* and at the summer assemblies that blood transfusions were right up there with murder, stealing, and adultery and it used Acts 15:20 and 29 to support its new position.

For the first time in 1923, and reinforced strongly in 1929, Club members were told smallpox vaccinations were an abomination to God. If you were a member in good standing, you couldn't allow the serum to enter your body or your child's. At the 1953 international assembly that Mama attended, she was delighted to learn that God had changed His mind and it was now okay to be vaccinated. Ironically, this was one of the many new truths shared at that assembly, providing Mama with evidence that Armageddon was just around the corner.

The Club has flip-flopped for years as to how Romans 13:1 should be interpreted. In this verse Paul tells Christians to be subject to the "higher powers." For twenty-seven years, the Club reported to its members that this referred to "secular governments." But as God is wont to do in Club theology, He changed His mind. In 1943, this new truth was announced: The "higher powers" were now "Jehovah and Jesus Christ." In 1964 God again changed His mind and said that the higher powers were the secular governments.

During my teen years, after one of our summer assemblies was over, Mama counted and identified all the new truths she had learned over the course of the four days. It was as if she had been to a dogma fashion show and knew now which interpretations were in style and which ones were out of date.

The eight-day convention at Yankee Stadium was announced to Club members a year in advance. And for the next twelve months, it was heavily promoted at meetings and in Club publications. If you considered yourself a good Club member, you knew you had to find a way to attend. This would be a spiritual smorgasbord and you couldn't afford to miss it if you were going to stay spiritually healthy.

Going to that assembly presented financial and logistical challenges for my parents. They didn't think their car could make the 6,000 miles and they didn't have enough money to pay for the expenses associated with such a long trip. But they were strong believers in prayer and decided to put it in God's hands.

Five months before the convention, things started to fall in place. Grandma Bean came to live with us in February, and the four months she paid for the mortgage and our groceries helped my parents build up an assembly nest egg. Brother Joe Jalotti, our congregation servant and a bachelor, bought a brand new four-passenger Willy's Jeep and told my parents in May that they could travel with him to the convention. My parents asked Grandma Bean if she would take care of us kids while they were away. She declined. Mama then asked her parents. Grandma said she'd do it if Mama brought us to their Idaho home.

In June my parents invited Brother Jalotti for dinner. After we kids were in bed, they had a long conversation about how to organize everything. They would drive two cars to Robin, Idaho, and leave my parents' car there. Since they had room for one more passenger in Joe's car, they decided to take Tim or me with them, but they couldn't decide which. They would drive day and night from Idaho to New York City, alternating drivers. They would eat homemade sandwiches, fruit, and vegetables along the way, and occasionally prepare hot meals over a Coleman stove.

Preparation for the housing of 100,000 out-of-towners that the Club expected to attend started in March. Club members living in the five boroughs of New York City went door to door asking homeowners for available rooms and beds. A month before the convention convened, they had secured thousands of clean, safe accommodations at reasonable rates. In addition, a large tented cafeteria would be set up on site to serve meals to all the attendees. Land was secured forty miles from Yankee Stadium and the site was prepared so that 45,000 people could move right in with their trailers and tents during the convention. It became a place fittingly called Trailer City. A direct telephone public-address line would pipe all the sessions live to this small, newly created Club city in New Jersey.

Toward the end of June, Brother Jalotti pulled me to the side at one of our meetings. With a big smile and his trademark little laugh that started most of his conversations, he said, "Dickie, I think you know that your parents are going with me to the convention at Yankee Stadium in July and that we have room for you or your brother. But they're having a hard time deciding which one of you should go. Personally, I think that assembly would do you a lot of good and I'd like to recommend that you go with us. How about you give it some thought and I'll talk to you about it in a week?"

Later, I asked Georgie what he would do if he were in my shoes. While no one in his family except his mother was going to attend, he saw it as a big adventure. He liked Brother Jalotti and thought driving across the country with him would be great. He wanted to see New York City and told me I'd be crazy to pass up the opportunity.

Eight days of Club meetings seemed excessive. But the opportunity to see and walk around Yankee Stadium appealed to me. After all, this was "the house that Ruth had built." Grandma Bean had taught me that. And being the baseball junkie that she was, I suspected that even she would sit through boring Club meetings if it meant spending time in a baseball shrine.

When Brother Jalotti asked what I wanted to do, I said, "Brother Jalotti, thank you for asking me. If you want me, I'd like to go with you."

"Dickie, first of all, let's get rid of this Brother Jalotti stuff. From now on, call me Joe. Now I'm going to tell your parents what I think about who should go with us. But in the end, they'll have the final say."

Mama broke the good news to me the next day. I don't think Joe ever told her that he had talked with me. She gave the impression it was her idea that I attend because I needed an infusion of spiritual food much more than Tim did. She told me that the experience would alter my attitude and behavior about the truth and help me to see the light.

We had been at my grandparents' house for two days when Joe arrived. The plan was for him to stay a day before we took off for Yankee Stadium. While he was there, I got cold feet and wanted to tell Mama that they should take Tim and not me. Joe seemed to sense it and asked me to show him around my grandparents' farm.

I was about to open the barn door to show Joe where Grandpa milked his five cows when he said, "So Dickie, you don't look like you're too excited about this trip we've planned."

It took me a while, but I finally responded. "Joe, I really love my grandparents. When I'm here with them, I feel like this is where I belong. If I could choose where I wanted to live, this is where it would be."

"Dickie, I know you've got some issues with your dad. And I know you don't always like going to the Hall or in the door-to-door work. But did you know when I was your age, I didn't either? It wasn't until I went to this big convention in Cedar Point, Ohio, many years ago that the lights went on for me. It was like my parents weren't telling me what to believe anymore; it was God's Holy Spirit directing me."

I was stunned that he seemed to know so much about me and what I was thinking. He was so soft-spoken about it, not like my parents, and he seemed to really care for me.

"Dickie, I believe what we have is the truth. But here I am thirty-three years old and still I have my doubts from time to time. I think that's normal and that's why the governing body organizes these yearly conventions. It's like a big shot in the arm, helping to get us all back on track."

I was speechless and looked away.

"Now Dickie, look at me and tell me what you're thinking."

"Joe, does Mama know you're talking about this to me?"

"No, Dickie. I just think that we're going to have a great time driving to New York City. The convention will get us all pumped up. Did you know the family we're going to stay with lives a block away from Ebbets Field, where the Brooklyn Dodgers play?"

Wow! He always knew what to say. But I was concerned that if Mama knew what I had been thinking, they would take Tim instead of me, so I asked, "Joe, you won't let Mama know we talked, will you?"

"Now Dickie, this little talk is strictly between you and me. How about giving me a smile?"

This was only the second man in my life who tried to reason with me, treating me like I had a right to my likes and dislikes. Grandpa was the first. I liked Joe. How could I not? And I wanted to spend more time with him.

On our two-and-a-half-day drive to New York City, Joe didn't disappoint me. He laughed a lot, and his laughter was contagious. He continually smiled, asked good questions, and took a genuine interest in everyone in our car. When we stopped in small parks along the way, Joe would play catch or take short walks with me. He cooked all the meals, putting an Italian spin on the dishes he prepared. When it was Joe's turn to drive, he'd tell me stories about things he did as a kid. Even when he slept, slumped over in his seat, I liked him.

One night, close to midnight, Joe took a wrong turn off the main highway. After several miles of driving on a narrow winding road, Joe brought our Jeep to a screeching stop, waking all three passengers. I first heard Joe's patented laugh and looked up to see a big cow not two feet in front of the car. She appeared to have no intention of moving. Joe rolled down his window, stuck his head out, and politely said, "Hey, Bossy, you ought to be moving on. Oops! I think I made the wrong turn a few miles back. No, you just stay right there. I'll back up and be on my way, or we'll be late for our assembly." And then he let loose with a huge laugh and apologized for waking us up.

This wasn't how Papa would have handled the situation had he been behind the wheel. Joe treated people and animals like he'd want them to treat him, and he never got riled up when things didn't go his way.

Early Saturday afternoon, on July 18, we arrived at the Brooklyn home where we would be staying for the next eight nights. We knocked on the door and were greeted by a very friendly, older Jewish couple. Inside, the first thing I noticed was their black and white television. The sound was turned way up and live images of the Brooklyn Dodgers danced across the screen. I could hardly believe my eyes. The man of the house saw me gawking and asked if I wanted to watch the game with him. I looked at Mama and she said it was okay. Watching Jackie Robinson, Duke Snider, Pee Wee Reese and the gang play baseball against the likes of Stan Musial, Enos Slaughter, and their St. Louis Cardinal teammates was a dream come true.

That evening, while the four of us were in my parents' bedroom, Joe reminded us that the convention would start early the next morning and end eight days later. There would be no morning sessions during the five week days, so we could visit places like the Empire State Building, the Statue of Liberty, and ride on the Staten Island ferry. In addition, he had organized it so that we would be able to take a tour of the Club's headquarters in Brooklyn Heights and its large, modern printing factory nearby. He was particularly excited about being able to see the Club's radio station (WBBR) and tower, located on Staten Island.

The plan was for us to take the subway to Yankee Stadium each day and eat all our meals standing up at the large Club cafeteria. The week-day series of lectures and testimonials would start after lunch and last for three-and-a-half hours. The evening sessions would begin at 6:00 p.m. and last for two-and-a-half hours. If all went well, we'd be in bed by 10:00 p.m. every night.

Finally, Joe asked us to hold hands while he prayed, "Jehovah,

Dickie and Mama at the top of the Empire State Building.

this may be the last great assembly we attend before you bring an end to this old world. So we want to be extra alert during the next eight days. And please, open up Dickie's heart and mind so that he, too, can hear and respond to your wise admonition."

Joe's prayer erased any second thoughts I had about going to the assembly. But a Club meeting takes on a totally different dimension when one is seated in the fresh air environment of historic Yankee Stadium with over 80,000 enthusiastic Club members, listening to skilled speakers deliver their messages through a state-of-the-art sound system. Some of those moments were electric. More than once, I felt the hair on my arms stand up and tingle, and I wondered if this was how God's Holy Spirit worked.

All the speakers were competent. And Hayden Covington was clearly in a league of his own. Having spent most of his career arguing and winning court cases for the Club in some of the most prestigious courtrooms in the country, his public speaking skills had been honed razor-sharp. He could work a large crowd into an emotional frenzy with the cadence and power of his words. Toward the end of one of his talks, he suddenly stopped, paused to promote what he had to say next, and yelled into his microphone. He sounded like an all-wise God should sound, enunciating each syllable of every word like it was being played on a fine musical instrument, branding each and every one of his words into my conscious mind, *"AR-MA-GED-DON* – will – be – the – WORST – thing – ever – to – happen – to – man-kind! GOD'S – *NEW*

122

– WORLD – will – be – the – BEST – **thing – ever – to – happen – to – man-kind... AND – IT – WILL – LAST – FOR-EVER!!"** When he stopped, the crowd went wild. The members clapped. They stood up. They clapped some more, louder and louder.

I felt the static energy in the air. I had goose pimples on my arms. I saw Joe looking at me. He clenched his right hand, which he held near his waist, and gave me a big thumbs up. He moved it up and down, as if to say, "Hey Dickie, can you feel God's Holy Spirit now?"

We ate our meals with Club conventioneers of all colors, nationalities, shapes, sizes, and ages, with whom pleasant small talk came easily. The people were always friendly and everyone wanted to know where everyone else was from. As Mama said, "When you're in this kind of environment with these kinds of people, it's about as close as you'll get to living in the new world and still be in this old one."

One of the most memorable aspects of the convention was the full water immersion baptism of 4,640 people. As men, women, and children rose from the water after being fully submerged, they seemed energized. Excitement and joy filled their eyes and I wondered if that, too, was God's Holy Spirit at work.

On the last day of the assembly, the Club's president delivered the keynote speech, "After Armageddon—God's New World" to a crowd of 165,829 people. There were 91,562 of us in Yankee Stadium, 25,240 in overflow tents, and 49,027 in Trailer City. Listening to him speak with such authority and conviction made me desperately want to believe him.

The eight days of that convention went by very fast. It seemed as if it had hardly started when we were saying our goodbyes. We had escaped into an insulated world of totally unique beliefs and a feeling that everyone we met was, or could be, our best friend. Even the New York City newspapers reported how remarkably clean, unprejudiced, efficient, thoughtful, happy, and orderly the Club conventioneers had been.

For the first time in my life, I felt good about going to Club meetings and spending time with Club people. While I hadn't abandoned my doubts, I hoped those might fall away in the months ahead if I went to all the meetings, regularly read the *Watchtower*, and went in the door-to-door work every week. I also hoped I might be just like Joe some day.

On our drive back to Idaho, we sang Kingdom Hall songs. Joe encouraged me to join in, even though I couldn't carry a tune. Once I got started, I felt the positive energy that singing can give a person and I thoroughly enjoyed it. Joe had also taped old copies of the *Watchtower* and *Awake!* on the inside of his back window to identify ourselves to other Club members. As we passed Club members' cars or were passed by them, the passengers enthusiastically raised their copies of Club magazines or books, broke into huge happy smiles, waved their hands wildly, and honked their horns. Every time, Joe would hoot and holler and wiggle with delight. It made it easy to think that all Club members were part of one big, happy family. And I was glad to be part of it.

A Dilemma
Chapter 18

I hadn't been home for two weeks when I was faced with a dilemma. The spirit, magic, and excitement of the Yankee Stadium assembly were all but a fleeting memory. The meetings I attended were just as boring and silly as ever. Going in the door-to-door work was the last thing I wanted to do. What had gone wrong?

Club members were often told that reading the *Watchtower* would cure anything from the spiritual blues to a mild depression. So I tried reading it several times, but that didn't do anything for me. I said silent prayers, asking God to help me get that Club spirit back, but for as much good as that did, I would have been better off talking to my bedpost.

Since I had three summer vacation weeks before I started the fifth grade, I decided to do more than just read Mama's two favorite Club books. I would underline in ink the answers to all the questions noted on the bottom of every page. This seemed to make sense because *The Truth Shall Make You Free* book had been rereleased at the big convention and attendees were encouraged to read it right away. It was originally published in 1943, but with so many new truths introduced over the previous ten years, it had been corrected and brought up to date.

I made a game out of the process of finding the answers in *Let*

God Be True and the newly rereleased book, hoping God's Spirit would take over at some point and give me that good feeling I had experienced at the convention. No thinking was required and I didn't challenge a thing. Within two weeks, I had underlined all the answers. Unfortunately, God's Spirit hadn't visited me even once. But something had happened. I had learned what the Club's core beliefs were and why it made those assumptions. I also had a better idea of why they appealed to Mama. And for the first time in my life, I could "talk the Club talk" if I had to.

At about this time I started to live two lives. It was never a conscious decision, it just seemed to happen. Around Mama and her Club friends, I tried to fit in, like I was one of them. At school, I was quite different. I tried to be more like the person I wanted to be. But in my heart of hearts, I really wanted Mama to be right. Perhaps with time, I'd see things just as clearly as she did. Maybe I'd even feel God's Spirit like Joe and Mama said people do when they're doing what He wants.

I turned ten in October 1953, and Mama believed I had turned the corner. I didn't balk at going to meetings or in the door-to-door work. I willingly got involved in Kingdom Hall activities and no longer challenged Mama's beliefs. But my mind hadn't stopped working. I still saw very clearly how silly and absurd some Club rules and beliefs were, but now I kept my mouth shut. I allowed myself to be entertained, as opposed to being irritated, by the often strange people who were attracted to the Club.

Two of the most unusual of those people were Minnie Temple and her mentally challenged daughter, Judith. They had started to attend our Hall early that year. And though they kept to themselves and hardly said a word, one would have been blind not to notice them.

Minnie was eighty-two, short and skinny, with wrinkled white skin and a constant smile. She wore drab Salvation Army dresses that were a size or two bigger than her tiny torso required. When she walked, she shuffled like Tim Conway imitating a 125-year-old man in constant motion on Carol Burnett sitcoms. She also professed to be of the *remnant*. These were Club members still alive here on this earth who believed they were selected by God to be one of the 144,000 and had the heavenly calling.

Judith was forty-six, big-boned, and had smooth white skin. She didn't look directly at people, never smiled, and seemed to be sad all the time. Like her mother, she wore hand-me-down dresses that never quite fit, although they were always much more colorful than the dresses Minnie wore. I never heard her talk, but she occasionally grunted if she wanted to get her mom's attention.

Normally they sat in the far back of the Hall. But at one of our Thursday night meetings, Minnie and her daughter showed up late. All the seats were occupied except for three in the front left row. Georgie and I were sitting in the second row on the right side and when Minnie and Judith were finally seated, we had an unobstructed view of the latecomers.

They hadn't been in their seats for five minutes when Judith started to fidget. She turned her body so that her legs and feet dangled into the aisle, resting her back on Minnie's shoulder. Then she proceeded to do the unthinkable—to pick her nose in public. And for the very first time, I saw her smile.

For the next few minutes, Judith picked, pulled, and extracted small bits of matter from her nostrils. She then carefully shaped and inspected each bit before dropping the tiny trophy into Minnie's outstretched and cupped hand. She repeated that cycle several times. When the well, so to speak, ran dry, Judith took all the unmentionables out of Minnie's hand and rolled them into a ball the size of a marble. She carefully inspected it, lifted it above her head, and dropped it into her mouth—then swallowed.

I closed my eyes, put my hands over my mouth, and audibly gagged. Georgie stood up, put his hand over his mouth, almost ran down the aisle, and opened the door to escape outside.

Mama was now aware that something was going on and gave me that "You'd better behave" stare. I struggled to regain my composure. I sat up straight and tried to look at the speaker. When I caught a glimpse of Judith, I felt sick and decided I had to get out of the Hall. I was hardly outside when Mama appeared, demanding an explanation. Fortunately, Georgie spoke up and told her what we had seen. Mama laughed and said, "Well boys, some interesting characters do come to the Hall. But I'll see what I can do so that the two of them always have seats in the back. You can stay out here a few more minutes, but when you come in, I want you to pay attention to the speaker this time."

Georgie and I stayed outside for several minutes. Georgie would share his take on what we had just witnessed and we'd howl with laughter. Then it was my turn and the laughing would start all over again. Finally Georgie said, "That was one of the grossest things I've ever seen. But it made my day to see that sad lady smile."

I agreed with Georgie and added, "Minnie must have known what Judith was doing because she held her hand out without taking her eye off the speaker. And she kept it there for ten minutes."

Shortly after Minnie started coming to our Hall, a fourteen-year-old girl came for the first time. Her name was Carol Harkey. Lena Edwards had been in the door-to-door work and talked with both the man and woman of the house. After listening to her spiel, they said that they weren't interested, but if she wanted to talk with their daughter that would be okay, since she was looking for a church to join. As it turned out, Carol liked what Lena said. They studied the *Let God Be True* book together, and soon after, Carol started coming to the Hall and she was baptized at a circuit assembly.

When Georgie and I got to know Carol better, we noticed that she had a short attention span and needed more love and attention than she was getting at home. And being so tall, skinny, and awkward, she wouldn't appeal to any of the boys we knew. Her one redeeming feature was a beautiful head of hair. Georgie used to say, "If you look just at her hair, she's a beautiful girl."

For the next four years, Carol entertained us with her off-the-wall comments and unpredictable behavior. One of her most memorable performances happened on a Thursday night. The first hour was uneventful. During the second hour, we had what the Club called the *service meeting*. Its purpose was to encourage and prepare members for the door-to-door work.

The meeting had hardly started when Carol walked up the aisle with her purse in hand and went into the bathroom. She stayed in there for over thirty minutes. When she came out, staggered gasps escaped from several people in the audience. Carol had cut most of her hair with kitchen scissors and it looked like a three-year-old had cut and styled it. Still, she smiled and walked tall as she strolled down the aisle.

It wasn't just people like Carol and Minnie and her daughter who entertained me at meetings. I was amused hearing some of the Club's more unusual beliefs explained from the pulpit. I often wondered why they thought it was so important to spend so much time on things that appeared to be so inconsequential.

One speaker went on and on about how we should dress at the Hall, as he seemed to think God really cared about such matters. Men or boys should never wear brush cuts or flat tops, although they should not wear their hair too long so as to be confused with a woman or a girl. God also didn't approve of facial hair or long sideburns for men and wanted them to wear suits, plain white shirts, and conservative ties. Colored shirts were a big no-no. Women and girls had to wear dresses that hung at least six inches below their knees. And the ladies were never to wear slacks or a pantsuit at the meetings or in the door-to-door work.

The silliest rule of all was that a baptized woman couldn't pray out loud if a man was present. But if ladies were meeting before going in the door-to-door work and wanted to petition God for His guidance on their day's work, the sister saying the prayer had to cover her head with a hat, scarf, a handkerchief, or even some tissue paper, if that was all that was available. Why was this so important? Because if one of God's angels happened to observe, he would be offended.

Papa once gave a talk stressing how important it was that the man should be the head of the family and that the wife be subject to her husband. He explained that this was how God had ordained things. Then he proceeded to cite Bible verse after Bible verse to prove his point. I thought that this message coming from him was a big joke. Mama was clearly the head of our family and not because she wanted to disobey God. Papa made poor decisions. It would have been a disaster for our family had he tried to run things.

Another speaker told us about the Bible story of Sodom and Gomorrah. Because the people who lived there were so wicked, God destroyed them all with fire and brimstone. While Lot and his wife were leaving the city, per God's advice, Lot's wife stopped to look behind and for her indiscretion, she was turned into a pillar of salt. The speaker tried to explain why it was relevant to us today, as we must never take our eyes off the prize of everlasting life in the new world. If we did, we could suffer the same fate as Lot's wife.

That little bit of information would have been sufficient, but he asked us whether we had ever wondered if any of those people who lived in Sodom and Gomorrah would be resurrected in the new world. I thought that question was silly. But apparently, that's not how the Club felt. He explained that in a 1952 issue of the *Watchtower*, some new truth had been revealed. After first reporting in 1879 that they would be resurrected, it was now believed they wouldn't be. Spending time on such silly stuff was not uncommon and it never failed to amuse me.

As I write today, I know that the Club reversed itself again on this issue in 1965 and reported that the people of Sodom and Gomorrah would be resurrected in the new world after all. Apparently the Club likes to spend time on this particular theological issue, for in 1988, it reversed itself again. At the moment, those people who were destroyed in those two sinful, disgusting cities will not be resurrected.

Yes, Club beliefs could be comical at times. But Georgie and I were not beyond doing some silly things ourselves. On one Saturday morning, we were in the door-to-door work together. Our goal was to place as many copies of the *Watchtower* and *Awake!* as possible. A half hour had passed with no success. Suddenly, Georgie stopped and said that he had an idea on how we could place more magazines. He wouldn't tell me what he had in mind, but cautioned me against laughing while he was doing the talking at the door.

He rang the bell and a woman answered. He proceeded to deliver our canned presentation with a German accent. Here was a dark-skinned Latino boy doing a perfect imitation and he had the lady's full attention. But the more he talked, the funnier it sounded. I wanted to laugh and tried to hold it. Then I just let loose, although I had the presence of mind to walk away.

In spite of my poor performance, the lady purchased both magazines for ten cents. Before our two hours of door-to-door work was up that morning, Georgie had placed sixteen magazines. I used a French accent and placed twelve magazines.

Once, a speaker asked all the boys in the Hall to come up on stage with him. He told us to think for a few minutes about who our heroes were. But first he wanted to explain what he believed was the critical ingredient of a real hero—courage. He told us that it takes real courage to knock on doors telling about God's kingdom and soon-to-come Armageddon, only to be rejected over and over again. He also told us that really courageous people believed and followed the Bible per the Club's interpretation, despite being persecuted for it. He challenged us to show courage by telling our schoolmates, relatives, and neighbors about the truth and God's new world. Then he started singling out one boy after another, asking who his hero or heroes were. Fortunately, I had some time to think before I responded. When it came my turn, I politely cleared my throat, grabbed hold of the handheld microphone, and spoke directly into it. "My hero is my mother." And I meant it, based on the criteria he had given us.

When I went back to my seat, I thought about the question that the speaker had posed. And while things were going well with Mama and me, I knew that my real heroes lived in books. First there was Little Lulu, my comic book hero. She was clever, brave, and could tell stories better than anyone I knew. And there was Freddy. He was a human-like pig that Robert R. Brooks had created and featured in several of his books. Freddy the Pig lived on Mr. Bean's farm and possessed exceptional organizational and leadership skills. He could solve some of the most difficult problems imaginable and lived quite well despite the fact that many people thought he was just a dumb animal. He was, in fact, far smarter than any human I knew.

Records and Rulings
Chapter 19

Mama thought it was an invention of God and it showed His wisdom. I, on the other hand, saw it as a man-made and creative way for the Club to exercise control over its members. Regardless of who was right, the record keeping and numbers game related to the door-to-door work was a way to set priorities at each Hall.

While engaged in the door-to-door work, members kept detailed records of the names and addresses of people showing interest and what literature they purchased. If no one was at home, the address was recorded on a special form and called on later in the week. After the door-to-door work was over, members recorded the number of hours they spent. And for some odd reason, participation in that ministry meant you were called a *publisher.*

Each week, all the publishers reported the number of hours they spent in the door-to-door work, making sure to sign their names. This information was dropped into a special box at the Hall, tabulated monthly, and recorded on a *publisher's record card.* Later, it was copied and sent to the Club headquarters in Brooklyn, NY.

But reporting hours wasn't enough. The Club also wanted to know how many books, booklets, magazines, and magazine subscriptions were placed, and how many *back calls* were made and *bible studies* conducted.

A back call was a follow-up call on someone who purchased Club literature. A bible study was counted for every unbaptized person who studied one of the Club's books with a baptized Club member.

To give some perspective, Mama once reported that she spent seventy-six hours in the door-to-door work for a month. She made twenty-seven back calls and held three bible studies, which included one with my sister Mary. She placed twelve books, twenty-two booklets, ninety-four magazines, and three subscriptions: two for the *Watchtower* and one for the *Awake!*

These were impressive numbers and well above the suggested Club goals. The Club recommended that to be considered spiritually healthy, each publisher in the congregation spend a minimum of twelve hours a month in the door-to-door work.

In 1954 our Hall started the year with ninety-two publishers. Nine months later, we were down to eighty. Our average hours dropped from eleven to nine per publisher. Back calls, bible studies, books, booklets, magazines, and subscriptions were decreasing as well. This information was recorded monthly and prominently displayed on a large scoreboard at the Hall for everyone to see. What made our drop even worse was that the averages for all publishers in the United States, reported in a small monthly paper called the *Informant,* were showing increases.

In October our circuit servant held a special meeting with our congregation servant, Joe Jalotti, to figure out why our numbers were dropping so dramatically. Generally when these things happened, Club members assumed there was an unclean person or persons in the congregation and believed because of this, God was blocking His Holy Spirit. And so the circuit servant's solution was to find the guilty party or parties and disfellowship them.

Within a month's time, Joe Jalotti announced at the service meeting on Thursday night that his brother Tommy was being disfellowshipped for conduct unbecoming of a Christian.

Papa later told Mama that Tommy was seen associating with homosexuals, and when confronted, he admitted to occasionally

134

participating in this lifestyle. He was asked to repent. When he refused, he was told that he would not be allowed to associate with the Club any longer. No one would speak with him, which included Joe and the rest of his family members. We were told that if we saw him on the street, we were forbidden to talk with him. He was to be shunned.

Mama was convinced that Tommy's sins had blocked God's Spirit and were the reason why our congregation numbers had dropped. She thanked Jehovah God for directing His earthly organization to make record keeping an integral part of the experience. She reasoned that without it, how would we have known something was wrong? But three months later, our numbers were still declining.

In February of 1955, someone at the Club's headquarters, with a recommendation from our circuit servant, decided that Joe was not a strong leader. Our Hall needed more housecleaning and a more aggressive congregation servant. Joe personally announced this information at one of our meetings and reported that a Brother Stuart Sanders would replace him. Stuart had worked at the Club's headquarters for the previous ten years and was considered a gifted troubleshooter who could solve the kind of problems we were having at our Hall.

Georgie and I were stunned at the news. Joe was likeable and never used guilt to get people to contribute more of their time or money to the Club. He always tried to appeal to the better side of people's nature.

A week later, Georgie and I had the opportunity to talk with Joe about his upcoming demotion. We wanted to know how he felt about it. He confessed that he was relieved that all that responsibility was going to be taken away from him and then said, "Boys, I can serve God in a lot of different ways. I don't need all this hassle. Let someone else do it and I'll help him any way I can. Besides, I've been single way too long, and I need to spend more of my time looking for a wife."

Georgie and I were impressed with Joe's candor. How could we not like someone so open, honest, and humble? Joe was definitely an exception and a good example for us.

A few days after Joe spoke with us, Georgie said, "Dickie, you know, I've been thinking a lot about what Joe told us. For him, that was probably the best thing that

Tim and Dickie shortly after Stuart Sanders came to Mama's Hall.

could have happened. You know, that looking for a wife stuff. If the Club is right, and Armageddon does come about like it says, and he doesn't make it, then the worst thing for him would be to be destroyed by God without ever having sex."

Over the course of the next three years, Georgie and I often recalled that observation. Because we were convinced that we wouldn't be among the Armageddon survivors, we were more concerned about not having our own experience.

But in the late summer of 1954, I wasn't thinking about that. I still wanted to capture the energy and spirit I felt at the 1953 Yankee Stadium convention. Both Mama and Joe were encouraging me to get baptized, as they believed that was the final missing piece of the puzzle in my life. And I wanted to believe them. But I also knew that I was taking a risk. Once I was baptized, I could be disfellowshipped for telling Mama or another Club member that I didn't believe in one or more of the Club's core doctrines.

I remember a man who came regularly to the Hall, participated at all the meetings, and spent over a hundred hours a month in the door-to-door work for years. He was held in high esteem by everyone in our congregation. Mama told me that he had brought many people into the truth. He also liked to read his Bible without using any of the Club's books or magazines.

Apparently, he read the Bible alone so much that he started questioning several of the Club's interpretations of Scripture. When he shared some of his newfound conclusions, he was reprimanded and told that he must meekly go along with God's organization. He should not pit human reasoning, sentiment, and personal feelings against the organization. He was then told that he must recognize not only Jehovah God as his Father but the organization in Brooklyn, the *Watchtower Bible and Tract Society* (the Club), as his Mother.

This was the breaking point, and he told them that he had to be true to his conscience. When he wouldn't repent and repudiate several of his new beliefs, he was disfellowshipped. At the Hall, he was called an apostate and deemed guilty of the greatest sin that a person could commit—losing one's faith.

That incident had occurred a year before and it didn't have an imminent or personal impact on my soon-to-be eleven-year-old mind. I wanted Mama to be right, and I wanted to catch the Club magic that I had experienced at the big convention in 1953. My baptism appeared to be the missing link.

Then I heard there would be a large baptism at a three-day *circuit assembly* the Club planned to hold September 10 - 12, 1954, at Gilmore Field. This was the stadium where the Hollywood Stars played and where Grandma Bean had introduced me to the bright, exciting world of baseball.

Several weeks before the assembly, I told Mama I wanted to get baptized. Her reaction was just what I expected: she was overjoyed. She hugged me. She shed some tears which really moved me. I could not have given her a better gift. I felt good about myself and was certain I was doing the right thing.

On a Saturday afternoon, September 11, 1954, I was seated on a wooden folding chair on the playing field of Gilmore Field. Eighty of us were to be baptized that day. People of all shapes, colors, sizes, and ages (at ten, I was the youngest) listened carefully as the speaker told us about the importance of full water baptism. We were informed that we were in the elite company of people like Jesus Christ and John the Baptist, who had symbolized their dedication to Jehovah God as we were going to do that day. He asked us several questions about our loyalty to God and His earthly organization, the Club. As a group, we shouted our response in the affirmative. Then he told us we were ready to be baptized.

We were escorted off the baseball field to a nearby swimming pool. Near the pool's edge, I was lined up in the middle of the group and could see the people in front of me walk toward the two men who did the baptizing. As each person came up out of the water, I recognized that look of joy that I had seen a little over a year before.

When it was finally my turn, both men securely grabbed hold of me and dipped me into the water. After I was fully submerged, they quickly pulled me up. When I could finally stand on my own two feet with water running down my eyes, they both smiled and congratulated me for the decision I had made to put Jehovah God first in my life.

As I walked out of the pool, I was caught up in the emotion of the ritualistic act. Something special had happened, although I didn't know for sure what it was. I certainly didn't see God's Spirit descending upon me, but I felt a strange calmness. I believed I had done the right thing and was confident that things would start to fall in place for me in the days to come.

I was then directed to a man sitting in a nearby chair. He asked me what my name was, how old I was, and what Hall I attended, recording my responses in a big notebook.

For the rest of that day and on Sunday, I had an odd feeling that all my past sins had been washed away and I was now right with God. If Armageddon had come on either day, I was pretty confident that I would be saved. I also expected something big to happen at any moment—but nothing did.

Unfortunately, as the days and weeks went by, my baptism didn't change a thing regarding how I felt about the Club. I had definitely pleased Mama and believed that made it worthwhile. I was also getting pretty good at making the best of a situation that I couldn't change.

I was fortunate to have friends like Georgie and Sheila. I could be totally honest with them, and their friendship helped me visualize the person I wanted to become someday. But I still didn't have a clue as to how I might make that someone a reality.

On Monday, when I went back to school, it was like my baptism had never occurred. I pledged allegiance to the flag of a country I had heard the speaker on Sunday claim was controlled by the Devil, and it didn't bother me in the least. Living two lives had now become routine. My transition between the two worlds was almost seamless.

Stuart Cleans House
Chapter 20

When he first walked into the Hall in March 1955 accompanied by a woman, he was not what Mama expected. She had imagined that our new congregation servant, Brother Stuart Sanders, would be tall, lean, single, and very regal looking. From her 1953 tour of *Bethel*, the name of the Club's headquarters, she had formed a mental picture of what the more than 500 bachelors working there should look like. And this brother, who had been married less than two weeks, definitely did not fit that description.

Stuart was thirty-five going on fifty, a few inches short of six feet, and weighed at least 250 pounds with most of his mass concentrated in his midsection. Even with the slightest gesture, his big tummy wiggled like jello and when he walked, his belly was in perpetual motion. He had thin, light-red hair, an odd oval-shaped head, unhealthy pinkish-white skin, piercing beady green eyes, and a serious perspiration problem. And his selection of suits, shirts, and ties would have made the late Chris Farley, of Saturday Night Live fame, look like a fashion trendsetter.

Irrespective of Stuart's appearance, when he talked or moved, he was a human dynamo. An unbelievable energy field was packed into his ungainly frame. He knew how to talk, entertain, and work a crowd. He was by far the best speaker we ever had at our Hall.

141

And while he could hold center stage and make people laugh, he was just as good at one-on-one conversations and in small groups. He could even be a good listener when he had to. He also had a special talent for getting people to talk about things they wouldn't ordinarily talk about.

Within the first two weeks, he met and charmed almost all of the publishers at our Hall, and Mama was his biggest fan. I don't think in her wildest dreams she imagined that God would send someone so good. And she wasn't alone in thinking that he breathed rich, fresh, spiritual energy into every meeting and social setting over which he presided.

He also met several times with just the kids at the Hall. He wasn't the least bit intimidating and seemed like he was really interested in our welfare. He told us that he wanted us to call him Stuart and his wife Gertrude. We learned that he liked baseball and enjoyed playing cards. But his priority was to serve God and to do what He required of him, and he hoped we felt the same way.

Stuart loved to cook and eat. His specialty was an eastern European spaghetti dish featuring spicy homemade sausages. At least twice a week for the first month at our Hall, he invited different families over to his small apartment, where he and his wife put on spaghetti feasts, making sure there was plenty of beer for himself and anyone else so inclined.

While our family was at his house for his signature meal, Stuart shared a story about himself and Gertrude that didn't match the image I thought someone in his position would want us to have of them.

He was more than halfway into the meal, having enjoyed several beers, when he proudly announced to a group of ten guests, which included me at eleven, Tim at ten, and Mary at six, "I don't know if you folks know it, but Gertrude was the fifth woman I asked to marry me in a span of three days." He then let out a big laugh, hesitated, looked over at his very red-faced wife, and continued.

"You see, I've always had this thing for the ladies and got myself into a little predicament. When I got called on the carpet for it, I was told that I better get married soon because the next time I got caught with my hand in the cookie jar, I'd be asked to leave Bethel (his home for the last ten years) with no place to go. In fact, the brother I talked with told me that if I could get myself hitched in a few weeks, they had this assignment at a Hall in Los Angeles that was right up my alley. So I got to making phone calls right away. Fortunately, Gertrude, who thought she was going to be an old maid before Armageddon arrived, accepted my offer and threw in her car and finances to boot."

As we drove home, Mama told Papa that she was impressed with Stuart's honesty and saw it as a good sign that he had taken them into his confidence. When I told Georgie about Stuart's surprising revelation the next day, he told me that he had heard the same story from two other families that had been at Stuart's house for dinner and wondered why he felt the need to tell a story like that to so many different people.

For the first six weeks, Stuart appeared to be just a normal, happy guy trying to get the lay of the land. He made no accusations and treated everyone with respect. If he was going to clean house, he was biding his time. But he did two things to set the stage for later events.

First, he appointed a judicial committee of three people (himself, Papa, and Roger Larson) and called it the congregation committee. Their role would be to investigate any wrongdoing that was reported at our Hall. And if necessary, they would interrogate and disfellowship the guilty party or parties. I thought his choice of people seemed rather strange. Neither Papa nor Roger was the head of his family and both lacked people skills.

Early in April, Stuart asked to speak with me in private. He was impressed with my speaking skills and my decision to get baptized at an early age, and he commented favorably on my averaging twelve hours per month of door-to-door work the past year. While he knew it was a few years away, he wondered if I had thought about going to Bethel someday.

I was dumbfounded and hardly knew what to say. My only

response was to ask what Bethel was like and why he thought I was a good candidate. When he was through answering my questions, I felt like I was being wooed and recruited to go to school and work at the House of God, which Bethel supposedly meant in Hebrew. Stuart claimed that more of God's Spirit was present at Bethel than at any other place in the world. He said that in his ten years there, he had been happy every single day. If it weren't for his weakness for the ladies, he would still be there.

Then he said, "Dickie, I'll tell you what we're going to do. I'm

Tim, Papa, Susan, and Dickie dressed for their door-to-door work.

going to start your training for Bethel service right now. I'm going to appoint you as our Hall's custodial servant. Your job every week will be to make sure that we have plenty of toilet paper and paper towels for the bathroom. I'd like you to clean the sink and toilet, and empty the trash, at least twice a week. In fact, I have a written list of things you'll need to do and a spot for you to check off when you've completed your duties. And you'll report to me once a month."

I was absolutely speechless. I felt as grown-up and proud as I had ever been. I was thrilled and flattered that he thought so highly of me. When Stuart announced my appointment from the pulpit a few days later, my head was swooning.

Toward the end of April, Stuart showed us another side of his personality that we hadn't seen before. It was like the kindly Dr. Jekyll decided to expose us to the mean, self-righteous Mr. Hyde.

144

He did so by opening the Thursday night meeting with an incredibly long and loud prayer. As soon as he started, I knew something was up. He screamed out to God like He was deaf and dumb, "Oh Jehovah God, I have some bad news for you tonight! Not all the publishers in this little Hall love you like I do." And he went on and on. He must have spit out venom for ten minutes. When he was finally finished, I looked up and saw that Stuart's face was blood-red, and that perspiration was pouring off him like he had been in a rainstorm. His white shirt was

Papa and Mama during Stuart Sanders' tenure at their Hall.

totally drenched and a small pool of sweat had formed on the carpet below his shoes.

He then told us that nineteen-year-old Michael Norris had been disfellowshipped for stealing cartons of cigarettes from his employer and selling them on the black market. He had been apprehended and released on bail, and a trial date had been set. While he had shown remorse to the congregation committee when they talked to him, they could not show him leniency because he had been stealing for over six months. Stuart went on giving details that only the hardcore gossip mongers at our Hall would have enjoyed.

Previously, when we were informed that someone was being disfellowshipped, we were told that it was because of "conduct unbecoming of a Christian." For the first time, we were getting the sordid details.

After the meeting, I overheard Michael's mother talking with another lady about her son. While eavesdropping, I heard her say,

145

"I'm just so grateful that Michael wasn't disfellowshipped for fornication." It was bad enough to listen to Stuart rant and rave and tell us far more than we needed to know, but I was stunned by this convoluted logic. How could anyone think that stealing was a lesser evil than premarital sex between a man and a woman? But in the Club environment, thinking skills were often a liability.

Over the next three months, Stuart announced the disfellowshipping of four more members at our Hall. He waited until the second one-hour meeting was over to give us the gory details, which meant we didn't get home until close to midnight.

We were also informed about three *probations*. Probation was an option that the committee had if they thought the person was repentant and a first time offender. It also helped if the guilty party confessed his sin before someone else reported it. While the sinner was identified, we were never told at the Hall exactly what he or she had done. Stuart would just say their conduct was unbecoming of a Christian. But because Papa was on the committee, he'd give Mama the details and she in turn would let little things slip to Tim and me. As probation was like a mild hand slapping, we could talk to the person like we normally did. And if he or she didn't repeat the offense during the next six months, the probation label was removed and all was forgotten.

The last four disfellowshippings and three probations were all related to sex—mainly younger people with overactive hormones who had fallen victim to a moment of passion.

Soon after Stuart announced his first disfellowshipping, he started giving us long guilt-trip lectures to get the publishers to spend more time in the door-to-door work. He told us about a ninety-three-year-old invalid woman who had what must have been every affliction a human being could have, but still averaged thirty-five hours a month of preaching. He reasoned that if she could do it, why couldn't we? The way he saw it, if you really loved Jehovah, you would somehow spend more time in the door-to-door work than you were currently doing. He also spiced up his routine by profiling a lukewarm publisher among us and making sure we knew this type of person wouldn't be an Armageddon survivor. And he never forgot to remind us that "broad and spacious is the road that leads to destruction, while cramped and narrow is the road leading to eternal life, and few ever find it." Georgie and I took to secretly calling him Doctor Jekyll and Mr. Guilt.

By the end of July, a remarkable thing happened at our Hall. We reported ninety-one publishers and our average hours per publisher for the door-to-door work were slightly over eleven. Stuart believed that his guilt trips, his "road is narrow" speeches, and his housecleaning techniques were responsible for those increases. And he had only just begun.

Unfortunately, I would also fall prey to his aversion for unclean things. My sinful conduct had started a little over two years earlier.

I was nine years old and taking my required one-hour Thursday afternoon nap. Because the meeting that night wasn't generally over until 10:15 p.m., Mama believed I needed the extra rest. But I couldn't go to sleep and just tossed and turned, while my brother Tim sacked out with ease on his bed on the other side of the room. As I fiddled back and forth, I discovered that a certain part of my body was even more restless than I was and wanted my attention. While lying on my stomach and in just the right position, I started to gently rock up and down. This repeated motion produced a very pleasant sensation. The more I moved, the better it felt. Before I knew it, my body began to shake, shiver, and then — boom. I never felt so good or so relaxed in my life. After that, it was like everything shut down and I wanted to close my eyes and go to sleep.

I didn't think that there was anything wrong with what I had done and felt comfortable repeating the experience a week later. I had done it for about two months before Mama realized how I was preparing for our Thursday night meeting. When we were alone in my room, she asked me point-blank, "Dickie, have you been playing with yourself?"

"I don't know what you're talking about," was my honest reply.

She clarified it by asking, "Have you been masturbating?"

147

"What does that mean?" I inquired.

Then she explained what it was and why good Christian boys shouldn't do it. She pulled out her Bible and read from Genesis 38. I learned about a man named Onan who displeased God by spilling his semen out on the ground and was destroyed by God because of it. After she was through, I told her that I wouldn't do it again. While I didn't do it the next Thursday, I did from time to time enjoy myself in this activity, thinking it was harmless and normal for people my age. Both Georgie and my friend Johnny Morrow had assured me of that.

In July 1955, while taking my Thursday afternoon nap at eleven years of age, Mama happened to come into my bedroom and caught me doing what Onan was guilty of. And Mama was not happy. She dove into a long lecture telling me how bad I was and what might have happened had Armageddon arrived while I was doing it. She said it was even worse since I was baptized now and had been given some responsibility at the Hall. She told me that I had to report my sin to Brother Sanders. But this is where I drew the line. She could rant and rave all she wanted, but I wasn't going to tell him.

A week passed and I wasn't about to budge. Then Stuart told me that he wanted to talk with me. He told me that Mama had told him what I had been doing and he had to remove me from my custodial role at the Hall. I was very upset with Stuart and Mama and looked directly into his beady eyes before blurting out, "Listen, I'm just a kid. What are you trying to do to me?" And I walked away. I wasn't going to allow Stuart to treat me like a criminal. When Mama asked what happened, I wouldn't look her in the eye and refused to talk with her for two whole days.

Devastated by her betrayal, I withdrew to the safety of my books for the next week. I lived in a make-believe world, imagining I was with my grandparents at their ranch in Idaho. And I began pulling my eyelashes out, one by one. With the exit of each hair follicle, I felt a twinge of pain, but it was a pleasant pain. If I was going to feel pain, I wanted it to be by my hands and not from Mama or Stuart. By the end of the week, I did not have one single eyelash left. And to make matters worse, I started sucking my fingers. It was a habit I hadn't entirely given up. While I had only been doing it privately and on rare occasions, it gave me comfort and helped me escape into a world of my choosing. Now, I didn't care who saw me and I was doing it all the time.

Unbeknownst to me, Mama had talked with Stuart on two occasions about how I was reacting. They agreed that their attempt to put the fear of Jehovah in me had gone too far. Their intentions were good, but they would have to backtrack on this one, or I could have some serious emotional problems.

Mama admitted to me that she had made a major mistake by telling Brother Sanders. It was a family matter and it should not have been shared, and she hoped I would forgive her. She confessed that masturbation by people my age wasn't unusual, but that she had been concerned that I might do it excessively and go crazy. It seems that while she was in high school, she toured a mental institution and saw several men doing it. I was grateful for her change of heart, but the wound was deep, and it would not quickly heal.

Stuart also talked with me, saying that he wanted me to have my old job back at the Hall. What I had done was a small sin, just a human imperfection. He did remind me that excessive masturbation or having sex with a girl were sins that I must never commit. My small sin, he claimed was one of those kinds of sins that Christ's death at Calvary paid for and I wouldn't be held accountable for it on Judgment Day. He told me that at Bethel, the cooks often put saltpeter in the food to reduce the sex drive for the young single men living and working there. He wanted to forget this incident had ever happened and hoped I would do the same.

But Stuart didn't learn from his excesses of supposed righteous indignation. When he decided to pick on Mama, he picked on somebody who could, and would, fight back. It happened in October, when he stopped at the house in the afternoon to get some documents that Papa had prepared for him. Mama was alone when he arrived. She invited him in and offered him coffee in the kitchen. I arrived home from school early and noticed Stuart's car in our driveway. I quietly came in the front door, sat down on the couch, and listened. Mama was probably just as shocked as I when I heard what he said.

"So Gail, tell me about Dickie's real father. It's pretty obvious to me that he is not one of Jack's kids."

"How dare you! Whether that's true or not, that is none of your business."

"So Gail, what are you trying to hide?"

"Stuart, please stop it!"

"Oh, so there really is a story here. What are you hiding?"

"Stuart, I'm going to have to ask you to leave."

"Gail, they tell me that leopards don't change their spots."

That's when I got up and walked into the kitchen. I didn't say a word and looked boldly at both of them. Stuart got up from his seat and said, "Thanks for the coffee and documents. I'll see you two at the next meeting."

Mama never said a word to me about what I had heard, but that was the end of her adoration for Stuart. He had stayed one day too long for her, and she wasn't bashful to let Papa and other Club officials know that she wanted him replaced.

But the straw that did Stuart in was his last disfellowshipping in January 1956. Our Thursday night meeting had lasted longer than normal and it was getting close to 10:30 p.m. Stuart told us that he had one last item on the agenda and it was a serious matter. One of our members had committed a grievous sin against the Holy Spirit and would be disfellowshipped that night. But for some strange reason he prolonged the identification of the guilty party. Months before, it had become apparent that Stuart loved his job as God's executioner, and tonight was no exception. He was savoring this moment.

Then, out of nowhere, he told us that it was Carol Harkey. What made it most unusual was that she was in attendance at the meeting that night. Without even thinking, I turned in my seat to look at Carol sitting three rows behind me, with her head buried in her lap, crying. Mama reached over and cuffed me, signaling that

I had to return my attention to the speaker.

Stuart's face was red, and sweat was pouring out of him as he told us why we wouldn't be able to talk or associate with Carol in the future. He provided unbelievable details about her sex life and why it didn't hold up to God's basic guidelines for living a clean Christian life. It was like he was getting turned on by telling us such explicit details.

While Carol may have made a mistake of judgment, she was a sincere and honest person. Only seventeen, she was uncomplicated and very vulnerable. Her parents were alcoholics and nonbelievers, and life had to be a challenge for her. She didn't have the best education and often made decisions that weren't well thought out. But she was trying to make a life for herself the best way she could and was bound to make some mistakes along the way. Why Stuart decided she needed to be disfellowshipped or have such intimate details shared, only he knew.

Stuart ranted about Carol for nearly twenty minutes. When the meeting was over, I couldn't get outside of the Hall to the fresh night air fast enough. Unfortunately, as I exited, Carol was in the same chair and position. She hadn't moved, or tried to leave, and everyone pretended that she didn't exist. When I met up with Georgie on the sidewalk, he was more than irate, calling Stuart as many off-color and body-part names as he could think of.

Finally, he made some sense when he said, "Dickie, I don't care what they do to me. I've got to go in there and help that poor girl. Are you with me?"

It was an act of defiance and the right thing to do as far as I was concerned. Georgie led the way as we marched back into the Hall and up to Carol. It took a while, but we finally coaxed her to her feet and helped her outside. While no one made an effort to stop us, the sad part was that it took two twelve-year-old boys to do what any thinking civilized adult would have done. Stuart was a tyrant, but because the attendees at the Hall that night believed his actions were approved by God, they abdicated basic human compassion.

Georgie walked Carol home that night. She only lived about two blocks from the Hall. When Mama finally confronted me, I was pleasantly surprised. She was not mad at me. She told me that she was proud of both Georgie and me, as we had done the right thing. She only wished she had acted quicker to help Carol. Mama could be like that at times. Unfortunately, her internal default mechanisms were hardwired with a Club motherboard that had atrophied most of the natural affection skills she once had.

When I talked with Georgie a few days later and asked what was said between Carol and him on their way to her house, he told me a very interesting story. "I kept telling her over and over not to worry and that you and I would always be her friends. We'd talk to her anytime and anywhere. I told her what a creep Brother Sanders was and that he should be taken out in the back lot and shot to death.

"It took a while, but then she got to talking, telling me that it was all a big mistake. It seems she met this guy at the Santa Monica pier and they hit it off right away. A few hours later, he asked her to come to his apartment to check out his record collection. Once she was there, he all but raped her, but Brother Sanders wasn't believing a word of it. She also said that your dad and Brother Larson weren't at the committee meeting. Brother Sanders brought two guys she had never seen before and they never said a word. Brother Sanders did all the talking."

While I was trying to absorb the revelation that Georgie was sharing with me, he switched gears without missing a beat. "You know, before I learned what had really happened, I thought I'd get a smile out of her if I asked her what sex was like and whether you and I would like it or not. I was going to say that we probably wouldn't end up experiencing it with Armageddon so close, but we at least wanted to know what it was like. Then I thought that's the last thing she needed. She was going through hell and didn't need that kind of crap."

Stuart was removed as our congregation servant less than a month later and reassigned to a position where he had no authority, except to preach in the door-to-door work. Within days after that Carol Harkey was reinstated. We were never told why or what really happened. We were only informed that her case had been handled improperly. Now, we were to welcome her back as our Christian sister and shower her with our love.

I was glad to see that the right thing was eventually done. But the reality was that eleven months passed before a monster was identified and removed. Part of that was due to the fact that all decision making in the Club was done primarily by an inner circle of old men who were cranky, insensitive, and isolated from reality. To them, God was a sexist who treated women like they didn't have a brain. He was an executioner, mean spirited at times, stern, and tough. And, He planned to destroy all those who didn't worship Him or acknowledge His earthly organization. With that kind of mentality at the top, someone like Stuart could easily blend in for a while. But even the Club had its limits.

Grandpa's Kisses
Chapter 21

Several months before and after Stuart's removal, I verged on the brink of an emotional breakdown. I had lost my self-esteem. I had gone from being one of the top students during my six years at grammar school, to being just a so-so student in the seventh-grade. Now at age twelve, I felt no purpose for my life, and any direction that I was given made little sense. My feigned belief in Mama's Club only made things worse. I wanted to stand up to Mama, but I couldn't.

While I clearly knew what I did not believe, that did me little good. What I needed was a good psychologist who could talk with Mama and me, and tell us how I could regain my self-confidence. But that wasn't going to happen. Getting help from a college-educated psychologist was a no-no. Club members believed that emotional problems were solved by reading the Watchtower and with help from an elder.

If things were going to turn around, I needed to find someone I could trust and something I could believe in—something that gave meaning to my life and a hope for the future. I also needed to be able to make a meaningful contribution to a world that Mama believed was destined for destruction. While none of this seemed likely to happen, things would change during our summer vacation in July 1956.

The vacation started like all previous trips to visit my grand-parents. I was very excited and more than ready, knowing that for three weeks we wouldn't attend a Club meeting. I wouldn't have to go from door to door selling the *Watchtower, Awake!*, or other Club literature. And I would get to spend time with normal people I loved, like Grandma, Grandpa, and my cousin Danny, in a place that I dreamed of living almost every day of my life.

The drive from our home in West Los Angeles to Robin, Idaho, started when Papa came home from work on a Friday afternoon in midsummer. Mama had the luggage packed and a small arsenal of sandwiches, fruit, celery, carrots, cookies, and thermos bottles filled to the brim with Kool-Aid. We would only have to stop for gas, potty breaks, or to replenish the radiator with water we carried in a canvas bag roped over the hood ornament on the front of the car. At midnight, we were in the middle of the Mojave Desert with all the windows rolled down, and all was well. Mama and Mary were slumped over, sleeping in the front seat of our faded green 1947 Plymouth. Susan and Tim slept like logs in the back seat with me. Papa and I were wide awake as he alertly steered us to the Promised Land.

Papa stopped for gas on the outskirts of Las Vegas, Nevada, not yet the big city it would become. Mama woke up and gently eased her door open, hoping none of us kids would waken. I quietly opened my door and stepped outside. It was warm and a soft, gentle wind greeted my perspiring forehead. The nearby lights flickered on and off, giving a surreal feel to my new surroundings. Although I should have been dog-tired, I felt wired and fully alive.

At first, Papa didn't notice that I was outside of the car. But when he did, he was quick to say, "Dickie, why are you up? You should be sleeping. Get back in the car."

Fortunately, Mama responded by saying, "Now Jack, leave him alone. If he can't sleep, he can't sleep."

Much later that day, as we crossed the Utah border into Idaho, I knew that we had less than two hours before we would be at Grandma and Grandpa's house. I still had not gotten a wink of sleep, but neither had Papa in what would be a twenty-four-hour drive from our house to theirs. As I contemplated our arrival, I thought about Grandma and how she would kiss me on the lips when I got to the front door. And as much as I loved her, I always dreaded that greeting. But I couldn't avoid it. Grandma's kiss was the price I would have to pay to live with them for the next three weeks.

As our car rolled slowly up the gravel road, the sight of the massive gap in the mountain, less than a mile west of my grandparents' property, overwhelmed me. Tears welled in my eyes, my stomach churned, and I felt lightheaded. This was a sacred landmark, a shrine that captured the mystery and majesty of creation. Even to this day, when I first see the Gap, I feel the presence of a grand, creative force. At each glance, I'm always washed over by gratefulness for the life with which I've been blessed.

The Gap

As we tumbled out of the car, I lingered behind. Mary was the first to get Grandma's kiss. Then Grandpa shook her hand. What a contrast in expressing their love. I was fourth in line to get Grandma's kiss, and when it was over I felt special and loved. Mama never showed that kind of affection. Next was Grandpa's handshake. He held my hand in both of his hands and vigorously shook them. It was Grandpa's way of saying that he was glad I was there. But still I wondered why Grandma kissed us and Grandpa shook our hand.

I felt comfortable as soon as we walked into their house. This

157

was where I belonged. Grandpa's unique and familiar body odor lingered pleasantly in the air. I felt safe and secure. For the first few minutes, the house was filled with lively, pleasant chatter about our drive and the status of relatives and common friends. Grandma excused herself to start dinner. Soon the engaging aroma of fried chicken trickled into the living room.

When we were asked to come to the dinner table, a large platter of steaming hot chicken breasts, legs, wings, and thighs greeted us. It was joined by a large white bowl of fresh, steamed green beans smothered in bacon bits; thin, fried slices of golden brown Idaho potatoes; puffy, mouthwatering homemade biscuits; creamy rich butter; homemade chokecherry, strawberry, and blackberry preserves; and large glasses of cold milk. As soon as everyone was seated, we began eating in earnest.

No prayer was said before dinner or any meal at my grandparents' house. I liked that. I always felt uncomfortable with Club members' mealtime prayers. First of all, a woman couldn't pray when a man was present. And when Papa prayed before a meal, the food always got cold before he finished his boring and meandering conversation with his God.

Our dinner that early evening tasted as good as it looked. After a dessert of lemon meringue pie, my lack of sleep for thirty-six hours hit me. I wasn't bashful about letting Grandma know I was ready for bed. My request made her laugh and she said, "Now that's a first for you. Normally, your mom has to ask you to go to bed several times before you're ready." Then she grabbed my hand and escorted me to the basement, where a large featherbed awaited me.

When I awoke the next morning, light was just beginning to find its way through the narrow basement windows. Translucent colors radiated from the large blue-tinted mason jars that housed Grandma's canned tomatoes, green and yellow string beans, and chokecherry jellies. I was mesmerized. Years later in Paris, while admiring Notre Dame's stained glass windows, I was reminded of that morning in 1956 when I experienced the surreal beauty of light and colors in my sanctuary.

After my short morning worship, I quietly slipped out of bed, making sure not to awaken Tim. I dressed and walked up the creaking wooden steps. No one was up yet. I looked for Grandpa's hats hanging on the wall of the indoor porch and found one of my favorites. It had his signature smell. I pulled it tightly over my head and went outdoors. To my pleasant surprise, Grandpa was saddling his horse, Silver, just outside the barbed-wire fence that kept the cattle and horses off the thick green grass surrounding the house. I began walking in Grandpa's direction when he spotted me. "Well, good morning, Dickie. You caught me just in time. Do you want to ride with me to check on the cattle?" His white-faced Hereford steers were pasturing on the other side of the Gap. I could hardly believe my good luck, and I let him know immediately that I was more than ready for a big adventure.

Making our way up to the Gap, I felt glad to be alive. The smell of high mountain sage filled the crisp air, and I basked in the bright morning sun. Once we reached the bottom floor of the Gap, the sun abandoned us. It was cold as we zigzagged our way through Grandpa's granite sanctuary. The sounds of fast running water coming from Garden Creek alongside the narrow road's edge and of our horse prancing in cadence on the loose gravel echoed off the canyon walls. It was music to my ears. Not a word was spoken between Grandpa and me on our ride. He wasn't one to make small talk. Although when he was among a group of friends or relatives, he loved to tell humorous stories about his six younger brothers and neighbors in Robin. Grandpa initiated little or no conversation on a one-on-one basis with me. I had to do that. Two miles from the house and twenty minutes later, we were on the other side of the Gap.

Grandpa spotted his cattle right away. After counting, he discovered that one was missing. We rode around the barbed-wire fence that was supposed to keep them in and found a section that had been trampled down. Fortunately, only one steer had gotten out. After repairing the fence, he told me, "Sorry, Dickie, but you'll have to stay here while I round up that son of a bitch." I'd heard that kind of language before, so it was no big surprise. When it came to an obstinate cow or horse, that's what Grandpa called it. If it was a particularly irritable animal, he'd say "why you goddamned son of a bitch." Other than that, Grandpa never swore. And because Club members were strongly and regularly advised never to swear, as Jehovah found those words disgusting and the use of them could bar your entry into the new world, it was a naughty pleasure for me to hear Grandpa do a little cussing.

Once Grandpa found the "son of a bitch" and corralled him with the other steers, he asked if I'd like to do some fishing at the head of Garden Creek, which was only a few yards away. "We just might catch enough brookies (brook trout) for breakfast this morning, Dickie. Wouldn't you like Grandma to dip those tasty morsels in flour and deep-fry them? Nothing goes better with eggs sunny side up." My mouth watered as I told him what a great idea it was.

But the fishing gods weren't with us that morning. The only bites I got were from wood ticks. I broke the silence by asking, "Grandpa, why do you think Mama is attracted to such a strange religion?" Grandpa jerked his head like he had a big fish on the line. At first, I didn't think he was going to answer me. Then he turned and looked directly at me for the longest time. Was I about to get a scolding? It looked like he was doing some serious thinking before he finally smiled and patted me on the shoulder.

"Dickie, you're not alone in thinking that your parents' religious views are a bit strange. What's unusual is that you are questioning their views. Most young people accept the views of their parents. It's our nature to conform, and most people believe what they're raised to believe. Now take me. My mother was born and raised a Mormon. That denomination answered her questions about life and helped give her life meaning and a hope for the hereafter. She liked that and wasn't about to change. My dad, on the other hand, was a nonbeliever. But he was happy that my mother had something that she believed in. The only time they had problems was when she tried to shame him into becoming a believer like her. Then he'd push back with a vengeance, telling her that religion got its

160

following from surrounding influences and atmospheres, not from study or thinking, and to stop pushing him.

"My father let my mother raise me as a Mormon. I was baptized as one because that's what my mama wanted. But even then, I pretty well figured out, at least for me, that religion was not what a person says they believe—but the way they lived their life. Unfortunately, the folks that make the biggest fuss about religious doctrines and why theirs are better than the next guy's were more often than not the biggest hypocrites. So when it was time to make my choice, I decided I wouldn't go to church or spend time trying to figure out all the stuff that supposedly makes God happy. I don't know if there's any evidence of life after death, but then I don't know if there's any evidence against it. Soon enough, we'll all find out. So I don't figure it does me any good to spend time thinking about such things."

He went on to tell me that one of the things that attracted him to Grandma was that she had religious beliefs and a childhood background similar to his. Grandma's mother was a Mormon and her father a Methodist. Differences in her parents' beliefs had caused a lot of tension and stress during her childhood. While Grandma had been baptized a Methodist, she had come to the same conclusion about religion that Grandpa had. And while the absence of religion had worked well in their marriage, my mama was probably more like her grandmothers and needed the structure, set beliefs, and association of a particular religious group. He just hadn't seen her need clearly when he and Grandma were raising their four kids.

Unfortunately, Grandpa couldn't do anything about it now, and if I wanted to blame someone for what she now believed and how she was raising me, he figured that he and Grandma were partly to blame. He told me that it wouldn't be long before I would be able to make my own choices in life. What I needed to do was focus on getting the best education I could get. School was very important. The better educated I was, the better chance I would have to lead a happy and successful life when I was ready to leave home and make decisions about how I would live my life and in what I believed.

Grandpa then looked into my eyes and he gave me a long stern look that said this conversation was between just him and me. God help me if any of this got back to Mama, Grandma, or anyone else in our immediate family. Grandpa was a very private person and what was said between the two of us stayed with the two of us. It is now fifty years later and I've never told a soul, until now. Hopefully, Grandpa will understand.

Mama (Gail Evans) at sixteen after graduating from high school.

During that vacation with my grandparents and one the following year, I learned more things about Mama. Grandma confessed to me that she believed Mama suffered from a melancholy similar to hers. Living so far away from civilization had triggered it. Mama wasn't like Grandpa, who could find sufficient spiritual sustenance from what Mother Nature offered and live happily in an uncertain world. Mama wasn't able to tolerate ambiguity. She needed well-defined beliefs and answers to her questions about God, His purpose for man, and life after death. She needed the fellowship of people who believed as she did to help her feel secure in an insecure world.

Years later, I learned that Mama had looked for love and meaning for life in all the wrong places during her teenage years. After graduating from high school, at age sixteen, she left home to live in the big city. First it was Pocatello, then Salt Lake City, and finally Los Angeles. A year before I was born, she had considered living as a plural wife with a polygamist group who claimed to be the true followers of Jesus Christ and Joseph Smith, the founder of the Mormon Church. Grandma was grateful that Mama had decided not to go in that direction. She wanted me to know that things could be much worse.

As I processed new information about Mama and my grandparents, I better understood how my life had come to be what it was. I didn't dislike it any less, but it helped make my situation more tolerable. And I decided that the best thing I could do was to focus all my energies on getting the best education I could get.

I asked Grandpa if he would recommend books or authors for me to read when I got back home. He told me that his favorite authors were Mark Twain, Carl Sandburg, Will Rogers, and Robert Service. When I told him that I had read *Tom Sawyer* and *Huckleberry Finn*, he laughed and told me that he enjoyed those stories as well. But he wanted me to try to figure out what these writers ultimately believed about life and the pursuit of happiness. He hoped this would help me improve my thinking skills.

My 1956 vacation was far from over. That night, after Grandpa had talked with me behind the Gap, we sat in my grandparents' living room while they told us several stories about Mama and her siblings growing up. As I relaxed, I unconsciously slipped the middle two fingers on my right hand into my mouth and sucked them. When Grandma saw me, she let out a gasp. "What in heaven's name are you doing, Dickie?" Tim told her that I'd been sucking my fingers again. Grandma looked at Mama for confirmation. She nodded her head "yes." Grandma asked if she could talk with me privately, and Mama agreed.

Grandma led me to her bedroom and asked me to sit on the bed. She closed the door and sat down on a nearby chair. "Dickie, I suspect that a lot of stuff is going on in your life to get you to start sucking your fingers again. But I just think that you're way too old to be doing that kind of thing. I have a thick wool sock that I want you to wear on your right hand whenever you're in my house. I don't think it will take long before you'll stop that silly habit." After putting the sock on my hand, she asked me to give

163

her a kiss and told me that we could join the others. I flinched, gave her a kiss on the lips, and went back into the living room. I had to wear that sock whenever I was in the living room late in the day or in my bed. But Grandma's cure worked. I never sucked my fingers again.

If that wasn't embarrassment enough, on the second night of our stay, I experienced some discomfort while taking my bath. I noticed a black spot on one of my testicles and it hurt. It hurt so badly that I was willing to tell Mama about it. As soon as she saw it, she recommended that Grandma look at it. This seemed a bit much, but I knew by then that I needed help. When Grandma inspected it, she knew right away that it was a wood tick. Left alone, it would eventually burrow itself under my skin. It needed to be removed immediately. Most likely, the tick had found its present home when Grandpa and I sat down to fish the day before. She pinched and pushed and, to my great relief, pulled it out.

During the last week of our vacation, my mother's sister, Norma, and her husband, Ralph, joined us. Mama tried on several occasions to convert them with her unique interpretation of the Bible. Both Aunt Norma and Uncle Ralph expertly articulated a rebuttal to Mama's Club beliefs. But Mama couldn't or wouldn't believe what they had to say. It dawned on me that at the core of Mama's belief system was that she had to change other people's beliefs to the way she believed. That was the Club way, and facts and data would never sway Mama. It embarrassed me to hear Mama expound so vehemently on her religious beliefs. Her weak argument could be best described in words that Abraham Lincoln once used: "It had got down as thin as soup made by boiling the shadow of a pigeon that had starved to death."

Fortunately, Mama and her sister didn't argue religion all the time. Every afternoon we'd set up a card table on the lush green lawn surrounding my grandparents' home and play pinochle. Papa partnered with Uncle Ralph, while Grandpa and I were teammates. Occasionally, Grandpa would get a big hand and announce that he was going to "shoot the moon," which meant he was going to take all the tricks. If he was successful, we could win up to 1,500 points and the game. While a bit unusual, he never failed to make his ambitious bids. Watching him play those high-stake hands were exciting and suspenseful moments. When it was obvious that he was going to take all the tricks, he'd slap that last card down hard on the table and break into a hysterical laughter, contagious to anyone within earshot. Once after "shooting the moon," he was so excited he jumped out of his chair, did cartwheels on the grass, and walked upright on his hands for several yards before proudly announcing, "Now how many sixty-year-old grandpas can do that?" Then he laughed and hooted for the longest time.

Every midafternoon at precisely the same time, a stiff wind swooped mysteriously down upon us from the Bannock Mountains to our west. The eerie but pleasant breeze lasted five to ten minutes before it suddenly disappeared. If I hadn't known better, it would have been easy to think Mother Nature was trying to tell me something. I never knew exactly what, although I suspected Grandpa heard the message clearly. He always stopped what he was doing, even if he was playing pinochle, to use all his senses to listen. He appeared to cherish those moments as if they were holy. I wondered if it was similar to how Mama believed that God's Spirit had changed the course of history by blowing through at Pentecost. Perhaps in Grandpa's world, this strong but controlled breeze helped him keep his faith, such as it was. The natural world spoke to him in many different ways.

During our time in Robin, I also spent time with my cousin Danny. He lived on the farm directly west of my grandparents'. We played games, fished, and explored the nearby woods, streams, and mountains together. Like Grandpa, we appreciated how special this part of the world was. No church or cathedral could equal its ethereal beauty. We never said a word about religion, although Mama asked me after the first week of our vacation if I had told Danny about the new world yet. When I told her "no," and asked her how she would like it if all Danny talked about was going to heaven and how great it would be to be there together someday, she said, "But he doesn't have the truth. You do." Mama always had to have the last word, but I wasn't about to talk religion with Danny. I knew he was a Mormon and believed that way because that's what his mother taught him. I respected that. What bothered me was that he probably thought I believed what Mama did, and I wanted to tell him differently, although I knew that wasn't a good idea.

Shortly after we were back in Los Angeles, I read Mark Twain's essay on "Corn Pone Opinions." I had never read anything like that before. I was particularly impressed with his notion that "Mohammedans are Mohammedans because they are born and reared among that sect, not because they have thought it out and can furnish sound reasons for being Mohammedans; we know why Catholics are Catholics; why Presbyterians are Presbyterians; why Baptists are Baptists; and why Mormons are Mormons. We know it is a matter of association and sympathy, not reasoning and examination; that hardly a man in the world has an opinion upon religion which he got otherwise than through his associations and sympathies."

I wondered what might have happened had I been raised by Danny's mom, Aunt Camilla, and Danny been raised by Mama. Would I have been a Mormon and Danny a happy member of the Club?

I had also come to the conclusion that kisses weren't all that bad, after all. Grandma kissed me once again on the lips when we left, and I liked it. That was her way of reminding me that she loved me. And I learned that I liked Grandpa's kisses even better. Every day during the three-week visit, I noticed that he kissed life to the fullest. Even when those "sons of a bitches" riled him up, it didn't last long and he was back to savoring each moment. He did everything with gusto, whether he was working in his wheat fields, walking his way down Garden Creek or Marsh Creek to look for that special spot where he'd catch lots of brook trout, laughing at the end of a good story, catching grasshoppers for fish bait, fixing fences, riding his horses Silver and Pinto, talking farm talk with his cronies in Arimo or Downey, hiking to the top of "Old Tom" (the highest point on the Bannock Mountains), playing pinochle, herding his cattle with his dog Rex, roasting marshmallows over a bonfire on the other side of the Gap, telling his grandkids there was a live mouse in his bicep when he flexed it, or simply eating a meal. And he didn't need or use alcohol or tobacco to help him enjoy life. He loved the natural world and heard its sounds. He found comfort in the soil and how it helped him earn a living. He respected the beauty and mystery of all things, whether they were living organisms or inanimate objects. Grandpa kissed life every day.

Mama's Letters of Recommendation
Chapter 22

When I started back to school at Daniel Webster Junior High School in the fall of 1956, I was eager for a new beginning and excited about my learning prospects. As Grandpa told me, a good education was critical to my future success. School was where I needed to focus my attention, and I had to avoid feeling sorry for myself because of my Club connection. Unfortunately, my schooling wasn't Mama's top priority.

It wasn't that Mama wanted me to stop learning. But if I had to go to school, she wanted me to take classes that helped me in the Club ministry or developed skills I could use in the new world. Basic math and English were fine. Mechanical or architectural drawing, typing, or a cooking class would do me good. It was higher math and science that she wanted me to avoid. She also didn't see what good would come from studying history, geography, or social studies. Athletic activities would be a total waste of my time. Fortunately, many of my classes were required for graduation and Mama didn't have a say. And for the next two school years, I made certain that whatever subject I took, I was at the top of my class.

While I tried to learn as much as possible in the eighth and ninth grades, my Club activities didn't stop. For my emotional well-being, I gave Mama the impression that while I had issues with some Club beliefs, I planned to live my life so that I could join her in the new world.

My speaking skills at the Hall continued to improve. Twice I was asked to speak at the local circuit assembly, where I had audiences of over a thousand people. Adrenaline rushed through my body as I forcefully recited what I was told to say. Preaching from this kind of pulpit, even if it meant that I had to tell some white lies, was like a mild drug that felt good for days afterward. It didn't hurt that Mama began to see me as a future Club leader. Though she knew I didn't yet have the gift of a full understanding of Club truths, my gift of the Spirit might just be public speaking.

While I felt an awesome sense of power addressing large groups, people didn't come to hear me. They came to hear the district servant talk about recent new truths that God had revealed to the Club's spiritual leaders in Brooklyn, New York. At one of those assemblies, the keynote speaker began his talk by asking us to open our *New World Translations of the Bible* to 2 Corinthians 3:1–3.

The *New World Translation* was a Club interpretation of the Bible and primarily the work of Fred Franz, the vice president of the Club. This Bible was a must-use for Club members. The fact that objective Bible scholars critically challenged the *New World Translation* for its self-serving interpretation didn't bother Mama or other Club members. Instead, they saw this as evidence of its accuracy since Bible prophesy predicted that God's true worshippers would be scoffed at during the last days. And the fact that it had a green cover as opposed to the traditional black binding was a good sign. Green was the color of life.

The speaker asked us to follow along in our green Bibles as he read, "Are we starting again to recommend ourselves? Or do we, perhaps, like some men, need letters of recommendation to you or from you? You yourselves are our letter, inscribed on our hearts and known and being read by all mankind. For you are shown to be a letter of Christ written by us as ministers, inscribed not with ink but with spirit of a living God, not on stone tablets, but on fleshly tablets, on hearts."

These *letters of recommendation*, we were told, were the people the Apostle Paul had brought into the truth. While Paul must have been proud of the vast number of letters, or converts, he was responsible for, these letters also served as markers for him. The more he collected, the greater were his chances of earning God's favor on his judgment day. And just as it was in Paul's day, so it was today. The more letters of recommendation we accumulated, the better were our chances of being rewarded with everlasting life. Then he asked us, "How many letters of recommendation do each of you have? If Armageddon came tonight, would you have enough letters to assure your salvation and life forever in God's new world?"

He went on to say how important the door-to-door work was. This was how we harvested our letters of recommendation. The more time we spent in this work, the better our chances were of acquiring these letters. If we currently spent ten hours going door-to-door, he encouraged us to spend twenty hours in the future. He recommended that if we could, we should try to *vacation pioneer*. This would mean spending seventy-five hours in the door-to-door ministry for one month out of every year. Ultimately, our goal should be to become *pioneers,* spending one hundred hours a month, twelve months out of the year, year after year, helping people learn the truth. He also told us about *special pioneers* who received their calling from the Club's headquarters and spent 150 hours a month preaching the good news of God's kingdom.

On our drive home, Mama told Papa how moved she was about the talk on letters of recommendation. She calculated that she had nineteen letters. After all, she was responsible for bringing the truth to Papa, us four kids, Pam and her three kids, Sondra, Henrietta's family of four, Opal, and Margie's family of four. Papa had only one, and that was Pam's husband, Ray. Mama figured that since Papa was the family breadwinner and had a full-time job, he would get some of the credit for Mama's letters of recommendation on his judgment day. But Mama wasn't satisfied with her nineteen. She wanted more. She tried vacation pioneering for one month and loved it. Six months later, she became a pioneer and served in that capacity for the next forty years.

Behind Mama's desire to pioneer was the high she received when she converted someone. And, behind each of Mama's conversions there was an interesting story. Probably none better than my parents' shared letters of recommendation: Pam and Ray Morrow, and their three children.

Their story begins in January 1952 when Pam Morrow and her son, Johnny, answered a knock at the front door of their small rented home on Bundy Drive in West Los Angeles. An attractive mature woman introduced herself as Ione Stafford and explained that she was there at the request of Pam's daughter, Brenda, who lived in Oregon. Pam immediately invited Ione inside.

Pam had agonized over the recent loss of Brenda's baby boy to a viral infection. What Pam didn't know was that Brenda had become an active Club member only a few months before. Shortly after losing the baby, Brenda wrote to the Club's headquarters in Brooklyn, asking them to send someone to witness to her mother. Brenda wanted that person to explain how she found comfort and hope in spite of the loss of her baby. She felt that her mother would benefit from hearing about God's promise of a new world where she would be able to see her baby grandson.

Now forty-four years of age and on her third marriage, Pam Morrow had been through a lot of pain. First married when she was only fifteen, Pam had Brenda at seventeen and a son, Bill, just two years later.

When Pam's first husband became insanely jealous and violent, she fled with her kids to find shelter at the home of an older couple living on a dirt farm in Odessa, Texas. In spite of the distance and remote location, Pam's estranged husband somehow tracked the three of them down and showed up at the farm unannounced.

At first Pam refused to see him. The old farmer threatened to shoot Pam's ex-husband if he didn't leave her alone. Hoping to avoid any violence, Pam finally agreed to a short meeting. They argued and her husband threatened that if she didn't come back to San Francisco with him, he would kill himself. He pulled out a small pocket pistol, grabbed Pam, and shot her behind the right ear. She dropped to the floor unconscious, bleeding profusely. He then put the gun to his mouth and fired, falling dead beside her. Four-year-old Brenda, and Bill, barely two, sat just a few feet away on the front porch and heard everything.

Realizing that Pam was still alive, the older couple wrapped her head in towels, gently placed her in the back of a horse-drawn wagon, and drove her to the only doctor into town. Somehow Pam managed to survive, but a piece of the bullet lodged behind her right ear for the rest of her life, causing some hearing loss.

In the mid-1930s, Pam married a merchant marine. In spite of his alcoholism, he was good to her and kind to her kids. One night he got drunk and fell off a pier, and was crushed or drowned between the pilings and the bow of the ship he was working on. Pam was a widow and single mother for a second time in less than ten years.

In the early 1940s, Pam and her girlfriend would go dancing at the Avalon Ballroom on Venice Beach. One night in 1941, Pam met Ray Morrow at the Avalon while on a double date with another couple. Ray was very handsome—and single—but was also very shy when meeting women. Pam managed to get his attention and they soon began to date. They were married in late 1942. Even though Pam was almost eight years older and still bore emotional scars from her past relationships, she found Ray to be a loving husband. Now ten years and three children later, Pam was finally enjoying a comfortable and secure marriage.

Pam listened as Ione explained the reason for her visit. The message was comforting and when Ione offered to conduct a free in-home Bible study with her, Pam immediately liked the idea, as did her eight-year-old son (my age), Johnny.

They decided that Ione would come by after school so both Pam and Johnny could study the *Let God Be True* book with her. Even though Johnny loved this learning environment, thinking he was studying the Bible, he would become restless whenever his mother and Ione would drift off and discuss more adult things. Whenever he got tired or bored, Johnny would stretch out on the couch next to Ione and she would occasionally rub and scratch his back.

Fifty years later, Johnny filled in the details of those early studies with Ione. "I remember how she would generously compliment me when I came up with the right answer. Her praise went right to my head. It really made me want to become a Club member so I could get more recognition."

Johnny also shared with me the events leading up to his family's conversion. "Dad didn't have any problems with Mom studying the Bible until he found out from co-workers and his brother that Club members didn't serve in the military, didn't salute the flag, and didn't celebrate Christmas. They convinced him that Club members were communists and didn't believe in Jesus. Riled up and angry, Dad insisted that Mom stop studying with Ione. The only thing that tempered Dad's anger was the fact that his stepdaughter, Brenda, had initiated everything and she and her family certainly seemed to be normal folks.

"About that time, Ione announced that she could no longer study with us. She was getting married and would be moving out of the area. She also informed us that because of where we lived, Mom should actually be studying with someone from the Mar Vista Kingdom Hall, not the Venice/Santa Monica Hall.

"She arranged for Gail Kelly, your mama, to take over the Bible study with my mother. I didn't study with your mama, but Mom did for a few months. I think Dad had told Mom that she could study, but he wanted her to leave me out.

"Dad decided to take a stand when Mom wanted to go to meetings at the Kingdom Hall. They got into some angry arguments over the issue. My mother finally explained to your mama that she didn't think she should continue studying for fear of damaging her marriage—something she would not and could not afford to do.

"Your mama shared her story of how your papa also became angry and threatened to leave her and the kids over the same issues. She suggested that her husband, Jack Kelly, could come over and try to reason with Dad.

"Initially Dad wasn't interested and told Mom that if Jack Kelly showed up at his door, he'd physically kick Kelly off the property. Mom accused Dad of being unreasonable and that he should show hospitality and at least hear the man out. Dad finally calmed down and reluctantly agreed to have a reasonable conversation, but promised that if he found out that Club members were communists or didn't believe in Jesus, then Jack Kelly should expect to fight.

"I wasn't present in the living room when your papa came to our home. We kids were moved to the back of the house into my bedroom in case there was any trouble. We could hear voices and some occasional shouting, but it soon became apparent that there would be no fight. All I know was that Dad actually liked your papa after that first encounter, so Dad agreed to study the Bible with him and ceased threatening Mom.

"As I look back, I think that my Dad and your papa were very similar. Both were of average intelligence, but not very social. Neither of them had a lot of friends. Both served honorably in the Army Air Force, but neither one was a willing warrior. Dad was a Chevy mechanic and your papa peddled pastries and coffee, so neither one was entrepreneurial. In many ways they were a perfect match.

"Dad always credited your papa for bringing him into the truth. Later, when Dad was trying to give up smoking, your papa encouraged him to not sneak around and hide the fact that he smoked, but rather be honest about it and continue to work at giving up cigarettes. Your papa never criticized Dad and always acted as if he were Dad's best friend. I think my father's conversion was more because of his desire for a friendship than because of any theological beliefs.

"As a result of the efforts of your parents, all five of us eventually became baptized *Jehovah's Witnesses*."

The Morrow family's conversion was only one of the many success stories that Mama loved to share with me. While much of this story was told from Johnny Morrow's perspective, converting people to the truth had now become Mama's one real passion, and pioneering was the best way for her to make that happen.

Once she became a pioneer, she constantly reminded Tim, Mary, and me that our goal after graduating from high school, if Armageddon hadn't arrived, was to be a pioneer. College wasn't an option for us. It was bad enough that the law required us to go to school for twelve years. Mama believed that higher education stuff at universities and colleges was a breeding ground for loss of faith, belief in evolution, and atheism. What we needed to learn could be taught to us at Club meetings and by reading Club literature. That was the only education we needed to become pioneers.

Due to the extra hours that Mama spent in the door-to-door ministry, several changes were made at our home. Mama no longer did the ironing, yard work, washing dishes, or housecleaning. That work was assigned to Tim and me.

Mama's pioneer life brought with it many more letters of recommendation. She was a dynamo at converting people. Surprisingly, most of her converts were very intelligent. But like Mama, they chose not to use data and facts when evaluating the Club's history and beliefs.

On three occasions during 1957 and 1958, Mama asked me to study the Bible with the sons of her potential converts. The first was Norman Borders. I knew full well that studying the Bible meant using the *Let God Be True* book to teach the person the basic Club beliefs. While I'd seen Mama study the Bible with people before, this would be a first for me. I told her that I didn't think I could do it. I didn't know what to say, and I wasn't about to say something like, "Hi, how are you? Would you like to study the Bible using this book?" But Mama insisted and said she'd tell me what to say.

Mama coached me to make small talk at first. Ask Norman if he ever wondered why so many bad things happened in this world, why people had to die, and if a Higher Being cared about people and their troubles here on earth. Young people were curious about those types of things. She said to tell him that God has a name—Jehovah. He was alone in the universe before deciding to make companions, which He called angels. This first creation was an angel he called

Michael, although He would change the name many years later to Jesus Christ. Then Jehovah made millions of angels, including one He called Lucifer. For thousands of years, all went well. That is, until Lucifer decided that he could be just like God, that he was God. He was so persuasive that he convinced hordes of angels to follow him. When Jehovah heard what was going on, He became very upset. He changed Lucifer's name to Satan the Devil, called his followers demons, and threw them all out of the main part of heaven. Unfortunately, when God made the first human beings, Adam and Eve, Satan and his demons had the power to influence humans. In fact, Satan and his minions still influence people. God gives everyone "free will" or the freedom to choose how they will live their lives, what they want to believe, and who they want to worship. While Jehovah would like them to worship Him, He doesn't want people to worship Him unless they want to.

Mama wanted me to tell Norman that death and all the bad things on earth have nothing to do with God. God is a God of love. He wants people to live forever. Death and badness are the work of Satan and his demons. But their days are numbered. Soon God will declare war on these evil spirits and their human followers at Armageddon. Those who love God and worship Him properly will be spared God's wrath and live forever on a paradise earth. I was then to explain how this was all Bible-based and he could learn more about it if we studied the *Let God Be True* book together.

I had heard all this before. These were Mama's fairy stories, and she and other Club members believed them like little kids who believe in Santa Claus. There was no way I was going to recite this baloney to Norman. But if he asked me to study the book with him, I could do that.

The plan was for me to join Mama on her weekly bible study with Olive Borders after I got home from school. She'd introduce me to Norman, give him a copy of the *Let God Be True* book, suggest we go to his room to get to know each other better, and perhaps I could explain why the book could help him get to know his Bible.

We arrived at his house and everything went as planned. Thinking his mother had prepared him for my visit, I asked if he wanted to study this book or if that was something his mother asked him to do. He told me that he had only learned about Mama and me less than an hour ago. He had no idea that his mom was studying with people from the Club, and he was pretty certain that his dad didn't know what was happening either. I suggested that we go outside and shoot some baskets while our mothers visited. On our drive home, I explained to Mama what had happened.

Several days later, I picked up the phone and had hardly said hello when a man started yelling. He didn't like Mama and he had no use for the Club. I had no idea who it was and I wasn't about to say a thing. This guy was nuts. I listened for quite a while. Suddenly he went silent. When he spoke again, his speech pattern had changed and he asked if I was a member of the Club. I replied, "Jehovah what?" He apologized and said he had the wrong number. As soon as I got off the phone, I told Mama. She was impressed with how I had handled the situation.

When Mama went back to study the *Let God Be True* book with Mrs. Borders, it appeared that no one was home. About to give up and go back to her car, Mama saw an envelope slide under the door. It was addressed to Gail Kelly. Mama picked it up and read, "Gail, I don't want you or any other Club member coming to my door again. After my husband explained to me how you deceive people into believing things that aren't in the Bible, we burned all the Club literature that you sold me over the last five months. I'm still upset with myself for allowing you in my home."

Later that day, Mama shared the letter with me. Now we knew who the angry phone caller was. It had to be Norman's father. Surprisingly, Mama wasn't upset over the incident and the loss of a letter of recommendation. Mr. and Mrs. Borders' reactions bolstered her belief that Armageddon and the new world weren't far away. This persecution was yet another sign from God to show that we were living in the last days. She often read Matthew 5:10, 11 to support that belief: "Happy are those who have been persecuted for righteousness' sake, since the kingdom of the heavens belongs to them. Happy are you when people reproach you and persecute you and lyingly say every sort of wicked thing against you for my sake."

Several months later, Mama asked me to study the Bible with the son of a woman she had been studying with for two months. This time, I knew the boy. I could take Club literature to a stranger, but not to someone I knew. That's not what I told Mama, but I tried my best to get out of it. However, Mama insisted I join her. While she studied with Mrs. Deam, Billy and I would go to his room and I was supposed to tell him what she'd wanted me to tell Norman. Mama even called ahead to make sure that Billy would be there.

If Mama had known what kind of kid Billy was, she wouldn't have let me spend time with him. But because Billy's mom thought it would do him good to study the Bible with me, Mama allowed it. Little did she know who would do the learning.

When we arrived at Billy's house, I was introduced to Billy's mom and Billy to Mama. Right off the bat, he charmed Mama, looking innocent behind his big glasses. He told her that he knew Georgie, and that I could probably teach him a thing or two. Then he invited me to his bedroom. What a mess. I had never seen such chaos. Hundreds of comic books were strewn all over the place, along with candy wrappers and empty pop bottles. I said, "So what's with this, 'He can teach me a thing or two' to my mother?"

Billy laughed. "Oh, you know how it works. Just tell adults what they want to hear and they won't give you any trouble. I talked with Georgie at school the other day and told him that my mother wanted you to study the Bible with me. He told me to play along and that you'd love to see my comic book collection. Oh yeah, did Georgie tell you about that kid who just moved here from Germany? He's at least two years older than we are. But before he came to the States, he was having sex with girls at his school almost every day." I sat there dumbfounded and nodded my head up and down like I knew about it, which I didn't. Then Billy said, "Let me show you two girlie magazines he gave me."

Billy and I met three more times for his bible study and never talked religion or looked inside a Club book. Once he showed me how to scare drivers as they were coming up the hill near his house. At twilight Billy and I hid behind bushes on each side of the road. A thick white rope lay harmlessly between us on the road. As the first car approached, Billy did a countdown. On the count of three, we both pulled the rope making it taut and very visible to the driver. The driver slammed on the car's brakes, swerved, and came to an abrupt halt. He opened his door, screamed obscenities, and spotted me. I started running. With an angry man in hot pursuit, I ran between two nearby houses, jumped a wooden fence, and eventually lost him. Fortunately, it was getting dark and the driver didn't recognize me.

On another occasion, Billy asked me to help him set fire to bags of dog poop we placed on the front porch of several of his neighbors' homes. He would douse the bag with lighter fluid, drop a match on it, and ring the doorbell several times. Then we ran for cover with twilight on our side. The real show started when the homeowner tried to stomp out the small bonfire. While Mama never had a clue as to what we were really doing, our entertainment came to an abrupt stop when Billy's mom decided she wasn't interested in joining the Club and asked Mama to stop studying with her.

The third attempt for me to have a bible study with one of Mama's converts was a success, or at least Mama thought so. She had studied with Margie Selby for over a year before Margie and her daughter started occasionally coming to meetings. Margie wasn't making the kind of progress Mama wanted because she couldn't give up her cigarettes, or at least that's what Mama believed. Then Margie asked Mama if I would be willing to have a bible study with her son, Tommy, who was two years younger than I was.

My first study with him started while we were on school vacation. We used the *Let God Be True* book and met once a week for an hour. I was supposed to say a prayer before and after we had our bible study, which I did. I'd ask the questions listed on the bottom of the page for that particular paragraph, he and I alternated reading the paragraph, and Tommy found and read the answers to me. It was like two robots doing what they were programmed to do and lacking any of the passion that Mama brought to and aroused in her students. Although for my efforts, I was able to report an hour in the door-to-door work, one back call and a bible study on the field service report card that I turned in weekly at our Kingdom Hall.

We had held four studies when Tommy first excused himself to go to his bedroom, leaving me to wait for him for fifteen minutes. The second time it happened, no one else was home. I decided to go to the bathroom. While sitting on the toilet, I noticed several cigarettes and a lighter stored in a drinking glass. The room reeked of tobacco and was most likely Margie's smoking room. I had never had a cigarette, but the more I looked at them, the more I was tempted. Finally, my curiosity got the best of me. I quickly brought a cigarette to my lips and lighted up. After several puffs, I decided I didn't like it, snuffed it out in the toilet bowl, and flushed. I stayed in the bathroom for several minutes before returning to our bible study.

Tommy came to only one meeting that summer and it wasn't because I asked him. I suspect he had no choice. Like me, he did what his mother wanted him to do.

The only break we took in our weekly ritual came in late July 1958, when a second eight-day international Club convention was held in New York City, at Yankee Stadium, the Polo Grounds (home of the baseball New York Giants), and Trailer City, New Jersey.

My family's financial condition wasn't good at the time. So Papa decided to stay home with my sisters, while Mama, Tim, and I would go to the assembly. We'd use our 1954 Ford station wagon to get there. Three people from our Hall wanted to go with us, and they were willing to pay for our gas and food along the way. One of them would do most of the driving, and we'd travel nonstop to avoid motel expenses.

Though I had my apprehensions about spending eight days at an assembly, I had a sense of adventure about the trip. Sure, I would have preferred to vacation with my grandparents, but Mama wasn't going to miss what she believed would be the greatest spiritual feast in the history of mankind. We would stay in a home of a nonClub member in the Bronx while we were at the assembly, and I'd get to see parts of the United States I'd never seen before. Our traveling companions would be fifty-year-old Hazel

The 1954 Ford station wagon that transported six people to and from the eight-day New York City assembly.

James, thirty-two-year-old Doug Stevens, and sixteen-year-old Donna Barnett, who was two years older than I was. And because Doug was joining us, we'd make a detour and stay overnight at his boyhood home in South Carolina.

Hazel was a short, plump, single woman who had recently moved to our Hall. Neither of my parents knew anything of her history. The only thing we knew was that she worked full time and was a recent convert.

Doug had been in the truth, as Mama told me, less than three years. Someone from the Club had knocked on his door, started a bible study, and within six months both Doug and his partner, Roger Tanner, were regularly attending meetings. When they were told that they must terminate their gay lifestyle, they prayed to Jehovah for guidance and immediately moved into separate apartments. Doug and Roger attended meetings at the same Hall we did. Like Mama, both Doug and Roger were pioneers.

Donna's parents had become Club members while living in Oregon two years before. They had recently moved to Los Angeles. When I first saw Donna walk into our Hall, I thought she was the prettiest girl I had ever seen. It didn't cross my mind that she was too attractive for someone like me. When we were introduced, I went brain-dead, tongue-tied, and red-faced. I'm sure she thought I was mentally handicapped. As it turned out, she had a boyfriend and wouldn't have given me the time of day even if I had been able to carry on a decent conversation.

Our drive to New York City was uneventful. Doug did most of the driving, and everyone seemed to get along. Mama and Doug were the most talkative. And Doug even told us about his old lifestyle and how Jehovah and the Club had been such a big help to him.

While we were driving through a corridor of lush green hills in Tennessee early in the morning, when the mist and sun work their magic on the landscape, Mama asked us to share what we planned on doing in the new world. Doug responded first. He wanted to be a carpenter and design and build high-end homes for Armageddon survivors. When I asked why he hadn't pursued that career in this life, he asked if that was a trick question. He said that we should spend most of our time and energies in the door-to-door work. He worked as a draftsman designing new homes, but only on a part-time basis so he could pioneer. Hazel wanted to meet a kind, loving man and have lots of children in the new world. Donna knew who she was going to marry in the new world, and she too wanted to be a good housewife and have lots of children. Mama wanted to live in a large, well-built home on a large grassy knoll overlooking a twenty-acre estate. Lions, tigers, and sheep would graze on her property and she would cuddle with them during the late afternoon. Doug liked that, but wanted to know why we'd need sheep in the new world since we'd all be vegetarians, forgetting that we'd need wool for clothing. Tim said he didn't know what he wanted to do or be in the new world and couldn't be coaxed into coming up with anything. I made up this thing about living in the mountains, riding horses, and farming.

Then I hit a sour note when I said, "I'm not certain that I'll be an Armageddon survivor." Of course, I wouldn't have dared tell them that I doubted Armageddon would ever happen. Telling a Club member that would have been worse than telling them I had gonorrhea. Doug was sympathetic and assured me that I wasn't the only one who thought that way from time to time. For him, the key was to spend as much time in the field ministry as possible, attend and listen carefully at all the Club's five weekly meetings and three yearly assemblies, read every issue of the *Watchtower* and *Awake!*, pray several times every day, and fellowship with only Club members.

It got real quiet after that. I think most everyone associated with the Club has a lingering fear that they might not make it into the new world. The Club-appointed leaders constantly reminded us that we should spend more time than we currently did in the door-to-door work, reading Club literature, and preparing for the weekly meetings. James 2:26 was often used to support their guilt-laced counsel, with the words: "Indeed, as the body without spirit is dead, so also faith without works is dead."

As we went further into the Deep South, I was shocked to see separate restrooms and drinking fountains for white and black people. It didn't appear that the white store owners ever cleaned the facilities for blacks. Grandpa had cleaner drinking tanks for his cattle. In this part of the world, Club members were segregated by race at separate Hall*s*.

When we arrived at Doug's boyhood home, his eighty-year-old mother warmly greeted us. What a kind and happy person she was. A new convert and one of Doug's letters of recommendation, she must have figured that there was something very special about this religious group if it could change her son's gay lifestyle. I wonder what she thought eight years later, when Doug and Roger moved back in together as a couple and were disfellowshipped. According to Club rules, she couldn't speak to Doug anymore.

The eight-day assembly had its own special dynamics. And though I didn't believe much of what I heard coming from many of the speakers, these men were skilled in using microphones. In an open-air baseball stadium, they managed to make it feel as though a supernatural force was roving around the place. The positive reactions coming from most of the attendees were contagious. I loved seeing Mama get so excited about the talks and releases of new Club literature. I was happy to be there, yet not nearly as happy as Mama.

Some moments I thought maybe this was the truth, and the Holy Spirit couldn't get through to me because I couldn't love God like Mama did. Her God seemed more human than godlike, and so demanding. Could He actually get jealous like people foolishly do? Could man's Creator become angry, and did He at one time require people to worship Him with animal sacrifices? Could He sanction war, death, and dismemberment of innocent people? Could He actually pout and rant when people listened and followed the Devil and his demons instead of Him? While Mama believed He could, I didn't think so. And yet, maybe I was too young to understand what Mama and most of the people at this assembly knew to be true.

I would have liked it if Jehovah could have been more like Jesus. Jesus seemed so kind, understanding, and wise. But then, according to Club beliefs, Jesus was God's first creation. They were not one and the same. Jesus came to this earth and died faithful to God as a ransom sacrifice for all mankind, which made possible his appointment as the king of God's kingdom in October 1914.

The main message at the assembly was that we were living in the time of the end. The year 1914 was the last normal year in human history. We were reminded over and over that 1914 marked the countdown for these last days. Armageddon would come to pass before all those living in 1914 had died. Every time we were told how fortunate we were to have this special knowledge of the past and present, the 250,000-plus attendees interrupted the speakers with long periods of enthusiastic clapping. We were informed that millions still living have not heard this message. While the time was short, we needed to get the good news of God's kingdom to these people. Most of the Club members were clustered in the bigger cities around the United States. We were challenged to move *where the need is great.* If we loved Jehovah, we should think about quitting our jobs and moving our families to more rural parts of the United States where there were few Club members. If we trusted Jehovah, He would help us find a way to make it work. We'd also be assuring our post-Armageddon eternal life. And if we wanted to know where in the States the need was great, a list of appropriate cities was available from any of the ushers after the session.

When this calling to serve where the need is great was first announced, I suspect lots of people were thrilled. What a wonderful way to show Jehovah God that they loved Him with all their heart, mind, and body. Then the reality of it should have dawned upon them. The family breadwinner would have to quit what most likely was a good-paying job. Selling a home, taking the kids out of school, moving a thousand or more miles away from family and friends, and finding a good-paying job in a much smaller city could be very daunting. The enormity and uncertainty of it all should have given a rational person some serious concerns. But in this setting, some people heard God speaking to them. And as one of the speakers said, if Jehovah God can provide food and shelter for the smallest of His creation, a tiny sparrow, surely He will see that you are taken care of. The key was to put your trust in Him, and He would take care of you.

Six days into the convention and while walking to our seats in Yankee Stadium, Mama saw our former congregation servant, Randall Shafer. She hadn't seen him since 1952. He had moved up in the Club hierarchy and was now a district servant. The two of them were excited to see each other. They shook hands, made small talk, and talked about Papa before Randall said, "Gail, I know you'll want to talk with Jack about it when you get home, but I want to encourage you to move where the need is great. I'd recommend that you go to either Columbus, Georgia, or Norfolk, Nebraska." He said he wanted to talk more but he was late for an important meeting.

As we traveled back home, Mama gave no indication to Tim or me what she was thinking with respect to this new Club calling.

We were home a month before Mama told me that we were going to have a family meeting. She and Papa had some exciting news to share with us kids.

Leaving Los Angeles
Chapter 23

Mama had that spacey "My religion is the only true religion" look in her eyes, and I knew immediately what she was going to tell us. Our family would answer the Club call to serve where the need is great. But I wasn't about to wait for a family meeting to confirm it. Though I felt like I had been punched in the stomach, I had enough energy to blurt out, "Mama, please don't tell me we're leaving Los Angeles. Mama, please don't tell me that." I started to cry like a baby, then ran to my bedroom and slammed the door as hard as I could behind me.

Mama waited several minutes before coming into my room. "Now Dickie, don't you worry about a thing. We haven't decided yet what we're going to do. But if we decide to move where the need is great, we want everyone in the family to have input. Your Papa and I will talk with you kids about it after supper tomorrow."

"So you haven't made a decision one way or the other. Is that what you're telling me?"

"Yes, Dickie, that's right."

But I didn't believe it. I knew Mama. We didn't have family meetings so the four kids could give input. That's not how it worked with Club families. We were supposed to listen and obey. Our opinions were only our opinions. If we didn't agree with Mama or the

Club, then we were wrong and that's all there was to it.

Several months before this, I graduated from junior high school. My last school year, the ninth grade, was a good year for me. I finished near the top of my class and made a favorable impression on all of my teachers. Two weeks before school was out for the summer, the guidance counselor called me into his office wanting to know which school I would be attending. When I told him Venice High School, he looked pleased, telling me that it was one of the best in the state. He encouraged me to take more math and science classes. If I did well, I could attend the college of my choice after I graduated. Perhaps I'd get a full-ride scholarship to UCLA or the University of Southern California. I swooned about the possibility and recalled Grandpa's advice about the importance of a good education and how it could ensure a future that made sense to me.

I had barely absorbed this good news when I had a mild panic attack. The palms of my hands were clammy as I thought about my Club connection and Mama's intentions for me. I didn't want my counselor to learn about it. But I'd take his advice and do the best I could during the next three years of school. Who knew what could happen? I'd be older and smarter. I'd get to know teachers and students who weren't tied to Club rules. And if Mama decided to disown me if I went to college as opposed to pioneering, I'd turn to Grandma and Grandpa for financial and emotional help.

But this plan would go up in smoke if I had to go to school in some small town in Nebraska or Georgia. I'd be isolated even more from normal, well-educated people who could or would want to help me get into a good college. I was now only two weeks away from enrolling in the tenth grade at Venice High School, and I suspected the worst news at our upcoming family meeting. Hopefully, when Mama and Papa thought about all the aspects of moving a family of six to a totally different environment, they'd have second thoughts.

Would Mama sacrifice my opportunity to learn at a top-rate school so she could serve where the need is great? I knew that she would if that was how this question was framed. But I was quite certain that she didn't have a clue about my college aspirations. The main issue for her was that Papa needed a good job to provide for our family, and those kinds of jobs wouldn't be easy to find in a small town.

We had our family meeting as planned. Mama told us that she and Papa were thinking about moving to Norfolk, Nebraska, although a final decision had not been made. If we did go, we could do it as early as mid-November of that year. We'd be able to see snow for the first time in our lives. Norfolk had a population of 10,000 people and no Kingdom Hall.

Papa told us that he had talked with Brother Tom Caldwell, who lived in the country on a 240-acre farm with his wife and five children twelve miles from a town called Pierce. He was the congregation servant for the thirty members who went to the Pierce Hall, including eight members who lived in Norfolk. He wanted us to come and believed our family's presence could be a real blessing for people who hadn't yet heard the truth. But he told Papa that finding a good sales job in the area wouldn't be easy. Montgomery Wards was always looking for capable sales people, but Papa would make at best a fourth of what he was then earning a year, although the cost of housing and living would be much cheaper in Nebraska.

Then they asked what we thought about moving to Nebraska. Tim, Susan, and Mary liked the idea. It would be a big adventure for them. I told everyone that it would be a big mistake. After listening to our comments, my parents said that there was one significant hurdle to our move. They would have to put our house up for sale, setting the price high enough to pay off the mortgage and still have enough money to live a full year in Nebraska in case Papa couldn't find a job. In their minds, Jehovah would make the decision. If He wanted them to serve where the need is great, He'd find a buyer who would pay the price they needed to get.

Our house wasn't on the market for a week when my parents received an offer higher than their asking price. The only condition was that we would have to move out a month sooner than my parents wanted. This was resolved when the next-door neighbors moved out of their house and agreed to rent it to my parents for a month. Things went so smoothly that Mama told everyone at the Hall about Jehovah's intervention in this matter. When Lena Edwards, Joe Jalotti, and his new wife, Louise, heard how God had directed our family to make the move to serve Him in Nebraska, they decided to serve where the need is great in Columbus, Georgia.

High school started in early September, and I submerged myself in school work. I avoided any and all conversation about the upcoming move. Shortly before leaving, Mama decided to have a long talk with me. She told me that one of the most compelling reasons for our move to Nebraska was to ensure my survival at Armageddon and my eternal life in God's new world. She claimed that for the last two years I had been going through a rebellious streak and that my pride was eventually going to get the better of me. I was putting too much attention on learning about worldly things at school that could only lead me out of the truth. Papa thought I was soon to become a juvenile delinquent because I liked to listen and dance to rock-and-roll music, which he believed was demonic. Mama wasn't so sure I would end up in jail, but she didn't like the fact that I was now trying to look like a delinquent since I started styling my hair in a jellyroll and ducktail.

Papa and I had had several altercations that year, and the language between the two of us had become very abrasive. On several occasions I openly defied him, challenging his poor thinking and bad parenting skills. I was now two inches taller than Papa and could hold him at bay when he tried to hit me. I started to regularly use the word "gee-whiz" when he told me that I shouldn't say "gee" because it was a shortened, derogatory use of God's son's name, Jesus. He also didn't like it when I used the phrase "good luck." He wanted me to say "good fortune." Club members believed that the word "luck" was rooted in the sinister underworld of gamblers who had no fear of God, and that Lady Luck was one of Satan the Devil's inventions to distract people from finding the truth. I constantly wished Papa "good luck" and he boiled with rage. I know he wanted to report my behavior to the congregation servant at the Hall, but he was afraid that his poor parenting skills would be exposed, and for this he could be removed as an elder. Something serious was about to happen, and Mama believed that our move to Nebraska would somehow solve our problems.

Mama, then into her preaching mode, tried to throw a kernel of Club truth my way—as if that would convince me that moving to Nebraska was something Jehovah had inspired. "You know Dickie, one of the things that convinced me that I'd found the truth was learning that the Club doesn't believe in hell. We don't have to scare people by telling them they'll burn in hell for eternity if they don't believe as we do."

I couldn't figure out what that had to do with this issue. And while I preferred to openly defy Papa and not Mama, I couldn't resist saying, "So you do what you do because you're not afraid of getting killed by God at Armageddon?"

Mama, who always had the last word, replied, "Dickie, I can only hope that our move to Nebraska will help you see the light because right now what you think and how you behave is hopeless."

Serving Time in Nebraska
Chapter 24

We arrived in Norfolk, Nebraska on November 30, 1958. It was cold and a light layer of snow dotted the flat, dreary landscape. I felt as desolate as our new surroundings. We had traveled from Los Angeles to Salt Lake City and Rock Springs, Wyoming, before heading due east. We had come close to Robin, Idaho, where my grandparents lived, yet we didn't stop to visit. I suspected Mama thought I might refuse to leave and want to stay permanently with my grandparents.

The trip was timed so that the moving van arrived in Norfolk the same day we did. Papa had rented an old, large, two-story home in the center of the city. Watching the movers bring in our furniture gave finality to the move and brought me to my senses. Sulking would not change our address. I would have to find a way to make the best of my time in Nebraska.

Mama went with me to sign up for the tenth grade. The high school building was new and modern, and I thought this might not be so bad after all. When I showed the principal the list of classes I'd taken in the eighth and ninth grade and started that year at Venice High School, he looked impressed, then apologized that Norfolk High School couldn't provide the kinds of classes I had taken in Los Angeles. He handed me a list of recommended subjects that would prepare me for college, although he wasn't sure that taking them would get me a scholarship. That's when Mama spoke up.

She explained what religious group we belonged to and why we had moved to Norfolk. She told him we were living in the last days, a grand worldwide preaching work was underway to help sincere honest people find the truth, and a new world was just around the corner. She wanted my education to prepare me for door-to-door preaching and life in the new world.

I shrank with embarrassment. Never had Mama talked to any of my teachers or a principal like this. If I had had even the slightest inkling of what she was going to say, I would have insisted that I register alone. I was fifteen years old, and Mama was telling a man who could have a positive influence on my future education something I didn't believe; and yet I sat there speechless. She took what power I had enjoyed for the last two years and chose what I would study. She was now in charge, and I wouldn't be taking college preparatory classes.

As Mama reviewed the list of classes that I could take and made her selections, the principal looked on in disbelief. He must have wondered how this young man from the big city taking college prep classes could be signing up for vocational agriculture (Future Farmers of America) and woodworking classes. It didn't fit. When he told Mama I would be required to take American and world history, Mama balked. She told him the only history lessons I needed were found in the Bible. He said it was mandatory by Nebraska law if I expected to graduate with a high school diploma. So Mama backed down. With my new curriculum in hand, I shelved my hopes for college.

A few months later, college again looked to be a possibility. Our football coach, Dell Miller, saw me playing in a pickup football game during gym class. I was quarterbacking and throwing long accurate passes. We played several times during the next few weeks before he asked to speak with me. He told me that I had the best throwing arm of anyone at our school. He wanted me to try out for the school's football team. He believed the University of Nebraska would become a national power and was confident that I was good enough to get a college scholarship. I told him that I would have to ask my mother. For two days, I fantasized that Mama would let me play, Coach Devaney from the University of Nebraska would see and recruit me, and I'd get into college.

When I finally approached Mama, I knew my biggest hurdle would be our two-hour theocratic ministry school and service meeting held on Friday night, because that's when the games were played. So I told Mama that if she would let me play, I would double the amount of time I spent in the door-to-door work. She told me "no" immediately.

When I reported the bad news to Coach Miller, he wasn't about to give up. He wanted me to practice passing the football and encouraged me to play as much pickup football as I could. He hoped Mama would change her mind for my senior year, although I knew she wouldn't.

I was angry with Mama for bringing me to Nebraska, and I was angry with her for not letting me play football. And yet, I transferred that anger onto Papa. That wasn't difficult to do as he was constantly putting his foot into his mouth and badgering me for the silliest of reasons. But what made matters worse was that his job at Montgomery Wards wasn't going well. He was barely getting paid enough for a single guy living with his parents, not nearly enough to support a wife and four kids. By the end of April, our family's cash reserves were almost depleted. We were down to rationing food portions to cut down on expenses.

Late one evening, I was very hungry and decided to sneak two teaspoons of peanut butter, although I hadn't been told directly that it was off limits. I got a peanut butter fix, sometimes twice a day, for almost a week. On Saturday afternoon, Papa came home early from work and caught me spooning the crunchy snack food into my mouth. He accused me of stealing, since I was taking food that belonged to the rest of the family, and demanded that I put it back immediately. I told him that he'd have to take it from me, that this wouldn't have happened if he had a decent job like he had in Los

Angeles, and that Susan had more common sense than he did. Then I calmly dropped the open jar and spoon onto the kitchen counter and walked slowly up to my bedroom.

I wasn't in my room for thirty seconds when I heard Papa running up the stairs. His face was blood-red and he looked like a crazy man when he appeared at my open door and started screaming. Though he wasn't coherent, I knew what it meant when he clenched his fist, cocked it back, and lunged in my direction. Before he could hit me, I grabbed hold of his fist and while falling back on my bed, I raised him up in the air with my knee, flipping him onto the wall next to my headboard. His head hit the wall with a thud, and he went down hard on the wooden floor. At first, he gasped for breath, and I was afraid he would stop breathing. When he regained his wind, and while still lying on the floor, he started yelling, repeating over and over that I wasn't his son. Mama heard the commotion in the basement where she was doing laundry, ran up the two flights of stairs, and told Papa to shut up and for me to get out of the house.

This time, Papa decided to report my conduct to the congregation servant, Tom Caldwell. When the three of us met the next day, Tom asked Papa to tell him what the problem was. Papa rambled on and on, and Tom patiently listened. Toward the end, some of Papa's comments were so inane that Tom raised his hand in the air and asked Papa to stop. Tom had figured out what was going on, and without asking me to tell my side of the story said, "Jack, this is not a congregational matter, and I would suggest that you do a better job in learning how your behavior influences Dickie's responses. I also know that both of you are having problems adjusting to life here in Nebraska. Perhaps it would work best for your family if you moved back to Los Angeles." Papa's silence was deafening.

Although I wouldn't learn this until many years later, Tom was one of the very few people associated with the Club who had the skills to counsel members when they experienced family or marital problems. Most congregation servants or elders were so poorly qualified to give good advice that they only exacerbated the members' problems.

I don't know what Papa told Mama about our meeting with Tom Caldwell. But a few weeks later, Mama said she and I needed to have a heart-to-heart talk. While I hoped she would tell me that we were moving back to California, I guessed correctly that's not what she had in mind. It seems that Brother Caldwell had told Papa about another brother in Freemont, Berger Anderson, who owned a janitorial supply business. Papa had interviewed with him and was hired. While he would have to be away from home for two or three nights a week selling in western Nebraska and South Dakota, Papa's income could exceed what he had earned in Los Angeles. And, in fact, it did. She told me that Papa was trying to be a better father to me, that I must do my part as well, and if we didn't solve our problems, both of us would be disfellowshipped.

For the three-and-a-half years that I lived in Nebraska, I was stigmatized for my association with the Club. The first year, I had no worldly friends. I spent any playtime I had with Club-affiliated boys who lived in either Omaha or Lincoln, almost a hundred miles away. I didn't have someone like Georgie or Sheila with whom I could be totally honest and share my inner feelings. But that would change in late August 1959, during a five-day district assembly in Rapid City, South Dakota.

The assembly was held in an open-air rodeo stadium. The grandstand's uncomfortable wooden bench seats, the hot muggy air, and absent protection from the sun made the three-hour stretches of sitting and listening a miserable experience—a self-inflicted persecution for God's sake.

On the third day of the convention, I met up with Glenn, a friend from Omaha, and we found a seat as far away from Mama as possible. We fidgeted and sweated for fifteen minutes before Glenn suggested we get out of the heat and find some relief under the grandstand seats. Eventually we found a spot where we could be alone and started talking. Glenn told me about some good-looking girls from his Hall and asked if I wanted to meet any of them during one of the assembly breaks. I told him that I really liked this girl I had seen in the refreshment booth on the north side of the stadium. He suggested we check her out when the session was over. Now I could talk a good talk about picking up girls, but I'd get all flustered and nervous when I tried talking to them for the first time. I'd have to make up some excuse because I didn't want Glenn to see how awkward I was around girls.

My thoughts were rudely interrupted when barely in my line of vision, I saw a ten-foot long two-by-four falling in my direction. I quickly jerked my head and the ten-foot two-by-four came so close to hitting me that a light breeze fanned my face on its descent. Landing less than an inch from my shoes on the soft powdery dirt floor, the fallen board kicked up a puff of dust. When I turned to see where it came from, there stood the very young lady I had been telling Glenn about. And she wasn't alone.

"Oh, I'm so sorry. You're not hurt, are you?"

"No, I'm okay," I replied, breaking into a big smile.

"I just tapped that board to get your attention. I didn't think it would almost hit you."

I quickly learned that this tall, attractive, and imaginative young lady was Helen Geerling. She and her friend Jeanie Crump had been working at the refreshment stand when they saw me and Glenn walk by. Helen immediately told Jeanie to get rid of her apron—they were going to meet some boys. They followed us under the grandstand and

Helen Geerling in 1959

were waiting off to the side when Helen spotted the two-by-four.

The four of us talked for almost an hour, totally free of the self-consciousness that often comes from meeting a person of the opposite sex for the first time, particularly during adolescence. We learned that both girls were from western Michigan. Helen lived in Holland and Jeanie, Grand Rapids. We laughed and had a lively conversation before I experienced a twinge of angst. I had to act now or I might not end up with the right girl. While Jeanie was nice, she was short and plump. Helen and Jeanie were like Mutt and Jeff. Since I was six-foot two-inches and Helen five-foot ten-inches, she was the girl I wanted. And it didn't take me long to figure out what to do.

"Do you girls mind if Glenn and I excuse ourselves for a moment?"

Helen's response was quick and encouraging. "No, take your time. We'll be here when you get back."

Once we were out of sight, I said to Glenn, "Let's flip a coin. If it comes up heads, I get Helen. If it comes up tails, I get Jeanie."

Glenn agreed, although I never told him I had a plan B if the coin toss didn't go my way. I flipped a quarter into the air and when it landed heads up on the dirt floor, I breathed a sigh of relief. I couldn't believe my good luck and headed back to the girls before Glenn could offer any resistance.

Without hesitating, I confidently asked, "Helen, how would you like to take a break from the convention? There's a nice park across the street where we can find some shade." I was so comfortable that it never occurred to me that she might turn me down. Fortunately, she accepted my offer.

For the next two-and-a-half days, Helen and I were inseparable. Helen was a happy person bursting with energy, and she possessed a real love for life. We never talked about anything related to the Club, and she took an interest in what I had to say, making me feel special and important.

I learned that Helen was seventeen, two years older than I was. And for the first two days we were together, she thought I was nineteen. She had traveled to the assembly with a Club couple and their two young children. Later I learned that she had been steadily dating a worldly boy back home in Michigan. Helen's mother, who had become a Club convert three years before, believed that going to a big assembly would allow Helen to meet some nice Club young man who could help root her into the truth. Helen was still struggling with the culture shock of going from a mainstream Christian church to meetings at the Kingdom Hall. She was further conflicted since her father and three older siblings were still nonbelievers.

During the hours I spent with Helen outside those convention grounds, I didn't waste my time thinking about how I would impress her. For the first time with a young lady, I participated in the pure joy of living without second-guessing myself. Together, laughter came easy and often. We shared our dreams about the future. With her, the trees, bushes, and flowers in the park that I had lunched among on the first day of the assembly were now greener, sweeter smelling, and more colorful. Songbirds of all kinds serenaded us. I again experienced the spiritual beauty of the natural world that I so much enjoyed when I was with my grandparents in Robin, Idaho. It was easy to imagine that someday my world might be bigger, better, and more to my liking if Helen and I were a team.

On Helen's trip back home to Michigan, she persuaded the couple she was riding with to stop and visit me and my family in Norfolk for a day and night. This dreary, small city came alive when I was alone with Helen. Clearly, it wasn't Norfolk that was causing my problems.

Once back home, Helen broke up with her boyfriend and started to attend all the Club meetings and go in the door-to-door work. She believed that this was what I would want her to do.

Over the next five years, we wrote letters frequently and spent time together on three occasions—twice at her home in Holland and once in New York City—and I never told her that I was a non-believer. I had learned to play the role of a religious hypocrite to appease Mama, and I believed I could do the same with Helen.

When Helen left our house that late summer of 1959, I had a

good idea of how I wanted my future to play out, although I didn't have a clue as to how I could make it a reality. But I did have some role models. Four young men, ranging in ages from nineteen to twenty-three, had come to live and pioneer in Norfolk in June of that year. They lived together in a basement apartment and worked part-time to support themselves financially. While they were fervent Club believers, I couldn't help liking them, particularly Daryl and Jerry Sutton, who had grown up in Omaha. All four had been raised as Club members, just as their parents and grandparents had been. But they seemed to enjoy life more than most of the Club members I knew. They could miss a meeting and not feel guilty about it. They didn't take the Club dogma so seriously and suggested to me that people at the Club headquarters weren't always right about some things printed in the *Watchtower*. It was, after all, just a group of imperfect men trying to do the best they could. While these pioneers believed in the new world and Armageddon, they weren't so sure that these events would happen in their lifetime. They also liked playing pickup football games with worldly young men and always asked me to be their quarterback.

After the games, everyone got together for food, drink, and conversation. The pioneers not only played with the worldly young men, they fellowshipped with them, and never once talked religion. This seemed both strange and refreshing. Mama would not have approved of me associating with worldly people. She believed they were under the control of the Devil, so they weren't capable of kindness or compassion, and definitely not trustworthy. In her view, we were better than they were. The four pioneers treated nonClub members as equals. I liked that.

The pioneers liked girls and went on dates, although no one was serious about any one girl. And each one of them planned to serve for four years at Bethel, get married after they left, have families, and live happily ever after as Club members in a world that Mama believed was awful. It didn't fit Mama's model, but it gave me something to think about over the next three years.

I also learned from Dave Martin, one of the four pioneers,

how to creatively count time in what Club members loosely called the door-to-door work. On this particular day, we met at the Hall at 8:00 a.m. for a fifteen-minute pep rally. Dave read from the Club's Yearbook, which records a Bible verse and the *Watchtower's* interpretation of it for every day of the year. Several people commented on the Scripture's application to Club members today. We talked about the Club book and booklets we would be placing that day, and Dave recommended a pitch that he believed would pique the householder's interest to want to purchase and read them. He told us that he planned to spend the whole day doing door-to-door work in the *rurals* and wanted to know if anyone in our group would like to join him. Working in the rurals meant calling on farm homes in the country where the houses were few and far between. The area he planned to work was a forty-five-minute drive from Norfolk. Mama raised her hand and it was decided that Mama, Tim, and I would join him. While I was a little shocked, as I'd planned to be back home before noon, it turned out to be an interesting day.

Dave's day in the door-to-door work had started at 7:00 a.m. when he left sixteen back issues of the *Watchtower* and *Awake!* at two nearby laundromats. He then stopped for breakfast, giving the waitress a tip and the latest copies of the *Watchtower* and *Awake!*, before meeting us at the Hall at 8:00 a.m. We knocked at our first farmhouse at 9:30 a.m., took a coffee break in the small town of Humphrey at 11:00 a.m., had lunch at 12:30 p.m., took another coffee break at 2:00 p.m., and we were back at the Hall at 4:00 p.m. Our day working in the rurals amounted to calling on twenty farmhouses. No one answered the door at ten of them; one farmer's wife purchased two books and six booklets from Dave; the other nine homeowners weren't interested. At the ten not-at-homes, Dave and Mama left twenty copies of the *Watchtower* and *Awake!*. On Dave's field service report card that he turned in once a week, he reported for that day: nine hours in the door-to-door work, the placement of twenty-eight magazines, two books, and six booklets, and one back call. Since Dave had left magazines with the waitress two weeks earlier, he rationalized that giving her the latest issues was a back call.

Mama never told me how creative she was with reporting her time in the door-to-door work. As far as she was concerned, that was personal — something between her and Jehovah. She could be very closed-mouthed when she wanted to. So when Mama asked to speak privately about a secret she had long kept from me, she had my full attention.

In February 1960, Mama told me what I had long suspected but never knew for sure. But before she would tell me, I had to promise that I wouldn't say a word about it to anyone — especially Papa and my siblings. Papa was not my biological father. My real father was named Dean Lowe Geddes. He had died only a few days before Mama told me of his existence when his truck turned over on an icy patch of road near Pocatello, Idaho. Mama had met Dean at a dance in Salt Lake City, Utah, late in 1942. He was tall, handsome, full of energy, fun to be with, and he made Mama laugh. They had dated for several months when Mama told him she was pregnant. He stalled for time and finally confessed that he was already married. He asked his wife for a divorce, but she wouldn't grant it because she was Catholic. And that was the end of the story as far as Mama was concerned.

Many things raced through my mind and I asked lots of questions. Why had Mama waited until Dean was dead before telling me about him? Was I ever adopted? How did Papa come into the picture? That winter day, I learned that I was born Richard Evans and that I was not legally a Kelly. Mama still believed that Armageddon would arrive before I turned twenty. And although I was now sixteen, she saw no need to change my name. In fact, she was proud that she had gotten a social security card for me without having to show my birth certificate. Her reason for telling me now that I had a different father than my siblings was so that I might treat Papa with more respect and maybe we wouldn't end up killing each other someday.

Knowing for sure that Papa wasn't my biological father improved our relationship. And I slowly began to admire how hard he worked at selling and how well he provided for our material things. He had been there for Mama when she needed him. I decided not to allow his peculiarities to irritate me and I stopped annoying him. He was who he was and he did the best he could with the talents he was given. We never again had a cross word between us.

I graduated from high school in May 1961. While I wasn't quite ready to leave home, I was determined to plot a plan of escape from Mama's pervasive control. I needed to break the stranglehold that Mama had on my life. But I needed lots of help from the Club for it to work.

Leaving Mama
Chapter 25

In May 1960 two of the four pioneers, Daryl Sutton and Larry
Shockley, were invited to live, work, and study at Bethel, the Club's
headquarters in Brooklyn. Not long after that, Jerry and Dave
moved away too, leaving a vacancy in capable men responsible
for directing the five weekly meetings and the door-to-door work.
Complicating matters was the Kingdom Hall's recent move from
Pierce to Norfolk. While Mama and several other women from
our Hall were more than capable of filling the vacated positions,
they weren't allowed to preach from the pulpit or act as ministerial servants as the Club taught that God finds this offensive and
women just don't have the emotional and intellectual toughness
to do a man's work. I believed, even then, that this was one of the
Club's most ludicrous teachings.

Before filling those positions, Tom Caldwell asked to speak
with me. I wondered if Papa had complained about me again.
Instead, he told me that he liked my speaking skills and wanted
me to start giving one-hour public talks, and not just at our Hall.
I was flattered and said yes. He told me what my first topic would
be, gave me a printed outline of the lecture (which came from the
Club's headquarters), and set a date—three weeks away. I learned
that I'd be able to count an hour in the door-to-door work on my

field service report card for my efforts.

I gave my first talk to a packed audience. I liked the adrenaline rush, and it appeared that everyone enjoyed not only the message, but my delivery–particularly Mama. Afterwards, several people told me it was one of the best talks they had ever heard.

When Tom Caldwell, who wasn't quick to hand out compliments, told me how well I had done, I was elated. That is, until he said, "Dick, I think you're ready to become a ministerial servant. I'm going to recommend that you be appointed as the magazine and territory servant and the Norfolk book study conductor. Now that you've given your first public talk, I think you're ready. Of course, you know that the appointment will have to be approved by the circuit servant and the governing body in Brooklyn, but I think it's just a formality. Congratulations." Then he shook my hand and hurried off to prepare for the next meeting.

This wasn't what I expected, but I was glowing from Tom's confidence in my skills. I knew Mama would like it if I accepted, but I'd have to give it more thought.

As the book study conductor, I would have to preside over the Tuesday night meeting at the Norfolk Hall where one of the Club's books was studied in smaller, pre-assigned groups. I'd prepare in advance by underlining the answers to the questions listed on the bottom of the page for every paragraph. Once at the meeting, I'd make sure a baptized brother, or I, opened and closed the meeting with a prayer. Then I'd read the questions for a particular paragraph, ask for a show of hands from those who knew the answers, and select someone to share it. We'd generally get three or four responses before I would need to ask someone to read the paragraph out loud and then we'd go on to the next paragraph. Occasionally, I'd ask someone to read a Scripture, as I thought that was the Club's unspoken policy to make it feel like the members were studying the Bible and not just a book.

As the magazine and territory servant, I would have to distribute the latest issues of the *Watchtower* and *Awake!*, which were published biweekly. Every member at our Hall would give me a standing order for the number of magazines they planned to purchase and place in the door-to-door work. They'd pay me three cents and place it for five cents. Members were encouraged to err on the high side because they could always give out-of-date issues free at not-at-homes, laundromats, and in the reception area of doctors' and dentists' offices.

The job also required that I organize and dispense a territory assignment card to members who wanted to go in the door-to-door work. Members couldn't knock on doors in just any part of town. They first had to check out a territory card, preferably for an area that hadn't been worked for at least the last three months. When a member had called on all the homes, he or she returned that particular territory card, and the territory servant recorded the date of its return. When a new housing development was built, the territory servant created a new card for the area.

I knew that as the magazine and territory servant, I wouldn't have trouble with my conscience. And the job would give me some diversion at the Friday night and Sunday morning meetings. It was the book study conductor position that troubled me. At the time, we were studying a book called *Your Will Be Done on Earth*. It made assumptions so far-fetched about the Club's activities fulfilling Old Testament Bible prophecy that I wondered about the sanity of the writer. The book was released at the 1958 convention in New York City and most likely written by Fred Franz. The author's name was not divulged, because once Nathan Knorr became president, the writers for Club publications weren't identified.

The basic premise of the book was that the Bible book of Daniel predicted events that would shortly precede Armageddon and the end of the first 6,000 years of human existence. It also wove biblical prophecy together with Club history. I saw the book as a litany of rants and miscalculations. The writer, who loathed anyone who didn't believe as he did, asserted that he'd identified the dates referred to as "times" in Scripture. For example, the *seven times* or *appointed times* (Daniel 4:16, 23, 25; Luke 21:24) were 2,520 years. These times began when Babylon burned God's sanctuary and destroyed Jerusalem in the fall of 607 B.C. (although all historians set the date at 586 B.C.) and ended in the fall of 1914 when God set up His heavenly kingdom and anointed His Son, Jesus Christ, to be the King of kings and Lord of lords. The *times, two times, and half a time* (Daniel 7:25: 12:7) began November 1, 1914 and ended May 7, 1918 when the Club's president, secretary-treasurer, and *Watchtower* writers were arrested (as some of the Club's literature was adjudicated to be in violation of the Espionage Act) and sent to the federal penitentiary for nine months. The two thousand and three hundred evenings and mornings or 2,300 days (Daniel 8:14) began in May 1926, at the London, England convention when the Club's president, Judge Rutherford, put world leaders on notice that they had offended Jehovah God by putting their trust in the League of Nations to bring about world peace instead of in His heavenly kingdom, in power since 1914. The 2,300 days ended on October 15, 1932, with the official publication of Rutherford's notice in the *Watchtower*.

A week later, I reluctantly accepted both positions, making me, at sixteen, one of the youngest ministerial servants in the state of Nebraska. However, I was careful to not give the impression that I believed any of the convoluted assumptions in the *Your Will Be Done on Earth* book.

Dale Larson, the circuit servant who approved my appointment, visited our Hall every six months. When he first started coming, he was twenty-six years old, had served at Bethel for eight years, was recently married to Sandy, a pioneer, and this was his first assignment in the circuit work. On his second visit to our Hall and at all subsequent visits, he and Sandy stayed at our home and slept in my parents' bedroom. They shared all their meals with our family unless other members invited them to dinner at a restaurant or in their home.

During Dale's visits, I had lots of conversations with him. Like Mama, he encouraged me to pioneer when I graduated from high school. While Mama wanted me to pioneer because the end of the world was near and a great preaching work needed to be done,

Dale's take on it was different. He told me that I couldn't get into Bethel unless I pioneered for at least six months. He had really liked Bethel and saw it as a wonderful learning opportunity. He knew a number of people who served at Bethel and went on to become missionaries, circuit servants like him, and district servants. But what he told me next piqued my interest.

Dale knew lots of guys who left Bethel to get married and have children, although that wasn't what he and Sandy were going to do. They planned to wait to have kids until after Armageddon, when they were living in the new world. Nonetheless, those guys leaving Bethel to raise families always found good, well-paying jobs because of their work skills acquired at Bethel. Many of them held key positions in the printing industry. Some of them were professional painters, gardeners, and cooks. He knew several guys who owned cleaning businesses and were making more money than most college graduates. In essence, he believed there wasn't a better technical school in the country.

After graduating from high school, I enrolled as a pioneer. I turned in my application for Bethel six months later. While pioneering, I worked part-time selling janitorial supplies and teaching sports at the local YMCA (Young Men's Christian Association). Several years later, the Club decided God didn't approve of the YMCA and told its members to disassociate themselves or be disfellowshipped. It seems that some new revelation made it clear to Club leaders that the only Christian organization recognized by God was the Club.

Meeting the time requirements in the door-to-door work was a real challenge for me, although I reported my time using the techniques I'd learned from Dave Martin. I met many of my quotas for placement of Club magazines, books, and booklets just like Dave. I had a regular route of lonely old men and women who enjoyed having someone visit with them. These were my back calls. I met my bible study quotas when I studied with non-baptized children of Club members. When I actually went door-to-door, I was never invasive like Mama. It was a sales job, as if I were selling Fuller

Brush or Avon products. If you wanted to buy what I was selling, that was fine. If you didn't, that was okay, too. Although it always bothered me that I was trying to sell something I didn't believe in or use.

I spent forty of my required one hundred hours a month writing letters to spouses, children, and parents of people I learned about in the paper's obituary column. In each letter, I'd share some Scriptures, the Club's interpretation of them, and a Club tract for the deceased's loved ones. This kind of door-to-door work was much easier. I would also write to my grandparents and cousins, Danny and Ronny, and count my time if I made even the slightest comment about something related to the Club. If it took an hour to write, that's how much time I reported on my field service report card.

I received my invitation to Bethel a year after becoming a pioneer. On a very impressive piece of stationery, I was asked to report to the Club's headquarters in Brooklyn Heights on May 10, 1962.

The first person I showed the letter to was Mama. She was very happy over a year before when I told her that I wanted to become a pioneer. But now, she was elated. She firmly believed that if I lived at the Club's headquarters for a few years, I would share the same passion she had for serving Jehovah God.

Only minutes past midnight, on May 9, I stood outside a nearly deserted train station in Norfolk, Nebraska, with Mama. She was fidgety and didn't seem to know what to say or do. My eighteen years of life with her were about to end. I could hear the faint sound of a train to the west—the sound of liberation. Mama's shackles were about to be broken. I had tried to run away from home many times since I was six years old, and now I would succeed. The train's brakes screeched and my freedom train lumbered to a stop. I hugged Mama, climbed aboard, and waved goodbye. I was finally leaving Mama.

A New Life at Bethel
Chapter 26

In the dead of night, my only traveling companions were the sounds and sways of a fast-moving train. Heading swiftly toward a new life at Bethel, it felt good to be alive. I knew I'd not sleep this night—an exciting adventure awaited me. Wound as tight as could be, my mind darted back and forth in time.

I thought about my grandparents. I hadn't told them I was going to Bethel. That's something Mama would eagerly do. They had visited us in Nebraska our first summer there. They looked old and much smaller without the backdrop of their Idaho ranch. Grandpa and I spent our time fishing and playing horseshoes. I wanted to tell him about my failed education plan and that I hadn't stood up to Mama on that first day of school. But the words never came. To make matters worse, Mama asked Grandma and Grandpa to attend a Friday night meeting and they reluctantly agreed. I wished they hadn't. They looked out of place and I felt ashamed for them to see me there.

After my grandparents returned to Idaho, I wrote to them every month. Grandma was the one who wrote back, never Grandpa. I wanted to tell them how many times I had dreamed about running away to live with them in Robin, but I didn't. I was too old now and would have to help myself if I wanted to change where I lived.

That's what I was doing now.

I thought about Mama. She had lived in Los Angeles as a Club member for eleven years and brought more than thirty people into the truth. And yet, after three years in Nebraska, she hadn't bagged a single convert. She couldn't get one person to attend our cramped, drab Kingdom Hall for even one meeting during her tenure in Norfolk. Of course, my grandparents' visit didn't count. Had she lost her touch? Were the people in Nebraska so different?

Her evangelizing skills hadn't changed. These were different people than the ones she witnessed to in the big city. These small-town Nebraska people had community. They were actively involved in their churches. What their neighbors thought about them mattered. And most of these people believed Club members were either uneducated apostates or wanna-be Christians.

Mama had such big aspirations. That's why we moved to serve where the need was great. But then, in her mind, she may have believed the move was a success since she had taken me out of the big city and all the trouble I would have gotten into. She had saved me from a sure death at Armageddon. Now she believed that I would do well at Bethel, be an enthusiastic convert like her, and one day become one of the Club's shining stars.

I thought about Helen: that she had become a believer, how our relationship had faltered, and my feigned piety in nearly three years of letter writing. We wrote letters almost every day for the first year. Helen told me about getting baptized. She was going in the door-to-door work and attending all five meetings a week. Helen's mother adored me, figuring I was partially responsible for Helen's transformation. I told Helen about my Club activities, but I didn't tell her what I believed about its core doctrines and policies. After a year-and-a-half, we were lucky if we wrote two letters a month.

I thought about when I fell in love with Helen all over again. It was spurred by her act of kindness in response to a crisis. On Saturday afternoon eight months earlier, as I walked home from my job at the YMCA, fire engine sirens blared, and I saw menacing billows of ugly black smoke above the tree line. Turning the corner on our street, I gasped. Our house was on fire. Dozens of gawking strangers were jammed into our yard and the street. Two heavily clothed firemen hosed the heart of the fire with a steady, sturdy stream of water from a cobra-like canvas hose. Finally, the flames were transformed into harmless, but acrid steam.

Two hours before, Mama had taken a pork roast out of the freezer, squeezed it into an aluminum pot, added a cup of water, turned the electric burner to high, and placed the metal pot on a red-hot burner to thaw the meat. When she realized that she needed a vegetable for the night's supper, she made a quick trip to the grocery store. But it wasn't quick enough. While she was gone, the water evaporated from the pan, hot fat around the pork sent sparks to a towel above the stove, and soon the whole house was on fire.

For the next three months, our family lived in a trailer home. I wrote Helen and told her what happened. A few weeks later, I received a package in the mail. In it was a gorgeous woolen knit sweater from Helen. She included a very touching letter, with not a word about the Club. She was concerned about me and worried that I may have lost most of my clothes in the fire.

Helen's act of kindness and her sweet words overwhelmed me. I thought about the wonderful time we had in South Dakota and Nebraska and how easy it was to talk with her. She exuded joy and a love for life. I wanted to cuddle up with her again.

The more I thought about her, the more I wanted to go see her. But I didn't have access to a car, and I wasn't certain things would work out between us. I needed help, so I called my friend Glenn. I asked if he wanted to travel with me to Holland, Michigan. He liked the idea.

We made our journey in January 1962 and it was a great success. Helen and I spent most of our time together talking. In one conversation, I shared a few of my concerns about Club theology, but I didn't tell her everything. I think because I was a pioneer, she thought my actions said more about me than a few doubts. Otherwise, we didn't discuss religion. We reveled in the joy of each other's company. And I decided anew that whatever differences there were between us, Helen was the person I wanted to marry someday.

When I arrived back home in Nebraska, I talked with Papa about the chances of getting a job with the company he worked for. I interviewed and was hired. I bought a 1957 Ford, and my career in selling janitorial supplies got off to a good start. But two months into my new job, I realized that I hated selling. While trying to figure out what to do, I received my invitation to Bethel. I told Helen about it, and she encouraged me to go.

Nestled in the aura of the train's pleasant vibrations, my mind drifted to what life would be like at Bethel. While it wasn't stipulated in my invitation letter, I knew the Club expected me to stay four years. I was told to report to the old Bethel home on Columbia Heights, directly across the street from the new Bethel home. The home I would be living in had ten floors, a tower, and two basement levels for the kitchen and dining rooms. The reception area on the first floor boasted a spectacular view of the East River's Buttermilk Channel and the lower Manhattan skyline. The new Bethel home had eleven floors. The living space between the two homes was 330,000 square feet.

As many as 850 people lived in the two Bethel homes at one time. One hundred of them came and went every five-and-a-half months to attend *Gilead*. This was the Club's seminary where missionaries were trained to serve in foreign countries or selected members were taught to hold key leadership positions. These students and the 750 people who worked at Bethel lived in dormitory-style rooms designed for two adults. Two large community bathrooms and showers were located on every floor. And since mostly men lived at Bethel, only a few floors were designated for women.

I knew that once I arrived at Bethel, I'd be evaluated for my work skills and assigned to work fifty-five hours a week at one of the homes, at one of the two printing factories a half mile away, or at the *kingdom farm* in Ithaca, New York, many miles away. Most Bethelites worked in one of the Club's two factories located at Adams or Sands Streets. The Adams factory had eight floors and the Sands factory thirteen floors, for a combined area of 350,000 square feet. In these factories, Bethelites printed the Club's books, Bibles, magazines, booklets, and tracts. About eighty people served at the kingdom farm where most of the food was produced for the Bethel family.

At midmorning I arrived at Grand Central Station, in the heart of New York City. Although sleep deprived, I can't remember a time when I felt more alert and rested. I gathered what little luggage I had and hailed a taxi. As we drove over the Brooklyn Bridge, the Adams Street printing factory, with its *Watchtower* billboard perched on the roof, served as a beacon: the Bethel homes weren't far away.

I was dropped off in front of a handsome, tall red brick building. I opened the wide, spotless glass door, walked up several steps, looked around the immaculate reception area, and informed the receptionist who I was. She said they had been expecting me and asked that I wait in a much larger reception room with a picture window of lower Manhattan. Someone was playing the piano—not one of the *kingdom songs*—which I took as a good omen.

I waited several minutes before a man from the Bethel home office came to greet me. He took me to room 204, my new home. I learned that my roommate was twenty-six years old, worked in the pressroom in the Adams Street factory, and would be leaving Bethel in three weeks. Two single beds hugged opposite walls and the tile floor was sparkling clean. I could hang my clothes on the empty side of the small closet. My roommate had his things crammed in on the other side. Each of us had a chest of drawers and a small desk, and we shared a mirrored cabinet over the sink. Looking out of the two windows in our room, I could see the well-maintained garden in front of the new Bethel home across the street.

Next, I was taken on a tour of both homes. I was particularly impressed with the industrial laundry and dry-cleaning department. I was to put my dirty clothes in a special hamper once a week and they would be returned clean the next day. Items that needed pressing were separated and hung up in my closet two days later. I met the barber, who was from Nebraska, and learned that I would get my hair cut every three weeks. The last stop on the tour was the commissary where I could buy incidentals at a reduced price. That was helpful, since after working fifty-five hours each week, everyone at Bethel was paid the same stipend of $14.00 a month. I could not have survived without Mama's financial help.

It was close to noon, and dinner was about to be served, so we went to the upstairs dining room. There I was assigned a seat at a ten-person table where I was to eat breakfast and dinner six days a week. I was introduced to my tablemates, and I could quickly see that they considered me to be nothing more than a *newboy*. These hardworking people were not in the mood for small talk or giving me a warm welcome. After the perfunctory hellos, I might as well have been invisible.

After lunch, I went to the Bethel home office and was told that I would be assigned a full-time job within the next few days. In the meantime, I could help with several odd jobs. They sent me to work right away breaking beer, wine, and hard liquor bottles into unrecognizable shards. This was done so that the worldly people who picked up the trash wouldn't see how much alcohol was consumed at Bethel, which was significant. It was explained to me that nothing should be done to bring reproach upon Jehovah's organization.

By mid-afternoon, with the sounds of breaking glass still reverberating in my head, I was escorted to a nearby five-story brownstone. Here my job was to clean the apartment on the second floor. About thirty minutes into my work, I realized I was cleaning Hayden Covington's home. He was the Club's attorney and a key-note speaker at the international assemblies in 1953 and 1958. But that day, in the presence of his redheaded wife and small children, Covington wore a suit that he must have slept in the night before, looked like he had been drinking, and rattled off expletives that Papa told me people with weak minds use to express themselves forcibly. This was my first exposure to the double standards for the Club's top officials.

On my third day at Bethel, I was assigned to be a waiter in the downstairs cafeteria. My job was to set the tables, serve food, clear the tables, and wash the dishes with a large, fast moving, automatic dishwasher three times a day, five-and-a-half days a week. I would have weekend duty every three weeks. And instead of eating at the table I was originally assigned to, I was to eat my meals with the kitchen and dining room staff after the Bethel family ate their meals.

I liked my co-workers in the dining room and kitchen. We didn't talk religion. Small talk came easy and we laughed often. I enjoyed the fast pace of my job. I treated the preparation and service of the meal as show time and the diners appreciated my attentiveness. There wasn't anything I disliked about my job, although there was one day I could have done without.

The kitchen overseer, Carl Hoppe, noticed that beef kidneys were piling up in the meat locker. So he decided that our Saturday afternoon dinner entrée would be kidney pies. He gave his assistant, Ralph, clear instructions on how he wanted them prepared, since he would be gone for the day. Shortly after Ralph started boiling the organ meat, his nose should have clued him in that this wasn't a good idea. But Carl had told him what to do, and Ralph, being a good soldier, did what he was told. When the meal was prepared and portions set on every table, the two dining rooms smelled like a herd of cattle had urinated everywhere. Most people coming down for dinner turned around and left. It took two days to get rid of that awful odor.

After two months of working in the dining room, I was transferred to the kitchen. For several weeks I worked in the bakery making bread and pastries, helped the head chefs prepare the main course and side dishes, cleaned vegetables and fruit, and helped prepare the salads. I also took my turn as the pot licker—the person who cleaned up the food-stained cooking pots and pans.

Within a month, I was assigned to be the veggie room overseer and held this job for the rest of my Bethel career. At eighteen, I was the youngest overseer at Bethel and had ten to thirty people working for me, depending on the time of year. Our department peeled potatoes, cored and peeled apples, sliced and diced onions, canned peaches and beans, and did our best to present the vegetables, fruits, and salads as culinary events. My specialty was making creative salads and dressings. I learned how to manage and lead people without bossing, a skill that served me well after leaving Bethel. I believed my work efforts were always appreciated and I can't remember a work day that I did not enjoy.

While working in the veggie room, I met lots of unique and interesting people. One was Ron Barnaby. He worked in the bakery and was very good at what he did. He was a good listener. And I could share my concerns about the Club without worrying that he would report me to the higher-ups. Ron was a nonpracticing gay. He was not attracted to women, although he had several lady friends. He was very effeminate and could not disguise it. That bothered him a lot. Reflecting Club attitudes, he worked hard to control his inner demons and believed that in the new world all would be well, he would fall in love with a woman, have babies, and no longer have to suppress the very essence of who he was.

It wasn't uncommon to meet district servants in the veggie room. These men, I would later learn, hadn't followed instructions from *the service department*, and unbeknownst to them, they had been called into the headquarters to be demoted. One of the most ironic experiences occurred when I was told that Randall Shafer would be working with me for a few days. He had been my parents' congregation servant in Los Angeles, moved up the ranks from circuit servant to district servant, and advised Mama to move and serve where the need was great. His transgression had probably been to use his thinking skills instead of the service department's printed black book policies on how to handle a delicate congregational matter. I didn't know for sure.

When he was introduced, Randall appeared happy to see me. We made small talk about the fact that he had known me as a boy. I think he knew what was going to happen. Harley Miller, the service department overseer, was delaying the bad news. When Randall was informed of his demotion to a circuit servant, he decided to call it quits and move back to Los Angeles. Mama told me several years later that Randall went back to the family furniture business and was a lukewarm publisher after that.

The service department at Bethel was the unofficial police force for the Club. Knorr had known Harley for years and trusted him implicitly to enforce policy that Knorr considered inspired from God. All congregational concerns were sent to the service department. All circuit and district servants reported to Harley and his enforcers.

Several years after I disassociated myself with the Club, a close friend, Marshall Overstreet, confided that while he was in a leadership position at the congregation level, it was reported to him that a ministerial servant had been molesting his then twelve- and fifteen-year-old son and daughter. The man's wife caught him in the act. Marshall shared this information with a circuit servant, who informed Marshall that while the man's ministerial servant status would be terminated, Club policy was to not report his transgression to the authorities. Several months later, Marshall was informed that another ministerial servant sexually abused his stepdaughters. Again, Marshall was told to keep the matter hushed up. When it happened a third time, Marshall decided to circumvent the circuit servant and call the service department at Bethel. When he was told to do as the circuit servant directed him, a bank of flood lights turned on in his head. He questioned God's oversight of this organization and left the Club three years later.

I saw firsthand how the Club treated its followers when Chuck Arnold joined me in the veggie room. He had his hand severed in a printing press. After it happened, Knorr informed the Bethel family of the incident, claiming it was due to Chuck's negligence. That's not what I was told by people who were there. But everyone knew that you didn't publicly challenge God's appointed leader and not pay the consequences. Chuck was fitted with one of the cheapest, ugliest prosthesis I had ever seen. And yet, he didn't complain. It was all I could do to hold my inner rage while he rehabilitated in my department.

My most memorable day in the veggie room was Friday, November 22, 1963. It was late afternoon, and I was sequestered in a circle of ten people peeling potatoes. Just before our work day was to end, the assistant home overseer walked in, asking if we had heard the news that President Kennedy was shot. In the sudden silence, everyone stopped what they were doing to get more information. And the spectrum of responses during the next fifteen minutes was vintage Club silliness.

Club members were constantly told what to think and how to feel. Their thinking skills atrophied over a period of time. And at moments like this, without knowing the Club's official position, members said the craziest things. Several people were elated, thinking that Armageddon wasn't far away, perhaps only a few days. Some said it was a sign from God that the end was near and we needed to be particularly vigilant.

As outrageous as those observations were, they were voiced by people who had undergone rigorous training. For my first six months, I was enrolled in a special school designed for all new Bethelites called primary. Here I spent twenty hours a week attending religion classes, doing homework, taking tests, and reading the Bible. The promotion of critical thinking skills wasn't one of the curricular agendas. The purpose for the intense training regimen was so that the Club could evaluate the new arrivals and determine where they could best help it promote the worldwide preaching work.

Not everyone graduated from primary. Those with poor study skills were doomed from the beginning. I was never sure what criterion was used, but if at any time during those six months the primary instructors determined a person didn't meet their standards, he was asked to leave Bethel immediately. Members in the Hall that the fellow came from would think he was a failure, leaving him with a stigma that there must be something wrong with him since he didn't have the "stuff" to make it at Bethel. Several young men didn't go back home when they were asked to leave.

After completing primary, it was the lack of work skills or ethics that involuntarily ended careers at Bethel. When this happened, Nathan H. Knorr, the Club's President, would tell the Bethel family who the guilty party was and share the sordid details before breakfast. Knorr, like Stuart Sanders, seemed to get an evil pleasure telling people details they had no business knowing about. It was obvious whom Stuart had learned his poor manners from.

Several people were escorted off the premises because they were caught stealing from a roommate. I never understood how someone could subject himself to the Club's rigid lifestyle and still think that God wouldn't notice he was a thief.

Laziness and drunkenness were reasons for dismissal, and we were always informed of who and why with lots of juicy details. The glaring exception was Covington. His heavy drinking was allowed to go unchecked for many years before he was disfellowshipped, though I don't know if that was the reason. He was reinstated a short time later, but it didn't stop his drinking.

As far as Knorr and the Club were concerned, the biggest sin of all was fornication. If caught having sex out of wedlock, the person was kicked out of Bethel and his story was the entrée for our morning breakfast.

A friend, Darrell Lyons, was introduced to Knorr's rants less than thirty days after he arrived at Bethel. He was eighteen, naïve, self-righteous, and sheltered. So when Knorr informed everyone that Brother and Sister Rothwell, who had been at Bethel for ten years, were expelled for engaging in oral sex, Darrell was embarrassed and confused. He wasn't exactly certain what the crime was. Then Knorr further informed everyone that the Rothwells had occasionally dabbled in anal sex.

Now Darrell was thoroughly confused, and wondered how he might bridge his knowledge gap of the libidinous. Perhaps he could go to the public library. But Knorr wasn't through. He then gave a blow-by-blow description of the married couple's sins and reminded everyone of the proper God-ordained mechanics of sexual union between a man and a woman.

Darrell tried to figure out how Knorr knew such personal details. What most likely happened was during an innocent conversation with someone, one of the Rothwells shared how they practiced birth control. When a Bethelite couple got pregnant, they were asked to leave. So they probably thought that helpful information would be appreciated if the couple wanted to stay at Bethel. But a Gestapo-like mentality was pervasive. If you saw or heard something you believed a wrongdoing, you were supposed to report it to the higher-ups. That's the way it worked at the congregation level as well.

After being snitched on, the couple would have had to meet with a committee of three elders. At the meeting, the couple would be asked if what was reported to them was true. If it was, the guilty party or parties would be obligated to share the details. This would allow the committee to evaluate the damages. And no one was kicked out of Bethel without Knorr knowing everything, especially the sordid details. While Knorr should have been ashamed of himself, no one had the courage to tell him that this behavior of sharing such details was simply wrong.

It irritated me when Knorr delayed breakfast in order to vent his righteous indignation, but what I really didn't like was the requirement to spend ten hours a month in the door-to-door work and attend all five of the Club's weekly meetings held in the Bethel Kingdom Hall. Fortunately, because I worked in the dining room and later the kitchen, I was not held to the same standards as other Bethelites. When I had a day off, instead of going in the door-to-door work, I explored the museums, libraries, and unique sights of New York City.

After my successful completion of primary, I was assigned to an all-black Kingdom Hall on 125th Street in the heart of Harlem. The members were generous and kind, and on Sundays I was always invited to someone's apartment for a home-cooked meal. The congregation servant frequently teased that whenever he looked at his audience, the four young Bethel brothers there looked like snowballs in a coal bin.

These appointments to the Kingdom Hall in central Harlem and my work in the kitchen/vegetable room were the consequences of unusual events and odd acquaintances.

I had been at Bethel for a month, enjoying my work as a waiter.

From what I could observe, cleanliness was next to godliness, and I liked that. But I didn't know that not all Bethel residents shared this value. The revelation came about when I was asked to open the dining room and the kitchen early in the morning to help get things organized for the day's breakfast.

My alarm went off at 5:15 a.m. I showered and shaved in the community bathroom and went back to my room to dress. My roommate was sound asleep and snoring loudly. I quietly walked down three flights of stairs to the spacious kitchen located on the second and lowest basement floor. When I turned on the column of lights, I looked in horror at a living wall-to-wall carpet of cockroaches covering every inch of the concrete and tiled floors. Almost instantly, like someone in the ranks yelled "fire," there was a mass exodus. Perhaps I had imagined it, as there wasn't a creepy crawler in sight. I turned off the lights and waited. When I turned them back on, the cockroaches were back, but not nearly as prolific. I decided to leave the lights on.

When Carl Hoppe, the kitchen overseer, reported for work, I excitedly told him what I had seen. He tried to hold his trademark stern, austere, old-school German expression, but a slight smile escaped for a half-second. Looking back, I'm sure that my naiveté was both amusing and refreshing. He told me how important it was that we thoroughly Lysol the floors, every inch of the floors, every day and sometimes twice a day. He explained how critical it was that we change the deadly chemicals in the cleaning solution every few weeks. Cockroaches were so good at adaptation that what might kill them one day would be gourmet cuisine a few weeks later. We could minimize the numbers of cockroaches that lived in the kitchen, but we couldn't rid them completely.

Several weeks later, I told the waiter overseer I reported to that I wasn't feeling well. After touching my forehead, he told me I should go to my room and lie down. He wouldn't be surprised if I had the flu. Later in the day, Carl inquired of my whereabouts and was told I had gone to my room sick. Believing I was faking it, he marched up to my room, opened the door, and walked in.

By now, I had the shivers and was sweating profusely. When I heard the door open, I turned on my side and looked up. When I saw Carl Hoppe standing in my room, I weakly asked, "What do you want, Brother Hoppe?"

He stood there for several seconds before backing away. And without saying a single word, he walked out of my room.

The next morning I felt well enough to report for work on time. At mid-morning I was told that Carl Hoppe wanted me to work for him, and that I was to report to his assistant for my assignment. Ralph told me that Carl was from the old school and trusted no one, but he had somehow taken a liking to my work ethics. I was not to take it personally that he had walked unannounced into my room.

While Carl worked at Bethel, he didn't live there. Ten years before, he and a woman who went to his assigned Kingdom Hall in the Bronx got married. Carl figured that he had enough seniority and with his standing at Bethel, his new wife would surely be invited to live with him there. But she did not want to give up her home and privacy. While she was a hard-core believer, she didn't think she'd like living at Bethel. It was too much of a structured environment and the women there were too standoffish. She would also have to work fifty-five hours a week at a job, most likely cleaning Bethel rooms. This was work similar to that performed by cleaning ladies in motels and hotels. And that is not how she wanted to serve Jehovah. Carl asked the Club's president if he could live with his new wife in her Bronx home and commute by subway to his job in the Bethel kitchen. Carl received the okay, and he was told that he wouldn't have to work on Saturdays or Sundays as a reward for his long service.

Shortly before I worked for Carl, I got to know Barry Morris, who worked in the kitchen as the butcher. Barry and I had come to Bethel at the same time so when my first roommate left, I asked Barry if he'd like to room with me. As we got to know each other, I decided that he wouldn't be someone to open up to with respect to my concerns with the Club. However, he liked to party and he was very generous. If you drank beer with Barry, he paid for it.

Barry's primary job was to cut meat for the meals served in the two Bethel dining rooms. However, he spent a good bit of time preparing special cuts for the fifteen to twenty men in the Bethel hierarchy. These guys and their wives, if they were married, would place their orders a few days in advance. Barry made sure they got the very best cuts of meat at no cost. The meat was always much better than what would be served to the rank-and-file Bethelite. These elite few also lived in apartments with their own kitchen, dining room, living room, and bathroom facilities, as opposed to the dormitory type rooms that other Bethelites lived in.

One evening there was a knock at our door. It was a newboy who worked in the home department. He told Barry that Nathan Knorr and the Club's treasurer, Grant Suiter, wanted a special cut of top grade sirloin for a party they were hosting. They wanted it right away. Barry was told that for his inconvenience he could cut some meat for himself. Before leaving the room, Barry asked me to join him in the kitchen for a party after he delivered the steaks. In the meantime, I was to ask two other Bethelites to join us, which I did. Our festivities officially started when Barry came out of the meat locker carrying four thick steaks, two six-packs of Rolling Rock beer, and a bottle of Scotch.

Not being an experienced drinker, I paced my beer consumption, making sure I focused my attention on the juicy medium-rare steak. Eventually, Barry broke open the bottle of Scotch and the party went downhill from there. It was all Barry and I could do to make it safely back to our room. However, one of the guys, Mike Danish, spent over an hour hovered over the toilet in the kitchen bathroom. He didn't make it back to his room until early in the morning. Fortunately, there was no damage done to the kitchen and no one had seen any of us in the latter stages of our drinking binge.

Unfortunately, Mike got to feeling guilty about what happened. While no one saw him stagger back to his room, he believed that it hadn't gone unnoticed by Jehovah. Confession was necessary to keep his good standing with God. So he met with George Couch, the home department overseer, and told him what had happened and who had partied with him.

No one from George's office spoke to me or Barry about the incident and I thought it was all but forgotten. Boys were being boys and no harm was done. It wasn't like we misbehaved all the time. However, when it came time for us to be assigned to a Kingdom Hall in the greater New York City area after graduating primary, all four of us were assigned to an all-black Hall. This was not normal. And it wasn't because of our skin color; 125th Street in central Harlem was not a safe place for anyone to be, let alone four nineteen-year-old white boys.

But that is how things worked at Bethel. If you got caught partying too loud and too late in your room, passed out in the hallway because you drank too much, or you happened to question one of the Club's leading men, it wasn't uncommon to "get the shaft." You weren't kicked out of Bethel for doing it the first time, but you were taught a lesson. As soon as news leaked out about our Harlem assignment to our fellow workers in the kitchen and dining room, Barry and I were bombarded with, "so what indiscretion do you owe the honor for that assignment?"

While the four of us didn't encounter any serious problems in Harlem, we never attended an evening meeting alone. We often played this game we called "count the number of times you hear the word mother f..." as we walked from the subway to the Hall. We never failed to hear it less than ten times before we reached our destination. Several times we were called "blue-eyed devils" by militant blacks, but without incident.

What a contrast in people when we stepped into the Hall. These were hardworking people who cared about us. Our congregation servant was particularly impressive. He shepherded a group of people who had come from a very negative environment. Like Mama, they needed the structure that Club rules and policies provided.

It seemed an anomaly to see so many African-Americans embrace a religion that for more than sixty of the Club's eighty-year history treated people with black skin as inferior. The Club's first two presidents were outspoken both on the pulpit and the printed page, claiming that Negroes were condemned by God because of Ham's indiscretion toward his father, Noah. At Bethel, no one of color served in the Club's hierarchy.

While I spent little of my time in Harlem, I was always learning something new. But my most significant learning experiences occurred while I worked at Bethel, where I met many fascinating people. It would ultimately be two of those people who would help me remove the millstone I had carried for sixteen years of my life, ending my Odyssey in Mama's Club.

Removing the Millstone
Chapter 27

After six months at Bethel, I felt very good about my accomplishments, and my self-esteem had never been better. I had successfully completed primary and impressed several of the Gilead instructors with my learning skills. I had a good job and was well-thought of by the people I worked for. I had plenty of good food to eat. And since September, I had been playing pickup football games on Saturday afternoons and rejoiced that I hadn't lost my passing ability. No one was bugging me to do more door-to-door work or place more Club literature. And I now had a circle of friends who shared my disbeliefs about many of the Club's doctrines and practices.

That was my biggest surprise at Bethel. When I arrived, I thought I was the only nonbeliever. I was relieved to discover I wasn't alone. While we doubters were a small minority, some of the guys I met were even angrier than I was. Most of us had come to Bethel to escape from and appease our parents, who hoped that God's Spirit would knock some sense into us while we lived at the Club's headquarters. But once here, we quickly saw that this was a man-made organization with old men at the top, who for the most part couldn't admit mistakes or take constructive criticism, had big egos and short tempers, lacked critical and logical thinking skills, and were significantly removed from the reality of the normal person making a living and taking care of a family.

One of the guys who shared my convictions was a young, unkempt man from Southern California. His family history went back to the early days of Russell and Rutherford. Tobin Trujohn's people were hard-core believers and they had the money to support their convictions. While Tobin hadn't pioneered like most Bethelites, he was invited because his family had clout from the dollars they invested in the Club. He partied every night, was Covington's equal when it came to sordid language capabilities, and respected no one in authority. He worked in the factory so I never observed his work habits. He dared to be kicked out of Bethel, yet he was there every night in our small circle of discontents. Then one day he wasn't there. I never knew what happened. And not to my surprise, Knorr didn't have him for breakfast.

Mama and Dick in front of the new Bethel home.

It didn't take long for me and my nonbelieving friends to realize that Bethel wasn't the happy, harmonious theocracy that the rank-and-file Club members believed it to be. Members from all over the country toured the home every week with a "we're in Mecca" look in their eyes. Mama, Papa, and my three siblings came to visit during my first summer at Bethel and treated me like a saint as opposed to the juvenile delinquent I was supposedly becoming when I lived in Los Angeles.

Once at Bethel, I saw that what is preached isn't always practiced. Unfortunately, some new, well-meaning Bethelites, with a twinge of self-righteousness, were slow to see this reality. These were the naïve, true believing Bethelites who invested fifteen to twenty years of their life before realizing too late that they had nowhere else to go. That's what one Bethelite told me. When I asked him if he had any advice to help make my four years go faster, he said, "Dick, you'll see a lot of shit here. Just don't stop to step in it." That's when I got to thinking that maybe four years were too many.

One of those people who couldn't leave was an old man we called Pete the Greek. He had been at Bethel over thirty years and always wore what appeared to be the same drab white food-stained chef's apron and pants. Everyone liked him. He had a great sense of humor and was constantly teasing, but he vehemently refused to talk shop—Club talk—during mealtime or work. Although twice a year, he'd have a change of heart.

The standard protocol for our mornings Monday through Friday was a fifteen-minute review of the *Yearbook*. Unless Knorr went on one of his frequent rants, the Club's president started by reading the Bible verse for the day and asking for comments from the ten people assigned to the table next to his. At least once every six months, all Bethelites were required to sit at the table and respond to Knorr's request. I did it four times while at Bethel. When Pete the Greek had his turn, I could hardly believe my eyes and ears. It was as if he'd had a temporary Club lobotomy.

Dressed in a nice suit and tie, Pete uttered the Club lingo as if he talked shop every day. He was like Elmer Gantry ranting on about this old world and the wickedness of anything not associated with the Club. What he said had no correlation with his day-to-day talk. His apparent reversal brought me face to face with my own duplicity, which was beginning to bother me more and more.

Six months after coming to Bethel, I graduated from primary and was eligible to study the *Watchtower* on Monday night with Fred Franz, the Club's vice president. He conducted the meeting with about 500 Bethelites in attendance. While it wasn't mandatory that I attend, I was told that if I was regularly seen and heard there, it would help me move up in the Club hierarchy. I was at the lowest rung on the ladder, and I had no ambitions to go any higher. But I was curious.

It was one thing to see Franz in the dining room with his mismatched jacket, pants, shirt, and tie. But to see him on stage in his embarrassing attire, I wondered why someone didn't have the guts to tell him he looked like a crazy man. When Fred went off on several tangents, spewing all kinds of silly things like he was in the early stages of dementia, I decided that the clothes fit the man. My first meeting was my last.

When the Fred Franz show was over, a special theocratic ministry school was held. I thought of the meeting as an audition. Each Bethelite was asked to speak for ten minutes on a specific subject and a panel of judges—Gilead instructors—decided if he had what it takes to be a traveling lecturer on the Club's elite *speaking list*. Fortunately, we only had to attend when it was our turn to talk, which was about every three months. To make the speaking list, we had to give three outstanding lectures, per the opinion of the judges. The better speakers made it on their fourth or fifth try, while many Bethelites struggled for years and never made it.

A week after my third talk, I received a notice saying I had made the Club's prestigious speaking list. At first, I thought it was a joke. When I showed the letter to George Couch, he confirmed its legitimacy and congratulated me. Walking back to my room, my head was filled with the sweet smelling elixir that disorients a person's mind, making certain that for quite some time I wouldn't be able to see the big picture.

I inhaled the same intoxicating aroma several months before. It happened during my first two-week vacation in the summer of 1963 when I spent a week in Nebraska at home and a week in Michigan to see Helen. While there, I was a celebrity at the Club communities in Norfolk and Holland—what with me being a Bethelite. It was a two-week high.

I could smell that elixir once more, and I got to thinking that it wouldn't be long before I, at nineteen, would be giving talks to thousands of people at Club conventions, captivating them with my speaking skills. I thought about calling Mama to tell her the good news. But in those days, long-distance calls were very expensive, so I did the next best thing: I talked with my roommate, my half-brother Tim.

A year after I was invited to Bethel, Tim received his invitation. I was having trouble with my roommate, Barry, and I didn't think rooming with Tim could be any worse. Surprisingly, things went well between us. Tim saw that I was well-thought-of by the Bethel staff and assumed I had changed. He wasn't the least bit self-righteous as was the case with Barry. While Tim saw the same double standard and hypocrisy I saw at Bethel, he rationalized that it probably was far worse at the headquarters of other churches. Ultimately, he preferred the pioneer work and left Bethel after two years to pursue that ministry. But after reading my notice about making the speaking list, Tim broke into a big smile, reached out his hand, and shook mine vigorously. He was very proud of me and added that I needed to let Mama know the good news. Soon after that, I began having a disturbing dream.

The dream was always set on an October day. The bright blue sky suddenly turned pitch black. The ground beneath me shook violently and I lost my footing. I fell to my knees and watched as thousands of thick lightning bolts began bombarding the streets and high-rise buildings. It was a constant, otherworldly 4th of July. Some bolts landed only inches from where I was hunkered down. Buildings began to collapse. A twenty-story building crumbled into dust in front of me. I covered my ears against the deafening sounds of multiple explosions. A huge fissure opened in the earth, consuming cars, buildings, and scores of screaming people. Dead bodies were strewn everywhere in pools of blood.

Then I realized this was Armageddon. It was happening just like Sister Edwards and Mama said it would. All those Club predictions were right. I knew my death was imminent. Since I never believed, I wouldn't survive.

The holocaust continued for several days, and still I lived. I didn't know why. The destruction was unbelievable. Perhaps God was taunting me for my hypocrisy so I could see and hear His awe-some powers. And then, as quickly as it started, it stopped. It was very quiet now. The sun and blue skies reappeared. I heard heav-enly trumpets blowing. The sounds were divine. It was music from God, getting louder and louder. Animals and birds, so numerous I couldn't count them, appeared from nowhere and began devouring the flesh of the deceased. I felt an inner calm unlike anything I'd ever experienced. The storm was over and positive energy radiated everywhere. I was in the presence of Jehovah God. I had survived Armageddon. Why me? I never believed in the Club's interpreta-tion of the Bible. And yet, I was a survivor. Why? And that's when the dream ended.

I had that dream several times over the next two months. I didn't have a shred of faith in any of the Club's predictions, and yet, I was dreaming about Armageddon and surviving. It took me a while to figure out the genesis of that dream. When I realized that I was in the early stages of living the lie that I would be preaching to people at large conventions, I decided that I needed to be hon-est with myself. I shouldn't be giving talks at Club assemblies, or anywhere for that matter. I had to leave Bethel and the Club as soon as possible. However, wanting to leave and being able to leave were two different things. Fortunately, I knew Charley and Bert, so I decided to ask for help.

I met Charley sixteen months earlier while working as a waiter. I was washing Sunday's breakfast dishes and heard the clashing sounds of pots and pans hitting the tiled wall in the pot licker's work area. As I walked over to see what caused the commotion, I heard, "F-you, Brooks. If you want it that clean, you clean the F-ing pot yourself."

While I knew Covington used that word, I didn't think people talked like that inside the Bethel home. I finally glimpsed the person who had screamed the obscenities, a five-foot, four-inch Charley MacGregor, mired in a disarray of big metal pots, pans, and bowls. As I gaped, he greeted me with, "What the F- are you gawking at, newboy?" I remained motionless, not saying a word.

"That's all right, kid. You're new here. But you'll learn fast that's the only way you treat assholes around here. Tom Brooks won't bug me anymore about how I clean pots and pans." Then he laughed his signature naughty laugh.

My quick evaluation of Charley was that he wasn't very smart. The kind of language he used reminded me of what Papa said about people with weak minds trying to express themselves forcibly.

Several weeks later, I was transferred to the kitchen and had the opportunity to work with Charley for a full day in the bakery. We also occasionally worked weekend kitchen duty together. While he definitely had a foul mouth when he got riled, I decided he wasn't stupid. He just hated the Club and most people in authority and didn't have a rational way of exorcising his anger.

In November 1962, Charley and I worked the weekend kitchen duty together. In private, he told me that before the year was out, he planned to leave Bethel and the Club, and that he had found a way to support himself in a style that would be the envy of most college graduates. For the last year, he had been doing odd jobs on the side for Bert Parker, a disfellowshipped ex-Club member who lived about a mile from the Bethel home. Now they were going to form a partnership to manage five-story, ten-family apartment buildings (brownstones) in Brooklyn Heights.

Before our weekend duty was over, Charley asked if I wanted to meet Bert, adding, "Perhaps if he takes a liking to you, he'll throw some odd jobs your way." I told him I'd like that and we made plans to meet him on our day off on Wednesday.

Charley and I hunched into our coats that cold day as we walked along the upscale Brooklyn Heights Promenade. At Atlantic Avenue, we turned left. Two long blocks away, where the buildings weren't in as good shape as those in the Heights, we arrived at Bert's brownstone. We walked down five steps to his ground-level apartment and into an area cluttered with worn garbage cans blocking his door. Charley kicked several cans out of his way and rang the doorbell. He pushed it a second time. Soon we were greeted by a muffled voice from the speaker, "Who the hell is it?"

Charley barked back, "Who the F- do you think it is?" He commenced into his patented laugh.

"You aren't those F-ing Watchtower people, are you?" was Bert's response, followed by a maniacal laugh and then a buzzzzzzzzzz.

Charley pushed the door in. We walked into a long, dim hallway. It was musty and dirty. I followed as Charley kicked aside litter and soiled clothes. He opened a door and we entered a kitchen peppered with the pleasant aroma of Italian sausage, garlic, oregano, thyme, and sweet tomatoes simmering in a big metal pot. Dirty dishes were piled everywhere. And there, sitting next to a table covered with a well-used red checkerboard tablecloth, was a short, potbellied, unkempt, balding, mafia lookalike. Charley introduced the man as "Bert Parker hisself."

"So do you F-ers want some beer?" Bert asked gruffly.

Before the morning was over, I got to know Bert pretty well. While he was definitely foul-mouthed, cynical, and black humored, underneath the dark shell was a person I believed I could trust. While Bert's lifestyle was nothing I cared to emulate, I envied his freedom. He was his own person, beholden to no one. I liked that, as well as the fact that before leaving, Bert offered me part-time work whenever I wanted it.

By June, I was working ten hours a week—nights and week-ends—for Charley and Bert doing odd jobs like cleaning, painting, and making small repairs. I was also getting good exposure to a poorly served market and the financial rewards that could be had for someone who was willing to work hard.

When I told Charley and Bert in September that I wanted to leave Bethel, I already had a good reputation in the Brooklyn Heights area for my work ethic and dependability. I knew that I could make a living doing this kind of work, but I wasn't interested in developing a partnership with Bert or Charley. Our value systems were worlds apart. But that didn't stop me from asking them if they knew of someone in another section of New York City who could use my skills.

In January 1964, Bert informed me that he and Charley had talked with a man on the west side of Manhattan who owned a number of brownstones. He needed a superintendent that he could trust and Bert told him about me. I interviewed for the job and before I left, I was told that the job was mine if I wanted it. The offer included a rent-free apartment on West 68th Street. But I first needed to get my house in order.

Now it was time to talk with Helen. She'd been working as a waitress, keypunch operator, and accounts receivable clerk. She was putting money in the bank and had just purchased a 1957 Chevy. She had also started pioneering. While we weren't engaged, there was general understanding that we would get married when my four years at Bethel were up.

This needed to be a face-to-face conversation. I could not do this over the phone or in a letter. I wanted her to come to New York City to see me. But she would not be able to stay at Bethel, since the visitors' rooms were occupied. So I asked a man from my Kingdom Hall in Central Harlem, if Helen could stay with his family. He and his wife loved the idea.

When Helen got off the train at Grand Central Station, wearing a thick wool red coat, she looked gorgeous. I took her to the house where she would be living for the next three days. I gave her a mini tour of New York City and later that evening, we talked. I told her that being single and separated by so many miles was no way for two people in love to live. I told her of my plan to leave Bethel and my new job in New York City. And I asked her to marry me. She accepted my proposal and three weeks later, we set April 11, 1964 as our wedding date. I did not yet tell her of my plans to leave the Club. I would do that after we were married.

Everything was in order, except for one piece of business I had to address before leaving Bethel and ultimately the Club. I had seen Bethelites, like Charley, leave angrily with their middle finger in the air, spewing all kinds of angry feelings. Many of them never rid themselves of that hate and bitterness before it started eating away at their positive values. While I certainly had internalized a lot of anger toward Mama and many of her choices as they affected my life, that was past history and I needed to put it all behind me. Besides, I couldn't do anything about it now except rant and rave, and little good that would do. I needed to learn as much as possible, apply that new knowledge wisely, and focus all my energy on finding worthwhile opportunities for my life, and now Helen's.

My stay at Bethel had been a good learning experience for me. Sure, I saw things I didn't like, but it also gave me a wonderful opportunity to get away from home and Mama, and find out who I was and what I was capable of doing. I had, at long last, found something that I could believe in—me. Because of my accomplishments and successes at Bethel, I had learned to believe in my good judgment, using facts and data rather than relying on emotion. What more could I ask from my experience?

My plan was to leave Bethel on April 1, 1964, and to give my notice of departure two weeks in advance. I wanted to announce my resignation to the president of the Club himself. When I told several of my close friends about my intentions, they thought I had lost my mind.

Knorr was not the kind of person someone could warm up to. He was a cold and distant little king and I believed that he, like so many people with too much power and authority, believed his own bullshit. Because he hadn't surrounded himself with people who were honest with him when he said or did foolish things, he was an impotent leader—an emperor without any clothes. All he could do was rant and rave about why people didn't believe and see the world like he did.

As bad as he was, I saw him as an improvement over the first two Club presidents, Russell and Rutherford. Those two were tyrants who ruled with an iron fist. They were self-serving dictators who loved power—at least that was my take on what I had read and heard about their tenures at the Bethel home I had lived in for almost two years. It also amused me that Russell left a power vacuum when he died. He had not named a successor and there was some jostling for the top position. Rutherford was the Club's attorney and a dark horse for the job. Because he was a good public speaker, definitely not the best theologian, he was asked to deliver a eulogy at Russell's funeral. I think he anointed himself when he told the grieving audience that President Charles Taze Russell was the greatest person to ever live since the death of the apostle Paul.

Knorr was not nearly as charismatic as his predecessors. He didn't have their stage presence or bombastic speaking style. Many Bethelites saw him as a brown-noser, even calling him Brownie behind his back. With only a high school education, he was an unlikely candidate to replace President Rutherford. He had been a good soldier, but Covington was a much better speaker and Franz a better Bible scholar.

In the last months of his life, Rutherford asked Knorr, Covington, and Franz to escort him to Beth-Sarim, his San Diego home. The three of them visited him several times when he was there. When Rutherford knew his death was imminent, he petitioned his three lieutenants to see him one last time. Like always when traveling by train, they went first class on a Pullman. Rutherford insisted on it. That's how Jehovah would want it to be. While Knorr, Covington, and Franz spent those last days with Rutherford at Beth-Sarim, they called him Pappy and Pap, as they had done for years. He was their surrogate father. Rutherford instructed them to stick together to fight the enemies of God after he was gone. Covington assured Rutherford that they would, adding, "Pap, we'll fight them till hell freezes over."

Franz reported Rutherford's last words and Covington's response at a Cincinnati assembly and the conventioneers confirmed their solidarity by bursting into a long, jubilant clapping frenzy.

At the time, Knorr, Covington, and Franz were bachelors. Rutherford liked that. He encouraged his followers to remain single. His own wife had been paralyzed from a stroke many years before. His predecessor's wife had been a thorn in Russell's side, accusing him of infidelity and taking him to court several times. Rutherford, like the apostle Paul, believed God was best served single. Wives were a hindrance if a man wanted to put God first in his life. Those kinds of beliefs seeped into and shaped the Club's policies on women that Mama believed were inspired by God.

What was most revealing about the inner workings of the Club at the time was a response to a question asked of Covington about Rutherford. The male interviewer knew there were rumors about Rutherford's philandering, so he asked about it. Covington became very agitated and tried to defend the man he believed to be God's ordained leader with another question, "If your wife was paralyzed, what would you do?" Rather than neutralizing the question, he had confirmed the Club leaders' double standards.

I slept very well the night before I planned to speak to Knorr. I calmly worked kitchen duty the next morning and watched to see when his tablemates got up to leave. He usually stayed until everyone at his table was gone in case someone wanted to speak to him. I moved quickly in his direction and asked if I could schedule time to talk. He gave me a stern look, crossed his arms, and told me that now was as good a time as ever. Several people stopped dead in their tracks to see why I was speaking to Brother Knorr.

Without the least bit of nervousness, I said, "I want you to know that I will be leaving Bethel in two weeks, and I'd like to tell you why."

Stiffening his already harsh demeanor, he glared as he asked, "So, why are you leaving?"

His presence was unnerving, although I was quick to react with, "Because I want to get married, and..."

He held up his right hand, signaling for me to stop and listen. "So after you're married for a few years, do you think that you'll leave your wife as well? Perhaps you'll tire of her like you have of Bethel service. I wonder if you know anything about keeping commitments."

It had taken me over sixteen years to find the courage to stand up for my convictions and take control of my life. I was prepared to make a proclamation of my faith, not to Mama, but to the Club's president. However, Knorr made it crystal clear that, at least in his eyes, my big sin was leaving Bethel before my four years were up.

What kind of a tirade would he make if I told him what I really thought about the Club? I decided that I wouldn't be bullied and said, "I've learned a lot at Bethel, and I'm grateful for the experience."

He gave me a hard stare. His eyes pierced right into mine, seemingly waiting for me to say something stupid. But I wasn't going to take the bait. I politely smiled, turned, and slowly walked away. With each step, I liked the person I had become better and better. When I reached the swinging kitchen doors, I could not have been happier. I had just removed the weight of that sixteen-year millstone and completed a rite of passage. The end of my Odyssey in Mama's Club.

Keith, Helen, Kim, and Dick Kelly in 1974

A family picture in June 2005. Standing: Helen and Dick Kelly
Middle Row: Jon Waalkes, Kim Waalkes , Annie Waalkes, Katrina Kelly, Amy
Kelly, and Keith Kelly
Seated on grass: Erika Waalkes and Hannah Kelly

After Thought

A year after my sister Mary Lyn was murdered, I completed my first draft of *Growing Up In Mama's Club*. While it was very early in my writing learning curve and many drafts later before this book could be published, I celebrated my accomplishment by writing a rhyme of where I was at that moment in time. That's how Mama honored significant milestones in her life and what she encouraged me to do when I was a child. Both of us have always wanted to be poets. Perhaps that will come in our next lives.

In 2002, during one of my infrequent telephone calls with Mama, we were having a nice conversation when she abruptly changed the subject by asking if I was happy—really happy. While I've answered that question in the affirmative many times over the last forty years, she still does not believe me. Mama cannot imagine how I can be happy not being a Club member, particularly since I was raised "in the truth."

This time, I decided not to give my perfunctory, "Yes, I'm very happy." Instead, I said I could best answer her question if she'd read a rhyme I'd written three years before. Perhaps it would help her see the world from my point of view. It reads as follows:

It Is What It Is

For most of my life, I believed all was well.
I had repressed anger, but thought none could tell.

Way down deep in my innards is where it resided.
For the most part it slept and was not often sighted.

For thirty-five years, working hard every day.
It was easy to think it was locked safely away.

But retiring from work and with not much to do,
Damned if old demons didn't start to scream boo.

At first, I tried walking ten miles a day.
It got me in shape, but it wasn't the way.

I went to a counselor to seek his advice.
It was my bad luck, he could only be nice.

I began writing memoirs to find out the cause.
While it was painful, it gave time for pause.

Was it Mama and her demands on me
To submit my life to Club theocracy?

Was it all of my shame for what Mama believed,
Or the guilt she dispensed, is that why I'm peeved?

An unhappy childhood, of that there's no doubt.
But what should I do, feel sorry and pout?

After thorough review, it was all about me.
It was there all the time, when I finally could see.

Life is today and what happens tomorrow.
One must let go of the past with all of its sorrow.

It is I who decided to go on mental rampages,
To dredge up the past and put contentment in cages.

Forgiving Mama was the big key for me,
It released hurt's grip and my epiphany.

Life is what it is, and I can't change a lot.
My thoughts and beliefs are all that I've got.

It is what it is and now easy to see,
I am as happy as I want to be.

A week after sending Mama my rhyme, she mailed the following response: "Dear Dickie, please note my little contribution to the world of poetry:

The Bible's true, of that I'm sure
Its counsel good, its pages pure.
Some may scoff and make up lies,
But only God can give the prize.
So what we say and what we do,
Are based on lies or what is true."

Today, at age eighty-six, Mama is doing well. Her faith and resolve in her new world to come is as strong as it has ever been. It doesn't bother her that she once taught me to believe that this world would be destroyed before I reached twenty or that she should now be living in paradise. I cannot make sense of that apparent contradiction. But I do know that the sixteen years I spent growing up in Mama's Club had a significant impact, for better or for worse, into shaping me into the person I am today.

My story did not end when I left Bethel and the Club. Ghosts from Mama's Club would haunt me for the next forty years.

A Glossary of Club Jargon
(Unique to my sixteen years in Mama's Club)

- ***144,000*** – The Club taught that only 144,000 people, made up of Jesus' apostles and disciples from the early Christian era, martyrs and reformers, and members of the Club before 1935, would go to heaven. This select group of angelic former humans (also called the "anointed class") would ultimately rule over a paradise earth, the *new world*, where millions of people would live in peace and harmony, and never die. Anyone considered to be good who died prior to Jesus' own death, including the ancient prophets and faithful men and women of old (even Noah, Moses, Esther and John the Baptist), would not qualify for this group, but would be resurrected and live in the *new world*.

- ***1914*** – One of the Club's core beliefs was that the year 1914 marked the "time of the end." In its literature and at meetings, members were continually reminded that a generation of people actually living in 1914 would see and experience the end of this old world at *Armageddon*. A select few would even survive it.

- ***Armageddon*** – The war to end all wars, a world-wide holocaust to be initiated by *Jehovah* God to destroy Satan the Devil, his demons, and all wicked people on earth. It was Mama's version of Hell and I was constantly reminded that I'd better follow Club rules or I'd be destroyed at Armageddon.

- ***assemblies*** – The Club had two three-day circuit assemblies and one four-day or five-day district assembly every year. In 1950, 1953, and 1958 the Club substituted the district assembly with an eight-day international assembly located in New York City. They were also called "conventions."

- *Awake!* – A semi-monthly news magazine. Its purpose was to help readers understand world events and science from the Club's perspective. Along with its companion magazine, the *Watchtower,* it was *placed* (sold) on Saturday mornings in the *door-to-door work.*
- *back call* – A second or a subsequent visit with someone who purchased Club literature, made to assess further interest. Members reported the number of back calls made in a given month at their local *Kingdom Hall.*
- *bad association* – Anyone not a Club member. If a member spent too much time with these people, it was believed that it would lead to his or her loss of faith.
- *Bethel* – The Club's worldwide headquarters and the name for the two hotel-sized buildings that housed up to 850 Club members, as well as the two big printing factories, all located in Brooklyn, New York. If you worked and lived there, you were called a Bethelite and considered a member of the Bethel family.
- *Beth-Sarim* – A twenty-room mansion in San Diego, California. Club members were told it was to be used to house and reorient ancient worthies and prophets, like Moses, Abraham, and David, after they were resurrected in the *new world.* This mansion was also to be used by resurrected faithful Club members who died before *Armageddon.* Official records showed that the Club's second president, Judge J. F. Rutherford, used it as his winter home. The property was unoccupied and rarely visited after Rutherford's death in 1942. It was quietly sold in 1948 and rarely mentioned by the Club after that time.
- *bible study* – A one-hour, in the home, question and answer review of a Club publication, primarily the *Let God Be True* book, which was a primer of the Club's core beliefs. Its purpose was to assist the prospective convert to accept *the truth.* If after six months the person hadn't attended at least one Club *meeting*, members were told to stop the study. Members

reported the number of bible studies they conducted monthly at their local *Kingdom Hall.*

- *book study* – A one-hour question and answer *meeting* using one of the Club's newest books. The book study was held on Tuesday night in a member's home and in groups of no more than fifteen people.
- *circuit assembly* – See *assemblies.*
- *circuit servant* – A man responsible for approximately twenty *Kingdom Halls* or *congregations* that he visited for six days, every six months. He helped to explain and enforce Club policy, while encouraging members in the *door-to-door work.* His work was reviewed by a *district servant* every six months. He ultimately reported to someone in the Club's *service department.*
- *congregation* – See *Kingdom Hall.* Prior to 1954, congregations were referred to as "companies."
- *congregation committee* – A group of three men at each *Kingdom Hall* who were appointed by the *circuit servant.* In order of authority there was the congregation servant, the assistant congregation servant, and the bible study servant. They had judicial powers and could reprimand and *disfellowship* members.
- *congregation servant* – The nominal leader or manager of the *Kingdom Hall* prior to the early 1970s. Before 1954 this position was called "company servant." See *congregation committee* and *servant.*
- *contribution box* – A collection plate was never passed during any of the *meetings.* Rather, a large contribution box sat conspicuously at the back of each *Hall* where members were encouraged to donate money to pay for the *Hall's* rent and upkeep. Contribution boxes were used at all of the Club's *assemblies.*
- *disfellowshipping* – The act of excommunicating a Club member. After being baptized, members couldn't challenge the Club's beliefs or its mandates on what was considered

Christian behavior. If they did—and didn't repent—they were disfellowshipped. When this happened, no one in the Club could talk or fellowship with them. They were shunned. No exceptions were made, even for family members.

- *district assembly* – See *assemblies*.
- *district servant* – A man responsible for the review of twelve *circuit servants* and the organization of a three-day *circuit assembly* held every six months. He enforced Club policy and reported to someone in the Club's *service department* located at *Bethel*.
- *door-to-door work* – Visiting people's homes in the hopes of recruiting them as new members. Initially, *placement* of one of the Club's magazines or books was the goal. The door-to-door work was also called *field service* or going *house-to-house*.
- *elders* – While I was growing up, this word wasn't used. However, in the 1970s, the Club started using the word to describe the leading men at each *Kingdom Hall*. In the book, I used the word for that purpose.
- *field service* – See *door-to-door work*.
- *field service report card* – Each month, Club members reported the number of hours they spent in the *door-to-door work*, the literature they *placed*, the *back calls* they made, and the *bible studies* they conducted on this card.
- *Gilead* – Located at *Bethel*, this was the Club's seminary or school. Its purpose was to train missionaries to live and preach in foreign countries.
- *Hall* – See *Kingdom Hall*.
- *the home department* – A department at Bethel responsible for the maintenance and operation of the two Bethel homes. This included the kitchen, dining room, laundry room, and house cleaning. While I was at Bethel, George Couch was the home department overseer – occasionally called the home servant.

- *house-to-house* – See *door-to-door work.*
- *Informant* – A monthly four-page pamphlet used to organize the talks and skits presented at the *service meeting.* It was later replaced with the *Kingdom Ministry.*
- *international assembly* – See *assemblies.* More often referred to as "international conventions." The two largest were held in New York City (at Yankee Stadium in 1953 and at Yankee Stadium and the Polo Grounds in 1958) and had reported crowds up to 253,000 attending in three locations.
- *Jehovah* – God's personal name. An early English rendering of a name of God used in the Old Testament based on the Hebrew Tetragrammaton of "YHVH" found in the earliest scriptures.
- *Jehovah's Witnesses* – I used "Mama's Club" throughout the book instead of Jehovah's Witnesses (JWs). This name was first coined by Judge J. F. Rutherford, its second president, in 1931. Before that, Club members called themselves "International Bible Students."
- *Kingdom Farm* – A farm in Ithaca, New York, responsible for producing most of the food consumed at *Bethel.* Fifty to sixty Club members lived and worked there.
- *Kingdom Hall* – The name Club members gave their place of worship rather than calling it a church. It was also called a *congregation.*
- *Kingdom Songbook/songs* – Club members didn't sing traditional Christian music. At three of their five weekly *meetings* and at *assemblies,* they sang songs from their unique Songbook.
- *letters of recommendation* – A metaphor used for the number of people Club members converted to the Jehovah's Witness religion.
- *the magazine work* – *Placing* (selling) the *Watchtower* and the *Awake!* for ten cents on Saturday mornings.
- *meetings* – The Club had five one-hour meetings a week. They were the *public talk* and *watchtower study* (on Sunday),

the *book study* (on Tuesday), and the *theocratic ministry school* and *service meeting* (on Thursday or Friday).

- *memorial* – The Club didn't have communion like most Christian churches. It believed that Jesus commanded his followers to celebrate the memorial of his death only once a year, using the Jewish lunar calendar to decide the day. It also believed that just *144,000* would go to heaven and that only members of this select group could partake of the bread and wine served during the memorial celebration. However, there was "a great crowd of people" whose hope was to live forever on a paradise earth after *Armageddon*. This larger group couldn't partake of the bread and wine, but were commanded to attend the memorial and observe the service.
- *millions now living will never die* – An advertising slogan originated in the 1920s by the Club's second president, Judge Rutherford, and used by Club members in their preaching work to increase sagging membership. By 1928, membership had fallen by nearly 75%, due in large part to Rutherford's false prophecy that Armageddon would occur in 1925. Surprisingly, by repeating the message that millions now living will never die, this gimmick led to great growth in the society's membership in the 1930s.
- *ministerial servants* – Young men or adult males at the Hall who didn't have the skills to serve on the *congregation committee* or to be an *elder*, but to whom a number of duties and responsibilities were assigned.
- *newboy* – For the first few months, while living at *Bethel*, I was often called "newboy" and not by my given name. This was also the case with other new *Bethelites*, aged eighteen to their mid-twenties.
- *new truths* – The announcement of a new interpretation of the Bible or a change in one of the Club's doctrines or policies, even when the Club flip-flopped on a policy or specific belief. New truths were announced in the *Watchtower* or at an *assembly*.

- *new world* – The Club's promised paradise that survivors and millions of resurrected faithful followers of God would turn this earth into after Armageddon. In the new world there would be no more death or sickness, and while it would take a thousand years, everyone would grow to perfection. It would be like heaven, but here on earth.
- *New World Translation of the Bible* – The Club's version of the Bible released during the 1950s.
- *not-at-homes* – When no one answered the door in the *door-to-door work*, members were instructed to write down the address and call on that home at a later date. Some of the more aggressive members left out-of-date copies of the *Watchtower* or *Awake!* at these homes.
- *overseer* – See *servant*
- *placard work/ministry* – In this work, a person fitted a stiff cardboard placard (often called "sandwich boards"), promoting a special *public talk*, over the front and back of their body, from shoulders to knees. They then walked back and forth on a busy city block passing out handbills for the talk.
- *place* – While Club members asked people to purchase its literature for a preset price, they were told they didn't "sell" the *Watchtower*, *Awake!*, or any of its books. Rather, they "placed" them while asking for a small donation to cover their cost.
- *pioneering* – Active Club members spent at least twelve hours a month going *door-to-door*. But members were reminded that God was best served if they could be a vacation pioneer, a pioneer, or a special pioneer. This meant that they would have to spend from 75 to 150 hours a month going in the *door-to-door work*.
- *primary* – A special six-month (twenty hours a week) school for first-time *Bethelites*. While the Bible was read and studied, the purpose for this schooling was to evaluate the new *Bethel* member's spiritual and intellectual aptitude. If the person didn't meet up to the Club's standards, he was asked to leave.

- *probation* – After being baptized, members couldn't challenge or question the Club's beliefs or mandates on what was considered Christian behavior. If they were found guilty of an infraction, and repented, they were put on probation. While those in attendance were not told exactly what they did, after a *service meeting*, it was announced that a certain member was guilty of "conduct unbecoming of a Christian." While other members could talk to them, those on probation had to wait six months before they could be reinstated in good standing, provided they didn't repeat the offense.
- *public talk* – A one-hour lecture by a male Club member held on Sundays before the *watchtower study*. This meeting was open to the public and to potential converts. The speech was usually very generic and presented the Club's teachings in a very simplistic manner, avoiding controversial subjects while emphasizing prophecies about *Armageddon* and the paradise *new world*.
- *publishers* – Members who spent time in the *door-to-door work*.
- *publisher's record card* – See *field service report card*.
- *the remnant* – A small group of members who professed to be one of the *144,000*, by partaking of the bread and wine at the *memorial*, believing that when they died they would be immediately resurrected to heavenly life. See *144,000*.
- *rurals* – An alternative to the *door-to-door work*. Instead of walking from *house-to-house*, members drove their car in the country from one farmer's house to another.
- *servant* – A member who held a responsible position at the *Hall* (i.e. the *congregation servant*) or in the Club hierarchy (i.e. the *district servant*). Toward the end of my sixteen years in Mama's Club, the word servant was replaced with *overseer*. (When I lived in Nebraska, I was the book study servant, and when I lived at Bethel, I was the veggie room overseer.)

- *the service department* – A department at Bethel responsible for disseminating and enforcing Club policies at the congregational level. *Circuit* and *district servants* reported to someone in this department. Club policies were documented in black books, which served as the department's Bible. While I was at Bethel, Harley Miller was the service department overseer.
- *service meeting* – A one-hour Club *meeting* held on Thursday or Friday night after the *theocratic ministry school*. Its purpose was to inform members what the Club wanted them to say, which literature was to be distributed, and the procedures to follow while performing the *door-to-door work*.
- *the Society* – See *Watchtower Bible & Tract Society*.
- *sparing the rod* – The Club taught that "sparing the rod" (failure to use corporal punishment) wasn't the proper way to raise children. Discipline in the form of spanking and slapping was common and believed necessary in order to prevent-spoiling a child.
- *speaking list* – The very best public speakers at Bethel were appointed to the Club's elite speaking list. This made them eligible to give talks at one or more of the annual *district assemblies* or at special *public talks*.
- *spiritual food* – The nourishment (Bible-based knowledge per Club interpretation) that members received if they attended and carefully listened to what was said at the Club's five *meetings* or *assemblies*.
- *territory assignment* – Before going in the *door-to-door work*, members were given a territory assignment card. On the card was a map with four to six city blocks.
- *theocratic ministry school* – A one-hour *meeting* designed to educate boys and men in public speaking skills. It was held on Thursday or Friday night and was the invention of the Club's third president, Nathan H. Knorr. During the *meeting*, five eight- to fifteen-minute talks, or Bible readings, were given. Afterwards, the speakers were publicly commended and counseled on how to improve. It was believed there was

a significant relationship to being able to speak well in public and one's success in the *door-to-door work*.

- *the truth* – The Club's interpretation of the Bible. If a person accepted as gospel what the Club taught, went to *meetings*, spent time in the *door-to-door work*, and was baptized, it was believed that he or she was "in the truth." "The truth" was also used by the *Watchtower* and members as a metonym for the Club itself.

- *Watchtower* – A semi-monthly magazine and the official house organ for the Club. The *Watchtower* announced new policies, clarified doctrinal issues and long standing policies, restated core beliefs, introduced *new truths*, etc.

- *Watchtower Bible & Tract Society* – The legal name for the Club. Members also called it "the Society" or "the governing body."

- *watchtower study* – A one-hour *meeting* that followed the *public talk* on Sunday. A portion of the *Watchtower* magazine was reviewed by using a question and answer format.

- *where the need is great* – At the international assembly in 1958 and for the next three years, Club members living in big cities were encouraged to "move and serve where the need is great." They were reminded that *Armageddon* was only a few years away and yet there were many people living in remote areas of the U.S. who had never heard *the truth*. Thousands of members answered the Club's call and left good jobs and schools, thinking *Jehovah* God would reward their decision and help take care of them and their families.

- *worldly people/boys* – Anyone who was not a Club member and considered to be "bad association."

- *Yearbook* – An annually published book that reported the Club's membership and attendance figures from the previous year. The book also quoted a scripture from the Bible with a short Club interpretation for every day of the year. Good members read from the Yearbook every day and discussed the daily verse with their family before breakfast in the morning.

A Short History of Mama's Club

Mama's Club was the brainchild of Charles Taze Russell, born in 1852. Charles went to Presbyterian and Congregational churches as a boy and was so committed to their teachings that he chalked Bible verses on the downtown sidewalks of Pittsburgh to draw attention to the punishment of hell awaiting the unfaithful. At sixteen, he began questioning Christianity, thinking he might be agnostic. Two years later, he cautiously attended a presentation by an Adventist preacher who believed Christ's Second Coming would occur in 1874. Charles said that presentation left him with a renewed zeal and an understanding that not only was the Bible the Word of God, but that all Christians had a responsibility to preach the gospel.

From 1870 through 1875, Russell met with a small group of people, which included his father and sister, immersing himself in an analytical study of the Bible. In 1876 Russell read a copy of *Herald of the Morning*, published by Nelson H. Barbour. Russell liked what he read and set up a meeting with the author. Barbour convinced Russell of several new views, the most significant being that the "Rapture" would occur in April 1878. Russell was so moved that he decided to devote his life to God in what he believed would be the last two years before Christ's return.

Russell encouraged Barbour to write a book. Russell wrote articles in Barbour's journal and ordained himself a pastor, though he never finished high school or attended seminary. He met twice with Christian leaders in Pittsburgh, telling them of the Rapture's imminence, with no success.

When the Rapture didn't occur, Russell did some soul searching. He concluded that he and Barbour didn't make a mistake. Jesus had returned, but it was a quick, unseen visit to resurrect the twelve apostles and other faithful men and women who had been asleep in death, taking them up to serve with him in his heavenly kingdom. Those who died faithful after his visit would be changed "in the blinking of an eye."

Through Barbour's journal, Russell began teaching his beliefs on the subject. Barbour was embarrassed by the failed prophecy, rejected Russell's explanation, and shared his differing views in the journal. A debate ensued, and as their disagreements accelerated, they decided to go separate ways.

Although he retained the bulk of Barbour's eschatological views, Russell, with help from his father and other financial backers, started his own journal, now known as the *Watchtower*. The first issue was published in July 1879. What was to become the Watchtower Society was incorporated in 1881, with William H. Conley, an Allegheny, Pennsylvania banker, its first president, Russell's father Joseph its vice president, and Charles Taze Russell the secretary-treasurer. (In the book I state that C. T. Russell was the first president, as that's what the Club tells its members.)

In 1884 Charles Taze Russell was elected the second president. His group, International Bible Students, had grown to hundreds of members throughout the United States. The message he printed in the *Watchtower* and shouted from the pulpit was: "the end of the world will occur in 1914."

In 1903 newspapers began publishing Russell's written sermons. They were syndicated worldwide, with an estimated readership of fifteen million in the United States alone. Aided by additional advertising, Russell was gaining notoriety rapidly. But not all was good. In 1893 four of Russell's associates wrote a manifesto, accusing him of being a liar and a dictator, and of cheating them out of money from books they helped write.

In 1879 Russell married Maria Ackley. In 1897 they separated following disagreements over the propriety of Maria's role in writing articles for the *Watchtower*, preaching, and traveling abroad as his representative. In 1903 she filed for legal separation. Three years later she sued for divorce, citing their marriage agreement of perpetual celibacy as being intolerable.

For three years a Brooklyn newspaper accused Russell of making exorbitant profits from selling "Miracle Wheat." Priced at $60 a bushel, Russell claimed it grew five times better than regular wheat. It was in fact slightly inferior. Russell sued the paper for libel, but lost.

Russell died on October 31, 1916. Per his Last Will and Testament, a rotating editorial committee made up of five elders was to make sure the *Watchtower* contained material written only by Russell during his lifetime. In January 1917, Judge Joseph Franklin Rutherford was elected the third president. Two months later, when it was clear that Rutherford had no intention of honoring Russell's wishes, a power struggle developed between him and four of the seven-member board of directors. Matters reached a climax that summer when Rutherford dismissed the dissident directors.

Within a year of his presidency, Rutherford wrote *The Finished Mystery*, which was critical of Christian involvement in war. For this, he was sent to prison in 1918 for violating the Espionage Act.

Upon his release in 1919, Rutherford, known for his loud, booming voice, started a lecture series predicting the end of the world in 1925. The earth was to be turned into a paradise, and he claimed that millions now living would never die. In 1922 Rutherford introduced the door-to-door work with members playing his recorded speeches on phonographs.

Rutherford distanced himself from many of Russell's teachings and stopped printing his books. He eliminated congregational autonomy and appointed "servants" from headquarters. Those decisions, along with his failed prophecy for 1925, led to a mass exodus of members. Attendance at the Memorial dropped from a high of 90,434 in 1925, to 17,380 in 1928.

The period from 1925 to 1933 saw many significant changes in the Society's doctrines. The editorial committee was disbanded with Rutherford having the final say regarding what went into Watchtower publications. In 1931, at a convention in Columbus, Ohio, Rutherford announced the new name of "Jehovah's Witnesses."

During his presidency, Rutherford allowed no dissent. If someone didn't say or do what he wanted, he had them "disfellowshipped" and labeled an apostate. Olin R. Moyle, the Society's legal counsel, was a good example. In 1939 he wrote a long, open letter to Rutherford outlining his concerns about living conditions at Bethel.

Moyle was shocked to see how often fellow Bethelites were severely reprimanded, condemned, humiliated, and given public lambasting for making a suggestion or saying something Rutherford disagreed with. He was appalled that Rutherford had spacious, well-positioned homes at Bethel, Staten Island, San Diego, and the Kingdom Farm, while all other Bethelites were provided small rooms, unheated even during the bitter cold of winter.

Moyle said it was disgusting to hear vulgar language and dirty jokes at Bethel, with Rutherford himself one of the offenders. He believed that under Rutherford's tutelage, glorification of alcohol and condemnation of teetotalers had become a way of life.

Rutherford responded to Moyle's list of concerns by placing all of his personal effects on the sidewalk. He was asked to leave and disfellowshipped. Weeks later in the *Watchtower*, Rutherford stated "every paragraph of that (Moyle's) letter is false, filled with lies, and wicked slander." He claimed that Moyle libeled the family of God at Bethel and identified himself as "one who speaks evil against the Lord's organization, as the Scriptures had foretold (Jude 4-16; 1Cor 4:3; Rom 14:4)."

In 1940 Moyle sued the Society over Rutherford's comments.

He won financial damages, in spite of two unsuccessful appeals by the Society.

Rutherford replaced Moyle as the Society's legal counsel in 1939 with a twenty-eight-year-old lawyer from Texas, Hayden C. Covington.

In January 1942, shortly after Rutherford's death, Nathan Homer Knorr became the fourth president of the Society, inheriting a membership of 115,000. He immediately eliminated Rutherford's phonographs. Within a year, he instituted the Theocratic Ministry School at local Kingdom Halls and created a missionary training school called "Gilead." He also initiated the doctrine of not accepting blood transfusions.

Knorr was in poor health the last few years of his life, so leadership of Jehovah's Witnesses was reorganized. In 1976 the power of the presidency was transferred by the Board of Directors to a Governing Body of seventeen men. Knorr died in 1977.

Frederick William Franz, born in 1893, became the fifth president of the Society in 1978. He attended the University of Cincinnati where he studied Biblical Greek. In 1926 he joined the editorial staff as a Bible researcher and writer. He died in 1992 at ninety-nine years of age, as one of the oldest men ever to lead a religious organization in the United States.

Franz was succeeded by Milton G. Henschel. Henschel was succeeded by Don A. Adams. However, since 1976, the Governing Body, with a membership that varies from nine to nineteen men, has made doctrinal and organizational decisions and supervised the writing of Watchtower publications.

A history of Mama's Club would not be complete without Hayden C. Covington's story. While going to law school in San Antonio in the early 1930s, he listened to Rutherford's recorded speeches on the radio. He was dissatisfied with the establishment so Rutherford's message was appealing. It had nothing to do with an interest in the Bible, but with professional admiration. They were both lawyers and Covington liked how Rutherford forcibly presented his message, imagining that what the "Judge" said was the truth.

After defending several Witnesses in court, Covington was impressed with their dedication and character. He started attending meetings. Covington was a crusader and needed a cause to defend. Because they were heavily persecuted, the Witnesses were exactly what he had been searching for. Covington decided to join, saying, "I'm going to fight with these people...and we're going to win."

When news of his successes in defending the Witnesses reached the New York headquarters, Covington was invited to Bethel to serve as the Society's general counsel. Upon Rutherford's death, Covington was elected vice president and a director. Three years later, because he didn't profess to be one of the 144,000, he was asked to resign from the vice presidency.

What distinguishes Covington's career was his record for the most Supreme Court victories in the United States. Thurgood Marshall, former Justice of the Supreme Court, litigated twenty-three favorable cases, while Covington had thirty-seven victories. A brilliant Constitutional lawyer, he argued numerous cases on behalf of Jehovah's Witnesses in defense of their religious freedoms and indirectly advanced the cause of religious and civil liberties on behalf of all American citizens.

Justice Harlan Fiske Stone, 12th Chief Justice, gave the highest compliment to Covington when he wrote, "The Jehovah's Witnesses ought to have an endowment in view of the aid which they give in solving the legal problems of civil liberties."

Covington was a fighter, and that was one reason why he did so well in court. He was good with words and very aggressive, but as the Society won more and more cases, there was less and less need to fight. In the early 1960s about all there was left to argue were fairly simple draft cases. Covington's aggressiveness was no longer needed, and when he began drinking heavily, he was asked to leave Bethel.

In spite of the great legal victories enjoyed by the Watchtower Society during and after World War II, recent years have found it embroiled in damaging and costly legal cases involving child abuse and molestation among its ranks.

Beginning in the mid-1990s, stories began to leak out about children and women being sexually harassed, molested, and even raped by Witness parents and congregational elders. The Society had a clearly stated policy that reports of abuse, rape, incest, or violence should be handled within each individual congregation and, for most cases, not reported to civil authorities. Abusers were often simply stripped of any ministerial positions they may have held and were either disfellowshipped or placed on probation. In some cases, "elders" were transferred to other Kingdom Halls or reassigned to other duties.

The Society has lost or settled many legal cases involving these crimes. Aside from its many failed prophecies and constantly changing theological teachings, child rape and abuse within the organization has been the most damaging issue that the Witnesses have had to face. Like the Catholic Church's similar problems with predatory priests, the Watchtower Society has paid out a lot of money in settlements, and as yet has not made any serious changes in its policies or organizational structure to deal with this major problem.

* More information about the history and beliefs of Mama's Club (Jehovah's Witnesses) can be found in the following books and websites:

Books
1. *Crisis of Conscience* – Raymond Franz
2. *Secrets of Pedophilia in an American Religion – Jehovah's Witnesses in Crisis* – Barbara Anderson
3. *Apocalypse Delayed: The Story of Jehovah's Witnesses* – James Penton
4. *The Four Presidents of the Watchtower Society* – Edmund Gruss

5. *Blood on the Altar* – David Reed
6. *Jehovah's Witnesses: Portrait of a Contemporary Religious Movement* – Andrew Holden
7. *Jehovah's Witnesses: Their Movements in False Prophesy* – Edmund Gruss & Leonard Chretien
8. *Awakening of a Jehovah's Witness* – Diane Wilson
9. *Thus Saith Jehovah's Witnesses* – Randall Watters
10. *The Gentile Times Reconsidered* – Carl Olof Johnson

Websites

http://www.freeminds.org/
http://www.silentlambs.org
http://en.wikpedia.org/wiki/Jehovah's_Witnesses/
http://watchtowerdocuments.com/
http://jwinfoline.com
Google: "Jehovah's Witnesses Discussion Forum"

Printed in the United States
104362LV00002B/262-336/P